DOING
Counselling Research

Second Edition

John McLeod

SAGE Publications

London • Thousand Oaks • New Delhi

First published 1994, reprinted 2002
This edition first published 2003

SAGE Publications Ltd
6 Bonhill Street
London EC2A 4PU

SAGE Publications Inc
2455 Teller Road
Thousand Oaks, California 91320

SAGE Publications India Pvt Ltd
B-42, Panchsheel Enclave
Post Box 4109
New Delhi – 100 017

British Library Cataloguing in Publication data

A catalogue record for this book is available from the British Library

ISBN 0 7619 4107 X
ISBN 0 7619 4108 8 (pbk)

Library of Congress Control Number: 2002107099

Typeset by Mayhew Typesetting, Rhayader, Powys
Printed in Great Britain by The Cromwell Press Ltd, Trowbridge, Wiltshire

For Julia

Contents

Preface   viii

1   Doing Counselling Research   1

2   Reading the Literature: Placing Research in Context   10

3   The Research Process: Stages, Tasks and Traps   22

4   Using Quantitative Methods   41

5   Tests, Rating Scales and Survey Questionnaires   55

6   Listening to Stories about Therapy: from Qualitative Research
    to Human Science   71

7   Systematic Inquiry into Individual Cases   99

8   Does it Work? Evaluating the Outcomes of Counselling   117

9   Exploring the Interior of Therapy: Method and Strategy in
    Process Research   145

10 An Ethical Framework for Research Practice   167

11 Critical Issues in Counselling Research   178

References   195

Index   221

Preface

This book has been written to encourage critical thinking and reflection on the nature and purpose of counselling and psychotherapy. Throughout the book, the words 'counselling', 'psychotherapy' and 'therapy' are used to describe a set of activities and helping processes that are basically the same. This usage arises from a belief that the distinctiveness of 'counselling' and 'psychotherapy' lies in factors such as professional socialisation and organisational setting rather than in any differences in types of client need or therapist strategy.

This book should be of value to those engaged in counselling research, and those engaged in counselling practice who wish to use research to inform that practice. Chapters 1 to 7 introduce some of the methods that have been used in studies of counselling and psychotherapy, while Chapters 8 and 9 examine the ways that these methods have been applied in two key areas of inquiry: therapy process and outcome. Chapter 10 reviews some of the ethical dilemmas raised by research in this field. The final chapter summarises and explores the main methodological themes and issues in counselling research.

The book is written from an interdisciplinary perspective, which views counselling as an applied discipline that draws its ideas and techniques from the humanities, theology, philosophy, sociology and anthropology as well as from the more familiar sources in psychology and medicine. Each of these contributor disciplines has much to offer in terms of methodological diversity.

Anyone who has had even the slightest involvement with counselling will know that it is a highly complex undertaking. What may on the surface appear to be a simple conversation between client and counsellor can be understood at many levels and from many perspectives. This book reflects that multi-faceted reality. There is no one right way to do counselling research. There is, instead, a diversity of methods and techniques. In a book of this length it would be impossible to provide enough information to equip the reader immediately to go out and set a piece of research in motion. Instead, the aim is to act as a bridge between counselling and methodology by explaining how different methodologies have been or could be applied to counselling issues, and by supplying enough information for the interested reader to find more detailed technical sources if necessary.

The reader will find that there are three strands running through this book. Firstly, there is information about basic research techniques such as reviewing the literature, using tests or analysing data. Secondly, there are examples of what is involved in applying these techniques in counselling research. Thirdly, there is a strand of epistemological debate. Epistemology is the branch of philosophy that deals with the question of 'How do we know?' This third strand introduces some of the underlying philosophical assumptions implicit in different types of counselling research. These three themes interweave throughout the book, reflecting the nature of the research process.

Doing Counselling Research has two companion volumes, also published by Sage. *Practitioner Research in Counselling* (McLeod, 1999) covers many of the same topics, but with greater emphasis on the kinds of research which can be carried out by working practitioners. *Qualitative Research in Counselling and Psychotherapy* (McLeod, 2001) offers an expanded coverage of methods and possibilities in qualitative research, which is an approach that is of particular interest to many counsellors. It also explores in more detail the philosophical and social issues associated with research in this area.

I would like to acknowledge the help and assistance offered to me at various stages in the preparation of this book by Lynne Angus, Sophia Balamoutsou, Michael Barkham, Tim Bond, Sue Cowan, Robert Elliott, Kim Etherington, Joerg Frommer, Stephen Goss, Soti Grafanaki, Kevin Hogan, Kate Kirk, Dave Mearns, John Mellor-Clark, Chris Phillipson, Krishnasamy Puniamurthy, Peter Reason, David Rennie, John Sloboda, Jane Speedy, William West and Sue Wheeler. Any responsibility for errors or misconceptions is entirely my own. I would also like to thank Alison Poyner at Sage, who has been a supportive and patient editor. Finally, I owe the greatest debt to my wife, Julia, and my daughters, Kate, Emma and Hannah. Without their love, affection and belief in me none of this would have been possible.

1 Doing Counselling Research

This book is written both for counsellors intending to carry out research, and for counsellors who read research in the hope of finding knowledge and understanding that will help them to improve their practice. The growth of counselling over the past 50 years has been accompanied by a steady development of strategies and methods designed to facilitate critical inquiry into the process and outcomes of this type of helping relationship. The aim of this book is to show that, in counselling and psychotherapy, systematic research can make a vital contribution to the quality of service that is offered to clients. For the purposes of this book, the position will be taken that there is a large degree of overlap between 'counselling' and 'psychotherapy', and many examples of studies of psychotherapy process and outcome will be included. Despite some differences in settings, client groups and professional affiliations, counsellors and psychotherapists are engaged in fundamentally the same kind of work. Although it can be argued that a distinctive research agenda can be identified for counselling (McLeod, 1994a), the greater quantity and influence of psychotherapy research has tended to dominate the field. It is easier to get funding for research with 'psychotherapy' in the title than for studies of counselling. So, although it is probably the case that more counselling than psychotherapy research is actually carried out, in the form of student dissertations, the majority of large-scale studies, and thus the majority of articles published in academic journals, go under the heading of 'psychotherapy'.

Why is research important for counsellors?

There is considerable evidence, mainly from surveys of counsellors and psychotherapists in the USA (Cohen et al., 1986; Morrow-Bradley and Elliott, 1986), that practitioners of psychological therapies do not read research articles, and do not consider research to be particularly relevant to their work. The reasons for this research–practice 'gap' are examined more closely in Chapter 11. However, given the scepticism about the value of research that is expressed in these surveys, it is useful to consider the role of research within counselling as a whole. The following are some of the most salient reasons for carrying out counselling research.

1 **Gaining a wider perspective**. Counselling is largely a private activity, conducted in conditions of confidentiality. Research studies allow counsellors to

learn about and from the work of other therapists, and give the profession a means of pooling knowledge and experience on an international scale.

2 **Accountability**. There is a significant level of resourcing of counselling from public finances, and this financial backing brings with it a responsibility to demonstrate the efficacy of what is being offered to clients. It does not convince the public at large for counsellors to assert that, in their personal experience, most clients gain a great deal from therapy. More rigorous, objective evidence is required. In recent years, stimulated by the work of Masson (1988), there have been a growing number of published accounts of abuse of clients by therapists, which has led to research into the prevalence and causes of this type of mis-conduct. Other writers have been highly critical about the benefits that clients gain from therapy. If counselling is to maintain its good public image, and continue to attract funding from government agencies, health providers and employers, then effective, research-based systems of accountability are essential.

3 **Developing new ideas and approaches**. Counselling and psychotherapy are new, emerging professions, and innovations in theory and technique are springing up all the time. Until the 1930s, the only form of psychotherapy that existed was psychoanalysis. There are now dozens of well-established approaches. Counselling is an activity in which innovations are generated by practitioners and then subsequently evaluated by researchers. This is the reverse of the situation in medicine, where laboratory researchers will create a new drug or piece of tech-nology which is then carefully tested in patient trials. Whereas in medicine there are legal safeguards preventing premature experimentation with patients, in coun-selling it is inevitable that new techniques and ideas will be in practical use before they are subjected to research scrutiny. Given that there is evidence that therapeutic interventions can do harm as well as good (Lambert, 1989), an informed awareness of the value of research in checking the value of innovations is indispensable.

4 **Applications of counselling in new areas**. Running in parallel with the development of new techniques has been the opening up of new client groups and areas for the application of counselling. There has been a significant expan-sion over the past decade in counselling in organisations, in primary health care and in response to disaster and trauma. The relevance and effectiveness of existing models in these new contexts is an important topic for research.

5 **Personal and professional development**. One of the chief sources of job satisfaction experienced by many counsellors is the sense of continually learn-ing about human nature in response to the lives and personal worlds that clients allow them to enter. As part of this process, practitioners may find themselves with 'burning questions' that can only be answered by carrying out research. The professional and career development path taken by experienced counsellors may lead many to seek to consolidate their professional identity by making a contri-bution to the research literature (McLeod, 1997; Skovholt and Ronnestad, 1992). The motivation to conduct research may therefore arise just as much from the personal needs of practitioners as from external organisational or social demands.

A fundamental theme running through these reasons for undertaking research is that, like other institutions in modern industrial-capitalist societies, counselling is, or strives to be, an 'open system'. The knowledge base of counselling is not fixed, dogmatic and immutable. Instead, criticism and questioning are encouraged, and most (if not all) information about counselling is in the public domain, accessible through libraries. Although some of the theories currently in use may *appear* solid and immovable, reflection on the brief history of therapy will show that pioneers such as Freud and Rogers had to struggle to get their ideas accepted in the face of what was the accepted wisdom of their time and place. And, inevitably, even the apparent certainties of psychodynamic or person-centred theory will in turn be overthrown. Research is important for counsellors in establishing the legitimacy of the profession. Hasenfeld (1992) has argued that all forms of welfare or human service must be perceived as legitimate not only by their clients but also by regulators, resource-providers and other 'stakeholders'. Like other human service professions such as medicine, nursing, clinical psychology, teaching and social work there is an expectation that members of the counselling profession will be able to offer a rational basis for their interventions through drawing on a research-based body of knowledge. This trend is reflected in the increasing movement toward university- and college-based training for these professions, with significant emphasis in these courses on research awareness and skills. Many of these developments are problematic for counselling, where much of the training has been provided by independent institutes and much of the practice has been provided by lay volunteers.

What is research?

There are many myths and fantasies about research. These often include vivid images of white coats and laboratories. People with practical skills and competencies may believe that research is something that is 'beyond' them. A very prevalent myth in the counselling world is that research is about numbers, impenetrable statistics and large samples and has no place for ordinary human feelings and experiences. It is hard to identify with the role of being a researcher. The researcher is someone who is an expert, who knows. Running through these images and fantasies is a sense of research as another world, a kind of parallel universe that takes what is happening in the real world and processes it through computers.

These myths, perhaps stated here in an exaggerated form, act as a barrier that stops counsellors becoming engaged in research. A more constructive point of view is to start from the acknowledgement that we do 'research' all the time. Each of us has a model or map of the world, and is continually seeking new evidence with which to verify or alter that model. A counselling session with a client can be seen as a piece of research, a piecing together of information and understandings, followed by testing the validity of conclusions and actions based on that shared knowing. Over dozens of clients and hundreds of sessions we build up our own theories of what different types of client are like and what is effective with them. These personal theories almost always have some connection to 'official' theories, but retain an idiosyncratic element originating in the unique experiences of the individual counsellor.

A useful working definition of research is: *a systematic process of critical inquiry leading to valid propositions and conclusions that are communicated to interested others*. Breaking this definition down into its component meanings allows some of the assumptions that lie behind it to be made explicit.

1   The concept of *critical inquiry*. Research grows out of the primary human tendency or need to learn, to know, to solve problems. These impulses are fundamentally *critical*; the need to know is the counterpoint to the sense that what is known is not quite right.
2   Research as a *process* of inquiry. Any research involves a series of steps or stages. Knowledge must be constructed. There is a cyclical process of observation, reflection and experimentation.
3   Research is *systematic*. There are two distinct sets of meanings associated with the notion that research should be systematic. The first is that any investigation takes place within a theoretical system of concepts or constructs. A piece of research is embedded in a framework or way of seeing the world. Secondly, research involves the application of a set of methods or principles, the purpose of which is to achieve knowledge that is as valid and truthful as possible.
4   The products of research are *propositions* or statements. There is a distinction between research and learning. Experiential knowing, or 'knowing how', can be a valuable outcome of an inquiry process, but *research* always involves communication with others. Learning can occur at an individual, intuitive level, but research requires the symbolization and transmission of these understandings in the public domain.
5   Research findings are judged according to criteria of *validity*, truthfulness or authenticity. To make a claim that a statement is based on research is to imply that it is in some way more valid or accurate than a statement based on personal opinion. However, every culture has its own distinctive criterion or 'logic of justification' for accepting a theory or statement as valid. For example, within mainstream psychology truth value is equated with statements based on rational, objective experimentation. In psychoanalysis, truth value is judged on the basis of clinical experience.
6   Research is *communicated to interested others* and takes place within a research community. No single research study has much meaning in isolation. Research studies provide the individual pieces that fit together to create the complex mosaic of the *literature* on a topic.

This broad definition of research is intended to demonstrate that there are many ways of arriving at valid propositional knowledge in the field of counselling. The definition does not imply that research must be 'scientific', nor does it make assumptions about what constitutes science. In technologically advanced modern societies, it is all too readily assumed that 'research' equals 'science' and that scientific methods represent the only acceptable means of generating useful knowledge. A great deal of research into counselling and psychotherapy has followed this route, in taking for granted the rules and canons of scientific method and constructing therapy as a sub-branch of applied psychology or as a discipline allied to medicine. However, there are strong arguments in support of the position that counselling is better seen as an *interdisciplinary* activity, using concepts and methods from the arts and humanities, theology, philosophy and sociology as well as psychology and medicine (McLeod, 2003). If this perspective is adopted, it is essential that research in counselling is defined in such a way as to give equal weight and legitimacy to methods of inquiry drawn from *all* these disciplines.

Another feature of the definition of research being employed here is that research is not taken to be only studies that appear in academic journals. There exists a broad continuum of research activity. At a very local level, a counsellor may critically review his or her work with a particular set of clients and report back their conclusions to a peer supervision group. Also at a local level, a counselling agency may analyse data on clients and outcomes for inclusion in its Annual Report. By contrast, international collaborative studies may involve 'cutting edge' developments in theory and practice. Relatively little research ever finds its way into academic journals. The majority of studies are disseminated as limited circulation reports and discussion papers, or are lodged in college libraries as student dissertations. Nevertheless, across this continuum of sophistication and ambition, all counselling researchers are faced with the same set of methodological and practical issues.

Tensions and dilemmas in counselling research

Although one of the aims of this book is to enable people to carry out research in the field of counselling, it would be misleading to represent counselling research as a straightforward matter of obeying a set of guidelines or following a recipe. There are serious splits and conflicts within the research community, associated with different conceptions of what comprises valid research methods. It is necessary for researchers to be clear about the choices they are making when they design and carry out a piece of research. These choices are influenced by values, philosophical considerations, practical resource constraints and intended audience.

Counselling research is conducted in the context of a massive on-going philosophical debate about the nature of knowledge. The field of *philosophy of science* has emerged in the post-war era as one of the most important branches of philosophy. Philosophers of science have attempted to analyse and understand the basic nature of scientific inquiry – how do scientists create knowledge that is so powerful that it has transformed the modern world? The most influential philosopher of science has been Sir Karl Popper. In a series of books, Popper (1959, 1962, 1972) argued that science progresses through a process of *conjectures* and *refutations*. Scientists devise theories or conjectures that are then tested through experimental methods in an effort to refute them. Popper asserts that no theory can represent the complete truth, but that the best theory is the one that can stand up to the most rigorous testing. It is in this way that scientists arrive at theories that have immense power and practical value. For Popper, the role of the scientist as a well-equipped, skilful *critic* lay at the heart of the scientific enterprise. From this perspective, academic freedom is important because any restriction on the potential to criticise diminishes the possibility of advancement in knowledge. For Popper, the weakness of systems of thought such as Marxism and psychoanalysis was located in their unwillingness to open themselves to criticism. Popper saw these theories as representing *closed* systems of thought.

The ideas of Popper can usefully be set alongside the work of Kuhn (1962), who observed that, although Popper was right in identifying the crucial role of criticism and refutation in scientific progress, in practice the dominant scientific theories were very rarely ever actually overthrown. Kuhn (1962) suggested that to explain this phenomenon, science needed to be viewed as a social activity. In the early years in the life of a new area of science, there would probably be many competing theories, as different researchers attempted to grasp a poorly understood domain of knowledge. However, as soon as one clearly adequate theory emerged that the majority of scientists in the field could support, these researchers came together to form a scientific 'community' linked through adherence to a shared 'paradigm'. The concept of paradigm is central to the work of Kuhn, and it is a complex idea. It is possible to identify more than 20 alternative uses of the concept in *The Structure of Scientific Revolutions*, the book in which Kuhn (1962) developed the core of his model. A scientific paradigm can be seen as consisting of the whole apparatus or web of knowledge employed by the members of a scientific community: theories, concepts, methods, common educational experiences, readership of key books and journals, participation in conferences and seminars. Kuhn suggested that, most of the time, scientists engage in what he called 'normal' science, which consists of working out a detailed analysis and application of the paradigm. Occasionally, however, it may become apparent that the theory or paradigm is not able to account for important phenomena, and the scientific community is precipitated into a crisis which is resolved through a revolution represented by the adoption of a new and more comprehensive theory.

The ideas of Popper and Kuhn represent a compelling analysis of the nature of scientific inquiry, and their model makes a lot of sense when applied to the history and evolution of sciences such as physics and chemistry. There are, however, major difficulties inherent in fitting counselling and psychotherapy research into this scheme. It is hard to imagine any theory of therapy that has ever, or would ever, be rejected on the basis of research evidence. Also, there are many competing theories of therapy: the field is far from achieving a unified paradigm. Some commentators have proposed that psychology as a whole, and therapy as a part of that whole, are at a pre-paradigmatic stage. So, although the philosophy of science developed by Kuhn, Popper and others might describe an ideal set of principles through which counselling and psychotherapy might make significant headway in creating more robust and satisfactory theories and techniques, it could be that the field is not yet sufficiently mature to enter this land of promise.

In opposition to these views, other voices have argued that any attempt by the social and human sciences to mimic the methods of the physical sciences is misguided and doomed to failure. From this perspective, it makes little sense to conceptualise people and social groups as objects that can be experimentally manipulated in the same way as physical entities such as rocks or metals might be. The very aims of traditional science, centring on the prediction and control of events, are seen as philosophically and politically inappropriate when applied to the study of human action, which can be regarded as intentional and reflexive. The search in the natural sciences for universal 'laws of nature' are similarly regarded as mistakenly applied to elucidating culturally embedded ways of knowing in which there are many local truths but perhaps no universal truth. The eighteenth-century French sociologist Auguste Comte was the originator of the idea of a 'positive' science, in which all phenomena from physics at one extreme to human behaviour at the other could be explained by a single set of natural laws. The 'positivist' philosophy of science created by Comte has been a significant force in shaping much of behavioural psychology. Von Wright characterises the three main tenets of positivism as being, first, that 'the exact natural sciences, in particular mathematical physics, set a methodological ideal or standard which measures the degree of development or perfection of all the other sciences, including the humanities' (1971: 2). Positivism also assumes a unity of scientific methods. In other words, the same methods are applicable in all fields of knowledge. Finally, positivist thinkers are only satisfied by explanations that are framed in terms of strict 'cause-and-effect' sequences, and reject any explanatory models that employ any notion of 'purpose'.

The focus for much of the opposition to the dominant *positivist* approach to research on people has rested with the proponents of a number of interpretive or *hermeneutic* ways of carrying out research (Taylor, 1979). The key figure in this tradition was Wilhelm Dilthey, who proposed that the study of persons could only be properly carried out through a distinctive *human science*. The method of hermeneutic inquiry has its origins in the efforts of biblical scholars to interpret the meaning of incomplete fragments of Scripture. This approach supplies the basis for a number of research strategies that rely on qualitative and interpretive methods. These strategies draw in general on the kinds of research activity carried out in disciplines such as the arts, humanities and theology, in that the task of the researcher is ultimately to place a 'text' (e.g. a transcript of a therapy session) in some kind of interpretive framework of meaning. The nature and scope of qualitative approaches are explored in more detail in Chapter 6. Some adherents of this type of research have described it as a 'new paradigm' (Reason and Rowan, 1981), to make explicit the contrast with previous methods that relied on natural science techniques and assumptions. Gergen (1985) uses the term *social constructionist* to refer to the way that the researcher socially constructs a reading or interpretation of the material.

The tension or polarisation that is being described here can be seen as fundamental to all fields of human inquiry. One of the few scholars successfully to have straddled both sides of this gulf has been Jerome Bruner, who argues that:

there are two modes of cognitive functioning, two modes of thought, each providing distinctive ways of ordering experience, of constructing reality. The two (though complementary) are irreducible to one another. (1986: 11)

7

Bruner calls these two ways of knowing the *paradigmatic* and *narrative* modes. He characterises the paradigmatic mode as logico-scientific, which 'attempts to fulfil the ideal of a formal, mathematical system of description and explanation'. The narrative mode, by contrast, deals in 'intention and action' and works with 'good stories, gripping drama, believable (though not necessarily "true") histori-cal accounts' (1986: 12–13). In reflecting on the role and methodologies of the human sciences, he observes that, 'in contrast to our vast knowledge of how science and logical reasoning proceed, we know precious little in any formal sense about how to make good stories' (1986: 14).

The differences between these two ways of knowing raise many fundamental questions within counselling and therapy research. Some of the specific issues that are encountered by researchers are:

1 Can useful knowledge be best achieved by accurate, objective measurement of vari-ables or by respecting the complexity of everyday language?
2 Is the aim of research the prediction of outcomes (e.g. a person with a particular diagnosis will be helped by a certain type of intervention) or the development of insight and understanding?
3 What kind of research is most relevant for practice?
4 What is the role of theory in research?
5 To what extent should the researcher aim to be detached and objective as against being an involved participant in the lives of research participants?
6 By what criteria are the validity of research findings to be judged?

There are no right or wrong answers to these questions, which reflect competing value systems, 'images of the person', ideologies and intellectual traditions. The ways that different counselling researchers have attempted to address these issues will be illustrated throughout this book. Some tentative pointers to new directions are offered in Chapter 11.

Conclusions

Doing counselling research occupies a position in the service of practice. It is hard to envisage what 'pure' research into therapy might look like. Counselling and psychotherapy are applied, interdisciplinary activities that draw on a rich array of primary disciplines, each of which represents a valuable source of concepts and methods of inquiry. The diversity and complexity of these tradi-tions, and the fragmented nature of therapy as an enterprise, means that coun-selling researchers are called on to reflect deeply on the methodological and philosophical choices that guide their work. Readers of counselling research, similarly, need to bear in mind that different studies may be expressed in quite different languages and voices.

There are perhaps several threads running through this initial discussion of the nature of counselling research. First, the driving force of research is the area between knowing and not knowing. Something is known but it is not enough.

Research that has meaning takes off from that point, which ultimately comprises a personal felt sense of a need to know. Secondly, research is a component of all competent counselling practice. It is not possible to be a good counsellor without possessing a spirit of openness to inquiry. Good research in the domain of counselling and psychotherapy always exists in a live dialectic relationship with practice. Finally, research is a collective activity. Each study draws on what has gone before, and its inevitable imperfections and inconclusiveness will be carried forward by someone yet to come. In the next chapter this final point, which relates to the importance of understanding the research literature, is explored in more detail.

Further reading

Hoshmand, L.T. and Martin, J. (eds) (1994) *Method Choice and Inquiry Process: Lessons from Programmatic Research in Therapeutic Practice*. New York: Teachers' Press. Well-known researchers write about their experience of doing counselling research, and the meaning it has had for them.

Polkinghorne, D.E. (1999) 'Traditional research and psychotherapy practice', *Journal of Clinical Psychology*, 55: 1429–40. A highly stimulating discussion of the relationship between research and practice; Polkinghorne argues that much research does not reflect the complexities of actual work with clients.

2 Reading the Literature: Placing Research in Context

Research can be seen as a complex form of collective learning. It is through research of one kind or another that the community of members of any discipline develop their shared capacity to act in response to problems. It is important to recognise that any piece of research always exists in relation to other investigative studies. No matter how original a new research question or technique might appear to be, it can only be asked or constructed on the back of all the questions or techniques that have gone before it. One of the essential tasks in any research project is, consequently, to become familiar with other relevant work in the particular area of interest. In other words, it is necessary, at some point, to read and review the literature, to map a context within which the study can be located.

What is the literature?

The 'literature' on counselling comprises the written materials, and also some published video and audio tapes, that represent in their totality the body of formal knowledge on the subject of counselling. This body of knowledge can be contrasted with the tacit, experiential or practical knowledge that is transmitted through an oral tradition. When people are trained as counsellors some of their knowledge comes through books and research articles, but most of what they learn is acquired through observation, reflection, personal experience and active experimentation. It is obvious that both types of knowledge, formal and tacit, are equally important in the field of counselling. No one would suppose that it is possible to learn the skills of counselling solely through books. Equally, it is hard to imagine a practitioner being able to gain an adequate ability to conceptualise or understand clients and the counselling process through first-hand experience alone.

The literature on counselling includes writings on theoretical, ethical and professional issues as well as research. The research literature therefore represents a sub-set of the counselling literature as a whole. This research literature is *structured* into various specialisms. For example, there exist specialist journals on areas such as group counselling, supervision and student counselling. The literature is not only structured but is also *dynamic*. It can usefully be viewed as a field of discourse, in which debates and themes ebb and flow over the years. The literature is *boundaried*. There are areas of overlap between the counselling literature and the bodies of knowledge generally considered as, say, 'medicine' or 'anthropology', and some important material may be found in unexpected places in these other domains. Finally, the research literature is *regulated* and censored in accordance with the prevailing norms and consensus regarding what is 'publishable'. To become a paper in an academic or professional journal, a piece of writing must be acceptable to editors and referees, who act as gatekeepers to the literature. In parallel to the official literature that is stored in the periodicals stacks of university libraries, there is an underground literature of unpublished papers and dissertations and limited-circulation reports and discussion documents. These more ephemeral items may be less polished, but can none the less possess considerable interest and information value.

The historical development of counselling research

A sense of the historical development of research in counselling and psycho-therapy can be valuable as a means of finding signposts to potentially relevant areas of the literature. One of the striking aspects of the literature taken as a whole is that issues that may appear to be currently fashionable or at the cutting edge of research have also been 'hot' issues at some point in the past. The recent interest in the experience of the client (e.g. Rennie, 1990) has its parallel in client-centred research carried out in the 1940s (e.g. Lipkin, 1948). Similarly, current research into 'non-specific' or general characteristics found in all forms of successful therapy (Grencavage and Norcross, 1990) can be traced back to Fiedler (1950) and Watson (1940). The explosion of studies of outcome and effectiveness that occurred in the 1960s and 1970s had its precursor in the 1940s (see Eysenck, 1952). Contemporary attention to the problems of inten-sive case-study methodology (Hilliard, 1993; Jones, 1993) represents a fasci-nating recapitulation of the dilemmas and challenges confronted by Henry Murray and his colleagues in the 1920s and 1930s (Murray, 1938). Inspection of the research literature reveals cycles of interest and attention to certain topics and questions. It can often be illuminating, therefore, to look in the literature beyond the mass of recent references that are the standard output of most on-line databases.

The literature includes many examples of questions that have gradually become transformed and redefined through a series of studies. For example, the concept of 'non-directiveness' that informed much of the early client-centred research has become replaced by ideas such as therapist 'reflection' in more recent studies. Research into the Rogerian 'necessary and sufficient' conditions of empathy, acceptance and congruence has for the most part been recast as the study of the 'therapeutic alliance'. These examples also illustrate the trend for concepts and constructs anchored in specific theoretical models to be superseded by concepts that are trans-theoretical and possess a broader currency. In Chapter 8 there is a discussion of some of the historical developments in research into the effectiveness of counselling and psychotherapy. A significant phase in the evolution of that area of research was the proliferation in the 1960s of analogue studies. An analogue study embodies an attempt to create conditions of experimental control and precision by assessing the effectiveness not of 'real' therapy occurring between actual counsellors and clients, but of specially constructed quasi-therapy episodes. In this type of research, participants are not clients in the sense that they might have sought help at a counselling clinic, but are people who volunteer to take part in a one-off 'experimental' treatment. The argument in favour of analogue research is that it permits extensive evaluation of specific intervention techniques without taking the risk of inflicting these techniques on people in crisis, and without subjecting genuine clients to the vagaries of research designs that involve being allocated to a no-treatment control group. The weakness of the analogue method is that it is difficult to generalise from these studies to actual counselling situations. In recent years, the tide of fashion has emphatically turned away from analogue studies, and there are relatively few examples of the use of this method in the current literature.

Another technique that has fallen out of favour is projective testing. Projective tests or techniques are assessment tools that require the participant to give a free, open-ended and creative response to an ambiguous stimulus such as an inkblot or picture (Semeonoff, 1976). The assumption is that the respondent will 'project' into his or her answer their characteristic ways of reacting to people and situations. Also, the emphasis on creative, playful responding is intended to gain access to fantasy material that is less open to conscious distortion or faking. However, despite the strong theoretical consistency between projective techniques and psychodynamic approaches to counselling and psychotherapy, and despite the fact that projective techniques were successfully employed in therapy research in the 1940s and 1950s, this set of techniques is now hardly used at all.

The presence or absence in the literature of studies implementing certain techniques or addressing certain issues is not just a matter of fashions or trends within the scientific community. Inclusion of topics in the literature is also determined by political and economic factors and pressures. Within the long list of issues that have *not* been investigated to any appreciable extent are: the relevance for counselling of social class, ethnicity, religious orientation and sexual orientation, the existence of ineffective or harmful practitioners, and organisational influences on counselling practice (see McLeod, 1994a). Telephone counselling, which comprises the largest source of counselling help available to members of the public, has received little research attention. Only in the past few years have the views of service users been widely studied (Rogers et al., 1993). What all this means is that, from the point of view of the practitioner or client, there are large gaps or absences in the literature in just those areas that may be of most importance to them. Researchers or readers of counselling research wishing to gain a fuller appreciation of the development of research in this field will find useful information in a number of sources. Malan (1973) surveys the history of psychodynamic research. Lietaer (1990) examines the history of client-centred research. Treacher (1983) looks at the field from a politically informed radical perspective. Hill and Corbett (1993) approach the evolution of therapy research from the point of view of counselling psychology. A comprehensive and authoritative historical overview is provided by Garfield and Bergin (1994).

Where to find the literature

The primary medium for the dissemination of research is the academic journal. A list of journals that either specialise in counselling and psychotherapy research, or at least occasionally include relevant studies, is provided in Box 2.1. This is a lengthy list, and it is clearly impossible for even the most comprehensive university library to subscribe to them all. Even if all these journals were assembled in one place, it would be a formidable task to inspect them all in a search for articles on a specific topic of interest. Fortunately, there is a range of strategies for finding relevant literature, discussed below.

1   **Review papers**. Experienced researchers regularly write articles summarising developments in research in their particular field. The *Counseling Psychologist* journal is essentially a review journal, with each issue structured around one long major review article followed by a number of shorter commentaries. There are also books that bring together authoritative reviews of the literature. The most important of these books has been the *Handbook of Psychotherapy and Behavior Change*, which has now reached its fourth edition (Bergin and Garfield, 1994). A useful review of the research literature on the outcomes of counselling and psychotherapy can be found in Roth and Fonagy (1996). Authoritative reviews of research in specific areas of therapy, regularly updated, are produced within the 'Cochrane' reviews database, for example the Bower et al. (2002) review of the effectiveness of counselling in primary care. Internet access to Cochrane reviews is available through university and NHS library systems. Finally, there exist bibliographies produced by researchers in specific areas, many of which are available on the internet.

2   **Research articles**. Any research report will include at least a brief review of previous research on that topic. The references at the end of an article can be followed up, and each of these sources will in turn provide other leads. One approach to gaining access to the literature, therefore, is to scan the contents pages of recent editions of journals, examine the references sections of relevant articles, and work backwards from what is to be found there.

3   **On-line searches**. Over the past ten years, there has been a dramatic expansion in the amount of bibliographic information held on computerised databases. Typically, an on-line database will use a terminal or PC to link the user with a vast annotated bibliography. The user gains access to sectors of this data by employing key words, which then call up lists of references on that topic. These references can be printed off or displayed either in terms of basic author, title and publication details, or can also include a brief abstract of the paper. Databases of special interest to those doing counselling research are *PsyInfo* and the *Medline*. However, therapy articles can also be found in some medical, nursing and humanities databases. Further information about procedures for

Box 2.1   Journals regularly publishing research in counselling and psychotherapy

American Journal of Psychiatry
American Journal of Psychotherapy
American Journal of Orthopsychiatry
American Psychologist
Archives of General Psychiatry
Arts in Psychotherapy
Behavior Therapy
British Journal of Clinical Psychology
British Journal of General Practice
British Journal of Guidance and Counselling
British Journal of Psychiatry
British Journal of Psychotherapy
Canadian Counsellor
Clinical Psychology and Psychotherapy
Clinical Psychology Review
Counselling and Psychotherapy Research
Counseling Psychologist
Counselling Psychology Quarterly
Counselling Psychology Review
Counselor Education and Supervision
Employee Assistance Quarterly
European Journal of Psychotherapy, Counselling and Health
International Journal for the Advancement of Counseling
International Journal of Group Psychotherapy
Journal of Behavior Therapy and Experimental Psychiatry
Journal of Clinical Psychology
Journal of College Student Development
Journal of College Student Personnel
Journal of Consulting and Clinical Psychology
Journal of Counseling and Development
Journal of Counseling Psychology
Journal of Critical Psychology, Counselling and Psychotherapy
Journal of Eclectic and Integrative Psychotherapy
Journal of Humanistic Psychology
Journal of Mental Health Counseling
Journal of Sexual and Marital Therapy
Journal for Specialists in Groupwork
Patient Education and Counseling
Professional Psychology: Research and Practice
Psychiatry
Psychological Medicine

Psychology and Psychotherapy
Psychotherapy
Psychotherapy Research
Small Group Research

using these methods can be obtained from college or university library or computer centre inquiry desks. Some thought may be required to obtain the desired
material from an on-line search. For example, key words will follow American
spelling, and often synonyms need to be tried out to gather information from
adjacent key-word lists.

4   Personal contact. Experienced researchers may be willing to give advice or
even copies of papers. The address of the senior author of the paper is routinely
included on the title page of journal articles, and usually these people will respond
positively to requests for off-prints of their current and past work. Some may be
willing to send copies of pre-publication work in progress.

These strategies (review articles, research papers, on-line searches and personal
contact) usually provide only reference details of potentially relevant sources. At
the moment, computerised delivery of the actual published content of journals is
not possible because of copyright restrictions. In order to get access to a hard copy
of a paper or chapter, the reader must find it in a local library, visit a distant library,
or make an inter-library loan. The latter two of these options may be time-
consuming and expensive. Again, library staff will advise on how these arrangements operate in individual college, university or research institute libraries.
Counselling practitioners who are not affiliated to an academic department will
find that most college and university libraries are willing to register them as library
users on payment of an annual charge. Some public libraries also allow access to
on-line searches and inter-library loans.

How to read a research article

There are major stylistic differences between research articles and journalistic
pieces published in popular magazines, and those unfamiliar with the conventions of research reporting will need practice in finding their way around the
formats used in the literature. Basically, magazine articles are written in such
a way as to entertain readers and induce them to purchase the publication.
Research articles, by contrast, are written with the aim of offering as comprehensive a summary as possible of the aims, methods and results of a piece of
research. It is assumed that, having read a research report, a sceptical reader
would in principle be able to replicate the study to ascertain whether its findings
were generalisable and valid. Research writing is therefore dense, formal and

Box 2.2   Sub-headings or sections in a research paper

Names and addresses of authors
Title
Acknowledgements
Abstract
Introduction
Research hypotheses/questions
Method
Subjects/participants
Measures/variables/instruments
Materials
Design
Procedures
Results
Discussion
Conclusions
Notes
References

often permeated with technical terms. It is not meant to be intrinsically inter-esting or a 'good read'. Of course, for the person who really wants to share in the findings of a study, it *is* a good read.

Reports on research carried out within the mainstream tradition represented by the quantitative, experimentally oriented strands of psychology and medicine tend to follow the kind of format outlined in Box 2.2. Although individual journals may impose slightly different variants on this structure, the headings listed in Box 2.2 represent a way of presenting research findings that is almost universally accepted. The rationale for this type of report structure is that each paper will begin (introduction) by identifying the general background to the study, the broad area of theory or practice within which it is located. The introduction then continues with a brief review of previous studies on the topic of the paper. This review leads in turn to a specification of the actual questions or hypotheses being addressed in the study. Ideally, the research hypotheses will clearly and logically be implied by the conclusions of the literature review. In other words, the literature review provides a rationale for carrying out the study. There then follows, in the method section, a great deal of detailed, descriptive information about how the study was carried out – who the participants were, what they were asked to do, how the data was analysed. The next section describes the results of the study, without any interpretation being placed on the meaning of these data. The final section of the paper comprises a discussion of the significance of the results in the light of theory and previous research, and then ends with a conclusions section in which the main findings may be summarised and any implications for theory, further research and practice are reviewed. At the very beginning of the paper there is an abstract, a summary of the study in about 300–400 words. The abstract gives readers of the journal (or those carrying out on-line searches) enough information to decide whether they wish to read through the whole paper. At the end of the paper is a references section in which details are given of all sources quoted in the text. The notes section allows the author to give information about unpublished sources or instruments. An appendix may include supplementary material such as interview transcripts or test items and instructions.

A good research paper will offer a linear, rational account in which the reasons for carrying out a study can be clearly seen to lead to a particular set of questions, which are then made concrete through the application of certain methods. The data produced by the method is analysed in a way that allows the original questions or hypotheses to be answered or tested, thus enabling a discussion of the light that these findings cast on more general issues. This kind of paper introduces a general issue, focuses more narrowly on a set of data that reflects a specific instance of that issue, and then finally broadens out again to reflect on what this new information means in terms of the wider context. The standard format means that readers know where to look in order to find pieces of information of special interest to them. It also allows lapses in logical and methodological rigour to be more easily identified. Finally, it is a structure that enables a great deal of information to be summarised within a typical length of between 3000–5000 words.

Although the structure described in Box 2.2 appears on the whole to be an effective means of reporting results from quantitative papers, it is more problematic as a pattern for reporting qualitative data. Research using qualitative methods inevitably produces a great deal of descriptive material which is difficult to accommodate within the standard structure. Also, the use of first-person reflexive writing which can be associated with qualitative methods does not sit easily in this kind of format. It is significant that in social anthropology, for example, qualitative ethnographic studies are normally published as monographs rather than research papers, because the greater length of a monograph permits descriptive material to be handled more sensitively.

Developing a critique

In Chapter 1, the ideas of the philosopher of science Sir Karl Popper were introduced as a way of reinforcing the idea that research is about debate and criticism. The most plausible theories and research findings are those that have withstood the most rigorous and systematic criticism. It is essential, therefore, to read researcher articles in a questioning and somewhat sceptical frame of mind. While accepting that there is some truth in any research report that has been carried out in good faith, the limitations and uncertainties in that truth can be brought to the surface through the application of some key questions.

1 How generalisable are the results? Are there aspects of the study, such as the way the sample is selected, that might limit the extent to which the results obtained will also apply in other situations?

2 Are the results reliable? To what extent might another researcher, or the same researcher at a different time or place, have produced the same results?

3 How adequate or convincing is the operationalisation of key variables or constructs? The notion of 'operationalising' refers to the way in which an abstract concept such as, for example, 'anxiety' is defined and measured in terms of a set of research 'operations' such as the items on a questionnaire or galvanic skin conductance readings. In a study of anxiety, then, the critical reader must ask whether the measure of anxiety that is used sufficiently reflects his or her understanding of anxiety as it is exhibited in the real world.

4 Are there other competing or plausible ways of explaining or interpreting the results? A researcher will usually interpret the data in a manner that allows him or her to claim support for a particular hypothesis. There may, however, be quite different means of accounting for what has been found. Ideally, a researcher should systematically consider alternative explanations, and give reasons for believing that his or her preferred explanation is the one that is most fully backed up by the available evidence.

5 In what ways does the study contribute to the development of theory and practice? How *significant* is the study, in addressing fundamental issues and debates? A piece of research may be methodologically rigorous but address a trivial question or fail to examine important dimensions of a topic.

These questions can be used to structure the critical or questioning reading of research papers. It is often valuable to reflect on what has been left out of a paper. Research reports typically include a mass of detailed information. It is the information that has been omitted, or has been included but 'buried', that can provide the pathway to different or alternative ways of seeing the material.

Reviewing the literature

In most fields of counselling and psychotherapy research, the literature will consist of a substantial number of journal articles and book chapters. In order to make use of the information contained within these publications, it is necessary to *review* the literature. There are several different ways of presenting literature reviews, each of which has its own distinctive strengths and weaknesses.

The *laundry list* approach to constructing a literature review involves stringing together sets of notes on relevant papers. This approach is similar in intention to the annotated bibliography. Its strength is that it enables the reader to learn about the various pieces of research that comprise the literature in a particular area. The limitations of laundry list literature reviews are that they neither allow exploration or analysis of the links between different studies nor enable identification of debates or themes across the literature as a whole. This kind of literature review has a role to play at the beginning of a study, as it permits the relevant material to be set out and displayed, but is not usually appropriate in a published article or thesis, where a more structured and critical review would be expected.

The *narrative* literature review tells the 'story' of the development of research in a field of inquiry. Narrative reviews are effective in situations where there has been a substantial amount of research, much of which has built on previous studies. The reviewer can then point out the ways in which specific studies remedied the defects of previous studies by introducing new concepts or methods. An advantage of the narrative structure is that it naturally ends with an account of the research that is currently being conducted, and does so in such a way that the reader will be able to appreciate why this contemporary work is both relevant and necessary. The other advantage of the narrative review is that it provides a solid platform for arguing that further research should now be undertaken. However, the narrative approach to structuring a literature review is ineffective when the field being reviewed has been fragmented with little sense of linear development or progress. Also, narrative reviews are not particularly useful when the aim of the review is to evaluate rather than to describe.

A form of literature review that is widely applicable is the *thematic* approach. This strategy involves the identification of distinct issues or questions that run through the area of research under consideration. Thematic literature reviews enable the writer to create meaningful groupings of papers in different aspects of a topic. This is therefore a highly flexible style of review, in which the complex nature of work in an area can be respected while at the same time bringing some degree of order and organisation to the material.

In some circumstances, the primary purpose of a review may be evaluative, such as in a review of the literature on the effectiveness of a particular type of counselling for a particular problem. In this situation, it may not be relevant to discuss in any depth how the studies were carried out – what the reader wants to know is how the results add up. A widely used approach employed in this context is the *box-score* review. A box or table is constructed which contains a list of the studies that have yielded results that are favourable, unfavourable or neutral in respect of a proposition. Often, the reviewer will identify the criteria (e.g. in terms of methodological rigour) that have been utilised to decide on whether to include studies in the table.

The box-score review is easy to understand and is an effective way of summarising a great deal of information in a confined space. Its weakness is that, when reviewing research into the effectiveness of therapy, studies that report large effects and those that report small effects are treated as equivalent, each earning one tick in the relevant box. The review strategy known as *meta-analysis* overcomes this problem by adding up the effect sizes (see Chapter 4) across all the studies that have evaluated a particular intervention. By examining the results section of each individual paper, it can be estimated by how many standard deviation (s.d.) units the people in the experimental group have improved (or deteriorated). The two major attractions of this type of review are that it permits an assessment to be made of the level of effectiveness of different interventions, and that it allows large numbers of studies to be brought together in one review. The classic Smith, Glass and Miller (1980) review of the benefits of psychotherapy, for example, included data from more than 500 studies. It would be impossible to encompass as many studies as this within a single thematic or narrative review, and it would be clumsy to do so using a box-score approach.

The final type of review involves *theoretical* integration of the literature. This is the most difficult kind of review to perform, since it requires not just reading and understanding each research paper in its own terms, but arriving at a fundamental re-appraisal or re-conceptualisation of a field of study. However, effective theoretical reviews can make an enormous contribution to the development of understanding of a topic. A good example of a productive theoretical review is the work on time-limited counselling by Steenbarger (1992). In this paper, Steenbarger constructs a theoretical model that facilitates the application of the results of a large number of research studies to practice.

Assembling a literature review

The issues involved in finding literature and choosing a structure within which it can be effectively summarised and communicated have already been discussed. The actual mechanics of assembling a review are also worth mention. It is essential to devise a system for keeping track of each item that has been read and the main elements of what it has said. Many people employ a card index for this purpose, writing the topic, title and reference details of each item at the top of the card, with some notes on the content of the paper on the remainder of the card. It is important to record the reference details at the time of reading the paper, since inevitably it becomes harder to trace these facts at a later date, and it can be very frustrating to have completed a paper or project but be delayed in finishing it off due to a search for one or two missing references. Increasingly, the widespread use of personal computers has enabled researchers to keep bibliographic data on computer files. Software can be purchased that will translate references into the formats required by different journals or publishers.

Conclusions

The intention of this chapter has been to offer a guide to reading and reviewing the research literature. One of the issues that has been implicit in this discussion has been the inaccessibility of much of the literature. It is hard enough for academics to keep up with the literature and know what has been published. In fact, some leading academic therapy researchers admit that it is *impossible* to read everything published in their field (Orlinsky et al., 1994). It is even harder for practitioners who might be eager to learn about the contribution of research to their clinical work. Presumably, the rapid development of information technologies will eventually make research literature databases and even copies of journals available on-line in homes and offices. At the moment, however, readers and makers of counselling research must employ a range of strategies and accept that the frustrations of placing research in context are matched by the occasional delight of finding the one paper that makes a difference.

Further reading

These books are useful guides to the intricacies of assembling a literature review.

Fink, A. (1998) *Conducting Research Literature Reviews: From Paper to the Internet.* Thousand Oaks, CA: Sage.

Hart, C. (1998) *Doing a Literature Review: Releasing the Social Science Research Imagination.* London: Sage.

McLeod, J. (1999a) *Practitioner Research in Counselling.* London: Sage. Offers an explicitly practitioner-oriented discussion of the process of engaging with the literature.

3 The Research Process: Stages, Tasks and Traps

Carrying through a piece of research is a complex task, one that involves a substantial commitment of time and energy. It is no surprise that the vast majority of counsellors and psychotherapists who have completed research studies have only ever done so in the supportive and structured environment of a Masters or Doctoral programme. There are a number of distinct stages in the life of a research project. In this chapter the various challenges that each of these stages represent will be examined.

Experienced researchers are well aware of a substantial set of traps and obstacles that can interrupt, slow down or sabotage even the most sensible pieces of research. Hodgson and Rollnick (1996) have constructed a list of things that can and often do go wrong with research (Box 3.1). These pithy observations convey some uncomfortable truths about applied research in areas such as counselling and psychotherapy. In particular, there are always dilemmas over role conflict, control and time.

To gather data on any aspect of counselling involves interrupting and dis-rupting, and adding to, the on-going work and activities of counsellors and clients. In most settings, there are few if any pre-existing expectations regarding the role of the researcher. The person doing research typically must negotiate entry and access, and rely on the goodwill of others.

Another truth implicit in the Hodgson and Rollnick (1996) list of maxims is the fact that it is never possible to devise a research design that will unfold entirely according to plan. There will always be crises. Good planning is necessary to minimise these unexpected turns of events so that they do not precipitate the total collapse of a study. Published research articles of necessity present a polished and rational account of the aims, methods and results of an investi-gation. The reality of actually doing the study may be quite different. Sociological researchers have written vividly about their experiences in the field (Bell and Newby, 1977; Douglas and Johnson, 1977), and the anxiety, confusion and uncertainty they have felt in the research role. Within the field of counselling research, Etherington (2000) and Grafanaki (1996) provide valuable accounts of the complexity of roles and values, and the level of personal challenge, involved in doing research which involves clients.

It is important to recognise that research is very demanding of time. The routine preparation, administration and analysis of research materials takes longer than might be anticipated, because these are tasks that require careful attention to detail. Also, the work of cognitive assimilation and comprehension of

Box 3.1   How to survive a research project: some predictable crises

Getting started will take twice as long as the data collection.
The number of available subjects/interviewees will be one-tenth of your first estimate.
Completion of a research project will take twice as long as your last estimate and three times as long as your first estimate.
A research project will change twice in the middle.
The help provided by other people has a half-life of two weeks.
The tedium of research is directly proportional to its objectivity.
The effort of writing up is an exponential function of the time since the data was collected.
At the finish you will have regrets.

Source: Hodgson and Rollnick (1996)

the meaning of data is impossible to do in a hurry: it takes time for these meanings to 'sink in'.

The research cycle

Research can be understood as constituting a cyclical process incorporating question-finding, planning, data-gathering, data analysis, writing and dissemination. Each cycle through these six stages, which are described below, will yield a research 'product' such as a talk, report or paper. Usually, a single cycle of inquiry will leave the researcher with more questions and with a surer sense of the techniques and strategies that might be employed to gather quality data on the topic. These outcomes trigger off another cycle of inquiry. The output of well-established researchers or research groups is built upon dozens of cycles of investigation. Accounts of the cyclical nature of two very different types of research can be found in Cunningham (1988), who writes about a very personal investigation of learning, and Strupp (1993), who describes the continuity in the research programme directed by him at Vanderbilt University. The books edited by Hoshmand and Martin (1994) and Dryden (1996) include further examples of how a line of research is built up over a number of cycles of inquiry. Researchers who are limited by time and resources to only one inquiry cycle, for example people doing research for a BA or Masters degree, may often feel frustrated at their inability to go on to do the study 'properly'.

Question-finding

Research is guided by questions. The aim of research is to be able to answer questions and to generate new questions that open up previously taken-for-granted areas of experience. But where do questions come from? Some counselling research is stimulated by 'burning questions' that arise from practical experience. Ross (1994) gives some examples of the interplay between research and practice in his own career as a student counsellor. But many other would-be researchers, particularly those faced with the demand to choose a research topic to be pursued for a college or university degree, become blocked and uncertain at this point. There are so many potential topics from which to select. Considerations of relevance, importance, practicability, legitimacy and interest value flood in, making the choice even harder.

One strategy for narrowing down the field and converging on a specific research topic is to think ahead to the end of the study and ask: who is it for? Who is the intended audience of my research? There are basically five audiences for counselling research: the person doing the research, other counsellors, managers and policy makers, the general public, and other researchers. The interests of these different audiences are not by any means the same, although they will to some extent overlap. For example, a piece of personal research such as the study by Sussman (2001) into the significance of psychoperistalsis and tears in therapy, by Ryden and Loewenthal (2001) into the influence of therapist sexuality on the experience of lesbian clients, will have the aim of discovering more about a phenomenon felt by the author to be important. By contrast, research that is intended to have an impact on counsellors' practice will be likely to rely on case reports, and include detailed descriptive material on clients and interventions. Policy-oriented studies require data that can be used to address issues of cost–benefit and cost-effectiveness. Articles for the general public need to include vivid examples and case histories. Research aiming to advance the literature must be explicitly linked to issues, theories and methods already identified as important in previously published work. The anticipated audience or 'market' for a piece of research can be seen to have an important influence on the way a study is carried out, the type of methods that are used, and the form in which it is written up.

Once the researcher has selected his or her audience or audiences, it is helpful to look at the kinds of research reports that have been published for that group. If the intended audience is identifiable and accessible (e.g. other counsellors in a professional association, the management executive of an agency, key contributors to the research literature) it can be productive to go and ask them about the kind of study they would like to see carried out. It is worth noting, with some regret, that at the present moment it is difficult to envisage clients as consumers of research, except in so far as clients or would-be clients will read popular articles in newspapers and magazines. An important factor in the choice of audience is the function that the research is intended to have in the personal or professional development or broader 'life projects' of the person carrying it out. The choice of research question is an issue that can usefully be worked on in personal therapy, or explored with supportive friends or colleagues. It is essential to be aware, for example, of the implications of tackling an investigation into a question that is very personal. With highly personal studies, the researcher may find it difficult to gain enough distance from his or her own individual experience to be able to grasp the bigger picture implied in the experiences of others. Also, it may be hard to write up autobiographical material that still evokes strong, raw feelings. There are other literary forms, such as novels, autobiographies or poetry, that are more appropriate in allowing a voice to the person. On the other hand, a research study that does not connect with any personal experience runs the danger of becoming dry and lacking in motivation and sparkle. Devereaux (1967) suggests that all psychological research topics are chosen because they hold an unconscious meaning for the researcher. If a research project is to be located within the context of the career development of the person carrying it out, then it is necessary to look at what this will entail in terms of how the findings might be presented to managers and interview panels, and to shape the study accordingly.

There are different types of research question. Sometimes questions may be intentionally open and loosely boundaried, as in qualitative research. Examples of this type of question would be 'what is the client's experience of a therapy session?' (Rennie, 1990) or 'what is the experience of being really understood?' (van Kaam, 1969). These are open, exploratory questions. In other research situations, for example in most quantitative research, questions will be formulated as precise hypotheses of the type: 'behavioural counselling will be more effective than client-centred counselling for students with study skills problems'. This is a more precise question, which seeks to confirm the truth (or otherwise) of a proposition, rather than opening up an area for exploration. In any study, it is unlikely that there will be just one question. Part of the work of identifying a research question is to unfold or unpack that question into its constituent sub-questions. Usually, the original, 'big' question that motivates a piece of research is too all-encompassing to be answered within a single study. It is only by deconstructing the question that it is possible to find a version of it that can be addressed meaningfully within the time and resources that are available. Techniques such as brainstorming (Rawlinson, 1981) or mind-maps (Buzan, 1974) may be helpful at this stage. An example of the deconstruction of a question would be to begin with a research question such as 'how effective is Gestalt Therapy?' Box 3.2 gives some of the sub-questions that can be derived from this central theme. It can be seen that many of these sub-questions look like practicable research studies, whereas the original topic would have called for a massive piece of research. 'Big questions' represent a lifetime of work, a career choice rather than a single study.

The task of breaking a question down is liable to generate a long list of many aspects of the topic that could potentially be of interest. Techniques such as brainstorming or mind-mapping tend to increase awareness of the number of meanings that can be associated with a core concept. It is a mistake at this point to fall into the trap of attempting to find or invent measures for all the variables that might be identified at this stage, or include them all in an interview schedule.

Box 3.2   Breaking down a question and finding a research focus

The 'big question': 'How effective is Gestalt therapy?'
Sub-questions:

1   Specifying the client group. 'How effective is Gestalt therapy with . . . depressed people, clients in private practice, students reporting exam anxiety . . . etc.?'
2   Specifying aspects of the therapy. 'How effective are the following elements of Gestalt therapy . . . two-chair work, dreamwork, art exercises . . . etc.?'
3   Specifying methodological issues. 'Can the effectiveness of Gestalt therapy be most appropriately assessed through interviews, changes in questionnaire measures, diaries kept by clients, Interpersonal Process Recall . . . etc.?'

Resulting in a focused and practicable research study: 'Effects of Gestalt two-chair interventions on anxiety levels in exam-phobic college students'.

To do so is to risk getting bogged down in a study that is over-complex and in which it is difficult to summarise all the results adequately, never mind analyse them in depth.

It can often be useful, at this stage in a study, to attempt to create a model of the topic being studied. A good model provides a visual depiction of the relationships between variables. It must be more than a mere listing of variables, but should indicate the possible cause and effect linkages, feedback loops, sequences and process linkages that might exist. A useful heuristic device that can facilitate model construction in any branch of the social sciences is to ask: what are the stages in the development of this phenomenon? Any human or social activity develops and changes over time. As a rule of thumb, a usable model will have fewer than seven elements. More than this number can make a model very difficult to comprehend. The mechanics of model construction are facilitated by using large pieces of paper, coloured pens, and a generally playful attitude.

Constructing a model at this point in a study has a number of advantages. It can help the researcher to be explicit about what needs to be observed and may enable decisions to be made about which areas or variables are of crucial importance (central to the model) and which can be omitted from the study. The model can also aid the 'reflexive' researcher to keep track of how his or her own personal understandings are changed through engagement with actual informants (the concept of reflexivity is explored further in Chapters 6 and 11). Perhaps most important of all, constructing a model enforces progression from a static to a process conception of the phenomena being investigated. Finally, the existence of a preliminary model will assist the researcher in communicating with a supervisor or with people who might be interested in supporting or sponsoring the study.

It can be helpful to start writing at this early stage of a research project. Wolcott (1990) recommends that at the beginning of a study the researcher should write out as much as possible of the final report. This allows him or her to get a sense of what they already know, and what they need to know. It is also a way of being able to externalise personal biases so that they can be tackled in the open rather than operating at an unconscious level. Keeping a research diary or journal is helpful as a means of recording hunches and ideas, and as an aid to reflexivity.

To summarise: the question-finding stage of a research study encompasses a range of tasks and potential traps. It can be valuable to apply some of the principles of creative thinking (Sternberg, 1988; Taylor and Getzels, 1975) to this phase of the work, which can be likened to a gestation period. There is evidence that creative solutions to problems often emerge from a process of immersion in a question, absorbing new information from every source possible. The key to the creative solution will often appear in an image, fantasy, joke or dream, reflecting a degree of loosening or 'unfreezing' of constructs. This is a process that takes time, but can be assisted through creativity techniques such as brainstorming and mind-maps. Counsellors and psychotherapists embarking on research may recognise the similarities between the task of question-finding and the work of therapy itself:

> creativity involves turning one's attention from the well-articulated explicit form in which one interprets something, to one's as yet unformulated felt sense of the whole situation – exactly what effective psychotherapy involves. The creative individual is the one who doesn't scorn his vague impressions, who can stand a few moments of attention to his conceptually vague but concretely felt impressions, and who formulates them. (Gendlin et al., 1968: 219)

It is helpful to begin writing at this stage as a way of capturing the personal meanings associated with the study, and also as a platform for later more formalised reports. This writing is a means of formulating the 'conceptually vague but concretely felt' new insights emerging from immersion in the research process. Leaving all the writing to the end is to risk losing these learnings.

Constructing a research plan

Once a research question or topic has been identified, the next stage is that of detailed *planning*. The various tasks to be undertaken at this stage are listed in Box 3.3. The question-finding and model-building aspects of this phase have been dealt with in the preceding section, and the issues involved in reviewing the literature are discussed in Chapter 2. These can be viewed as preliminary to the formulation of a detailed research plan. The critical facets of the planning stage are selecting a research design and working out how it will be realised in practice.

> ## Box 3.3 Tasks in planning and designing a research study
>
> Identifying the topic or interest, and audience
> Filling in the background. Reviewing the literature. Not re-inventing the wheel
> Formulating a researchable question or hypothesis
> Looking closely at the question. Identifying sub-questions. Creating an initial model
> Deciding on a general research approach
> Deciding on the scale and design of the study
> Deciding on the research sample
> Negotiating access to informants and research sites
> Deciding on which techniques to use to collect data
> Anticipating the nature of data analysis
> Deciding whether or not a pilot study is required
> Assessing the research plan on ethical grounds and developing procedures to ensure informed consent and confidentiality
> Checking that there is consistency and coherence between the aims of the research and the data-gathering and data-analysis techniques
> Working out a timetable and costing
> Finalising a research plan, writing it out and having it approved by stakeholders (e.g. colleagues, managers, supervisor, Ethics Committee)

Research design

The concept of research design is a major topic in its own right, and several books have been written about the innumerable design variants that can be employed in different situations, including in therapy research. The reader interested in exploring this subject in more detail is encouraged to consult Robson (2002) for general principles of research design, and Heppner, Kivlighan and Wampold (1999) for a thorough discussion of design issues in counselling research. Examples of many different research designs are provided in later chapters concerned with outcome studies (Chapter 8), process studies (Chapter 9), quantitative approaches (Chapter 4), qualitative methods (Chapter 6) and case studies (Chapter 7). It may be helpful, however, to follow Horowitz (1982) in reducing these designs into three general types: contrast group studies, relational studies and descriptive studies.

Contrast group studies are controlled experiments where the researcher randomly allocates subjects to different conditions. This type of design allows rigorous testing of the causal effects of different conditions or interventions and usually involves a certain amount of manipulation on the part of the researcher –

for example, assigning clients to different types of intervention. *Relational* or *correlational studies* involve the examination of the level of association or correlation between different factors. For example, in a survey of counsellors, it might be interesting to look at the correlation or association between theoretical orientation and attitude to supervision. Finally, *descriptive studies* involve careful observation and classification of 'what one finds' within a single case, or through a series of interviews with a group of people.

Another consideration that needs to be taken into account when selecting a research design is the theoretical context of the study. This context will encompass the counselling theory that will inform the study, and also the stance that is adopted in relation to theory of knowledge or philosophy of science. As discussed in Chapter 1, the positivist and constructionist views of science generate contrasting prescriptions for methodology. The theory of counselling that is espoused will also influence the choice of research design, since particular forms of research are considered more acceptable than others within specific schools of therapy. For example, the 'new paradigm' methods described in Chapter 10 are consistent with the world-view and values of humanistic psychology, but would not sit easily within a behavioural approach. There have been some examples of research designs that have crossed these philosophical boundaries. The most significant of these programmes has been the body of research that has employed the methods of experimental psychology to test the validity of Freudian theory (Kline, 1981). This combination of positivist methods and hermeneutically inspired theory has been productive in generating data but has been dismissed by analysts as missing the point (Rycroft, 1966). There are many traps surrounding the subject of research design. It is easy to become preoccupied with the need to come up with the perfect design. However, the hope of finding a perfect research design is best viewed as an irrational belief – all research plans have their weaknesses and limitations. It is often helpful to look closely at studies that have already been published, and borrow design features from studies that appear to have been successful in producing knowledge that is relevant and appropriate.

In planning a study, it is essential to give careful consideration to its scale or scope. The length of time available to carry out the study is an important factor. For example, longitudinal studies, in which the development of factors is tracked over long periods, are rarely carried out because they cannot be completed within the time limits of most college courses or research grants. Research designs that involve negotiating access to clients through their counsellors, advertising in the media for informants, or building up trust with informants, are all highly time-consuming. The scale of a study also refers to the number of participants or subjects that are used. Where quantitative, statistical methods are employed, the 'power' ratio of the tests being used will determine the number of subjects that need to be included in each condition. For example, the assumptions for the chi-square test, a technique for testing differences between two samples where the measure is on a nominal scale (see Chapter 4), are not operative if there are fewer than five subjects in any sub-group. It needs to be remembered that in reality some subjects will drop out or produce unusable data, so it is sensible to aim for more than the minimal number of subjects necessary to satisfy statistical power requirements.

Where qualitative methods are employed, different considerations are relevant. The goal of qualitative research is to produce intensive, authentic descriptive accounts of experience and action, and if too many informants are recruited, it will prove impossible to do justice to their contributions in the research report. Also, in most qualitative research it is necessary to transcribe tape-recordings of interviews or conversations, and each hour of recording will generate around four hours of transcribing.

Other factors that may have a bearing on the scale of a study are the extent of cooperation offered by others and the cost of tests, tapes and other research materials. It should be kept in mind that large numbers are not necessary for valid research. In Chapter 7 there is a full discussion of various case study designs that rely on just one participant or therapy dyad.

Sampling

Having decided on the number of subjects or informants that are to be sought, the next task is to determine the sampling strategy that is to be used in selecting them. The research sample can be defined as the people who actually participate in a study. The research population represents the total set of people from whom the sample is drawn. There are a number of strategies for constructing samples that provide a representative and unbiased sub-group from that population. Random sampling (e.g. including every third person on a list of clients who have used an agency) is a standard approach that is used in many research situations. However, there may be occasions when random sampling would not turn up enough representatives of particular groups that were of theoretical interest. For example, there are relatively few people from non-white ethnic groups among the population of clients in most British counselling agencies, and so if random sampling were used in a study of the ethnic origins of clients in such an agency it would be unlikely to yield a large enough sample of people from Black and Asian ethnic backgrounds. In this situation it is more effective to introduce stratified sampling, in which the population is divided into sub-groups or strata, and a random sample selected from each stratum.

Random and stratified sampling are only possible when the researcher has a fair amount of knowledge and control regarding the research population as a whole. In a study of drug users who do not visit a drug clinic, for example, very little can be known about the research population. In this situation, a researcher might employ the sampling technique of 'snowballing', which involves starting with one or two representative informants who are known, and then being introduced by them to other members of the relevant population. In this instance, the researcher must use whatever relevant information is available from inform-ants (e.g. their opinions about how many drug users avoid the clinic) to estimate the extent to which an unbiased sample has been achieved.

There are other situations where the investigator needs to build in to the research design methods of checking on the representativeness of the sample. If a researcher is carrying out a mail questionnaire survey of members of a professional association, perhaps to assess the proportions of members who espouse different theoretical orientations, he or she may decide to aim for a random sample of every tenth name on the membership list. In this type of research, it is inevitable that not all of the people who receive the questionnaire will return it, so it is important to calculate the degree to which the sample achieved is representative of the population as a whole. The standard means of doing this is to compare the demographic characteristics of the pople who filled in questionnaires with the demographic data held on the membership records. If the people who completed the questionnaire have a similar enough age, gender, experience and job profile to the total membership, then the sample can be considered satisfactory. In cases when this kind of comparison is not possible, another approach is to contact some of the people who did not return the questionnaire, for example by telephoning or writing to them, and look for any systematic differences between them and those who have complied.

The concepts of sampling discussed so far have relied on the assumption that an adequate sample is as close a mirror to the larger population as can be practically achieved. However, within qualitative and case study research the focus of the investigation will be on the intensive analysis of one or at best a few cases. In this situation the notion of representativeness has a different meaning. In qualitative research, examples or cases may be selected because they are typical, because they are extreme cases (e.g. comparing the most and least successful cases from a set of people who all received the same type of therapy) or because they are theoretically interesting (Strauss and Corbin, 1998).

In formalising or making explicit the type of sample that is to be used, it is helpful to specify in advance the inclusion and exclusion criteria that are to be used in selecting research participants. For example, a study of the effectiveness of counselling may include every person applying for therapy during a six-month period except (exclusion criterion) those who report suicidal thoughts in an assessment interview. The more clearly that inclusion and exclusion criteria can be stated at the start, the less likely it will be that unwanted biases will creep in as the study proceeds.

Access to research participants

Sample size is an abstract idea that can only be put into practice through some process of gaining access to informants or subjects. It can often be frustrating and difficult to negotiate approval to interview or test potential research participants. Not only counsellors but also the managers and administrators of human service agencies tend to be protective toward their clients. Most state-funded clinics and agencies employ formal procedures such as Ethics or Research Committees for evaluating requests for access to clients. These committees often apply strict criteria and safeguards, and may meet infrequently. Involvement with such bodies can be helpful for the researcher in forcing him or her to be as clear as possible about what will be demanded of participants, and what steps will be taken to prevent harm, but this stage of research planning can also bring about long delays. Voluntary and private sector agencies, and private practitioners, less often employ formal vetting procedures, but their ad hoc decision-making arrangements may cause even longer delays.

Whether they insist that the request be written up as a formal proposal, or are satisfied with discussing the issues in face-to-face meetings, the person or group from whom research access is being sought will want information about the aims, scope and design of the study as a whole. They will also be interested in knowing how much of their time will be taken up with the study, and what arrangements there will be for maintaining confidentiality (see Chapter 10). They will want to see copies of any questionnaires, interview schedules, letters to participants and informed consent forms. Finally, individuals or agencies collaborating in research will usually seek confirmation that they will be given copies of any written reports, will be consulted over any press releases or other media coverage, and will have the right to comment on or veto drafts of any published articles. They may wish to be acknowledged in publications.

Given the large number of issues that must be successfully handled if access is to be granted to use clients or other defined groups in research, it is no surprise that much research is carried out with populations to which it is far easier to gain entry: colleagues, friends and college students. Another strategy for minimising access problems is to re-analyse data already gathered by someone else, or build an extra component in to a study for which approval has already been granted.

Selecting instruments

At some point in this planning process, it is necessary to identify the techniques or instruments that are to be employed in the collection of data. Many different data-gathering techniques have been used in counselling research, and examples of these methods can be found in other chapters of this book. There are some principles that can be used to guide the selection of research instruments. In most cases, it is an advantage to utilise instruments that have already been employed in other studies. In fact, an important aspect of the literature review is to survey the usage of different data-gathering strategies and instruments in the particular field of inquiry. If an instrument or technique has been used in several studies, and has attracted a literature on its validity, reliability, norms, acceptability to users and other properties, so much the better. If no such standard tool exists, and it is necessary to invent a new test, rating scale, questionnaire, coding system or interview schedule for the sole purpose of being used in a study, then two issues must be borne in mind. Firstly, there are established procedures for test construction (these are summarised in Chapter 5) that should be followed. Secondly, it will be essential to carry out a pilot test to check on the value of the new instrument.

The number and type of research instruments being used must be balanced against the amount of time that research participants are willing to give to the task, and the time and expense of coding and analysing the resulting data. It is inconsiderate, and possibly unethical, to ask research participants to supply data which will not be used. Very often published articles in the public domain only give a general outline of what is included in a test or rating scale, and researchers wishing to make use of these tools must contact whoever holds the copyright of the instrument. Some research instruments can only be used by people with special training, or with the permission of the author or a licensing body. The possible existence of such constraints should be checked out before making a commitment to use any particular technique in a study. When thinking about the choice of data-gathering technique it is also necessary to think about how the instrumentation fits in with the underlying theoretical rationale for the study. Does a rating scale or interview schedule furnish adequate information in relation to the constructs it is supposed to measure or themes it is designed to explore? At the same time it is necessary to think about the kind of data the instrument will generate, and how this data is to be analysed. For example, it is a mistake to design a questionnaire that yields categorical or nominal 'yes/no' answers, and then expect to carry out complex statistical analyses on separate items. The more ambitious or sophisticated statistical tests can only operate with parametric data (see Chapter 4) supplied through interval-scale measurement achieved through the use of items with 5-point response scales or multiple item tests. There are many other ways in which the researcher must anticipate just how the data being generated match the aims of the study. For example, if it is intended to examine age differences in the sample, then a suitable question must be provided for respondents to indicate their age.

Ethical issues

Throughout the planning stage of a study it is valuable to keep under review any possible ethical implications of the investigation. Chapter 10 gives more information on a range of ethical issues that may arise in counselling research. The most common issues are: confidentiality, avoidance of harm to participants, and procedures for dealing with distress caused to participants. A valuable strategy that a researcher can employ to sensitise himself or herself to possible ethical or moral difficulties is to experience the study imaginatively from the points of view of all potential participants, e.g. clients, counsellors, people excluded from the study, interviewers, observers, etc.

Completing the plan

At some point in the planning of a study it will almost certainly be necessary to carry out a pilot study. Usually it is more helpful to run through the study with a few well-motivated pilot participants who are willing to give feedback on instruments and procedures, rather than to administer the data-gathering techniques to large numbers of people who might not be in a position to comment thoughtfully on the task. A pilot study can provide information on how long it takes participants to complete the research instruments, whether any items or instructions are unclear, whether anything obvious has been left out, and whether the task evokes emotional reactions. In de-briefing pilot participants, it is often more effective to ask them for their advice on whether, in their view, other people would have any difficulty with the task, rather than requiring them to admit to any problems with it themselves. Another benefit of a pilot study is that it gives the researcher some practice in controlling the research situation, and can enable her or him to be (or appear to be) more confident or authoritative when the time comes to gather the actual data that will be included in the study.

Central to an effective research plan is careful costing in terms of time and money. Right at the start of the planning stage it is helpful to construct a rough timetable outlining the dates by which different research tasks will be accomplished. As the plan crystallises, these target dates can be made more specific. It is important to be realistic not only about the amount of time that various tasks will take, but also about other competing demands on time, such as work, holidays and family commitments. Careful costing is necessary if the researcher intends to negotiate in advance for the resources that might be needed to carry out the study.

The final stage of a research plan is to bring everything together into a formal proposal. In many research situations there will be external groups or bodies who will need to approve the plan before it can be put into action (Strain and Kerr, 1984). These external monitors might include academic supervisors, the Ethics Committee of a hospital, or the executive of a funding body. Each of these groups will have their own criteria or expectations regarding the information that should be included in a proposal. A list of the types of headings that are often used in research proposals is given in Box 3.4.

Box 3.4   Sections in a research proposal

Aims and objectives of the study
Review of the literature on the topic
Research questions
Design of the study
Research sample: characteristics, inclusion and exclusion criteria, access
Ethical issues
Procedures for data collection
Method of data analysis
Dissemination of results
Timetable and costing
Equipment
Qualifications and experience of researcher/research team
Tasks and time commitment of members of research team
Names of referees

Data-gathering

The data-gathering stage of a study is the point at which the robustness of the research plan is tested in practice. Will people return questionnaires or turn up for interviews? How often will the video or tape recorder break down? It is during data collection that the researcher is conventionally 'busy', interviewing people, administering tests and collating data. There are many different methods of gathering data in counselling research, and the choice of technique will depend on a range of factors such as the aims of the study, time constraints, what will be acceptable to participants, and researcher knowledge and skill. These methods are discussed in the following chapters. An important principle to be taken into consideration when selecting data-gathering techniques is that each method has its own distinctive strengths and weaknesses. For example, a psychological test will yield normative scores, but will not give access to the richness and complexity of personal experience. Face-to-face interviews, by contrast, can be used to generate sensitive qualitative data, but are more liable than questionnaires to be influenced by the personality or interpersonal style of the interviewer. In many research situations it is useful to employ a *multi-method* approach, using different techniques of data-gathering to address the same phenomenon. In this way, the limitations of each method can be balanced against the strengths of others. Ideally, the data gleaned from different techniques will converge on the same conclusions.

Data analysis

It is important to give careful thought during the planning stage of a study to the way that the data will eventually be analysed. There are few things more frustrating than taking great trouble to gather data and then finding that it cannot be analysed appropriately. For example, it is common for researchers to gather far more data than they have time to analyse properly. If a qualitative study is being attempted, data analysis may involve many hours transcribing and analysing each case in depth. This will restrict the number of cases that can be dealt with, and so a research design that specifies a large sample is inconsistent with the form of data analysis envisaged. In quantitative or statistical studies, large data sets may be handled with ease by a computer, but the researcher still needs to have the time to enter the data and interpret the output, and sufficient space available in the final paper or dissertation to present all the tables of results.

In quantitative research, a range of technical or statistical data analyses issues may arise. Not all statistics software packages are able to perform all of the tests or operations that might be necessary, so it is essential to check the menu of the particular package that is to be employed. The more powerful packages are capable of almost any analysis, but occupy large amounts of memory, and will operate extremely slowly on some personal computers. However, even the most sophisticated statistics software can only work with the data that is fed into it. Statistical tests are designed around assumptions regarding the type of quanti- fication they can deal with. There are major differences between the kinds of statistical operations that can be carried out on parametric and non-parametric data sets (these terms are explained in the next chapter). Also, if the numbers of subjects in a particular sub-group are too small, it may prove impossible to achieve meaningful statistical analyses. Similarly, in some situations missing data (e.g. participants forgetting to answer a question) may lead to statistical difficulties.

The researcher or research team must make decisions about when to analyse the data. Usually, all the data is gathered and then analysed at one time. This approach is sometimes driven by a feeling that if the researcher knew the way the results were going, he or she might exert an unconscious influence on later research participants to conform (or otherwise) to this trend. By contrast, in many qualitative studies, the researcher will analyse data as it is gathered, with the explicit intention of sensitively altering the kind of questions that are asked of later informants to accommodate what he or she has learned from earlier ones.

Studies in which both quantitative and qualitative data are gathered present distinct issues in analysis. There are different rules or 'logics of justification' associated with these different approaches. For example, it could be argued that it violates the rationale for qualitative research to gather personal and experi- ential material and then to quantify it. There are a number of analytic strategies for dealing with this type of 'pluralist' approach to research, which are discussed in Chapter 11.

The main point being stressed here is that the method of data analysis is a research planning and design question, to be thoroughly worked out before any data is ever gathered. As with many other research design issues, it is valuable to look closely at good-quality published studies, to learn how experienced researchers have tackled the problems in research situations similar to the project that is being planned.

Writing up

Good researchers are also skilled writers. There are a large number of interesting and worthwhile counselling research studies that have never been published or disseminated because the people who carried them out were unable to cope with the task of writing. Many students on counselling training courses are well able to write essays, but become blocked and anxious when faced with the task of writing up their research dissertation. Usually this is because they have had a lot of practice in writing essays, during the course and in their previous job or education, but have had no prior experience of constructing a research report. Writing a research report is a complex task. Different types of information – technical, descriptive, analytical – must be combined. Somewhere in the report will be new knowledge, which must be introduced and explained to the reader.

Box 3.5   Suggestions for easing the pain of writing

Start writing at the very beginning of the project. Keep writing all the way through.

At the start of a project, write a draft without data. This will clarify what data you need to get. It will also give you a record of why you are doing the study.

Write regularly. Find a time and place for your writing. Get in a rhythm.

If you get stuck on one section, go on to something else. When you return to the original piece, you will probably be able to see much more clearly what needs to be done with it.

Ask other people how they write. Be prepared to learn.

Think about your audience or readership. Imagine you are telling people what you have found. Use seminars, teaching and talks to structure your ideas on your topic.

Writing means re-writing. Accept that whatever you write will need to be revised.

Write in the active tense.

Edit out unnecessary adverbs and adjectives. Use fewer words.

Use sub-headings.

Ask other people to look at what you have done. Any passages that are unclear to your readers are by definition unclear. It is not enough that you understand what you mean – the aim is to communicate to others.

Writing is a form of thinking. You do not have to have everything worked out before you start writing. The act of writing will help you to clarify what you mean.

Get it out of the door. Your research is doing nobody any good while it remains in your filing cabinet.

Behind all this, there can often be an exaggerated image of the level of expertise and intelligence that is required to carry out research, accompanied by a self-image that falls far below this exalted standard. These problems may be exacerbated by the fact that much research, particularly in colleges and universities, is carried out in isolation. The researcher finds himself or herself alone in a room with notes, data and a deadline.

There are a number of solutions to these difficulties, some of which are summarised in Box 3.5. There are several very useful self-help books that have been produced for students and academic writers, such as Becker (1986), Wolcott (1990), Richardson (1991) and Bell (1993). Parry (1996) and the final chapter of Cozby (1985) are also helpful. The fundamental message of these texts is that academic or research writing comprises a set of skills that must be acquired through practice, trial and error, observation and consultation with others.

Dissemination of results

There is a range of ways that counselling research findings can be disseminated:

- talks to local groups;
- papers read at national and international conferences;
- workshops;
- sending copies of a report to key individuals and organisations;
- selling copies of a report;
- articles in the popular press (newspapers and magazines);
- articles in professional journals;
- papers in academic journals;
- books and chapters in books.

Each of these outlets employs its own criteria for what is acceptable or relevant. Researchers must adapt their style of writing to accommodate the expectations of editors and readers of these publications. It is essential, therefore, to look carefully at the kinds of articles that have previously been published in a journal or magazine, or the types of books that have been produced by a publisher, to gather information about where to send a report of a research study, and what it should look like when it is sent.

Academic and professional journals exist to make information available in the public domain, so it is always desirable to publish research findings in these places, even if other dissemination strategies are also used to reach a wider audience. There is a wide range of academic journals carrying papers on counselling and psychotherapy research (see Chapter 1), and so it is important to find the most appropriate journal for any specific study. Journal editors will normally respond constructively and helpfully to a letter describing the topic and asking whether they would welcome a paper on it. All journals include a statement, often inside the front cover, of their aims and terms of reference. Journals have different requirements regarding layout of articles and referencing formats, which should be checked before the article is written.

Virtually all journals send out papers to blind peer review. The title page (which carries the name of the author) is detached from the paper, and it is sent to three or four expert readers for comment. These referees then make a recommendation to the editor, who makes the final decision on whether or not to publish the paper. All this takes time, but it ensures the quality of what is published, and also means that writers can expect to receive detailed and well-informed feedback on what they have submitted. The majority of papers submitted to academic journals are not accepted in their original form, but are revised once or twice in the light of referees' comments. At the end of most published papers there is a sentence giving the date of submission and re-submission(s) of the article. It can often be facilitative to send off a paper to a journal in order to get feedback from referees. Many writers get trapped in their personal search for perfection, and are unwilling to send off an article unless it is 'perfect'. It can free such people to re-frame this process, so that what is being sent to the journal is not the final, 'perfect' version, but merely a 'good enough' version that can be used to elicit comment. It is important to be aware that it is not acceptable to send off the same article to more than one journal at a time. Journal reviewers and referees work voluntarily, and the system would break down if their workload was increased by multiple submissions. When submitting an article to a journal it is worth looking at the paper from the point of view of a prospective editor or reviewer. Garfield (1984), former editor of the *Journal of Consulting and Clinical Psychology*, supplies some valuable insights into the decision-making processes of editors.

Conclusions: completing the research process

It can be seen that there are many skills and tasks involved in the successful completion of a research study. A number of general themes emerge from this chapter. Doing research calls on a wide range of competencies, encompassing critical thinking, imagination, time-management, planning, self-discipline, organisation of paperwork, and writing. It is unlikely that anyone entering the research field will initially possess all these competencies at a sufficient level. To become an effective researcher requires not merely having a passionate interest in knowing more about a topic, but also being willing to learn about research methods and procedures. Doing research also draws upon a substantial commitment of time and resources. Some of the time spent on research needs to take the form of an intensive immersion in the project. It is hard to design or write up, or carry out certain types of analyses, without having lengthy blocks of time to devote solely to the task. Some research tasks can be done, and are perhaps better done, on a part-time basis, but other aspects of research require the full investment of the researcher in the work, if the eventual outcome is to be satisfactory. The final theme running through this chapter relates to the fundamental role of *collaboration* in research planning and implementation. There are many points in the research cycle where other people are needed, to provide information, teach skills, offer support and give critical feedback. Initiating and carrying through a research study can be viewed as a valuable and challenging form of personal and professional development, which involves negotiating and working together with people in a variety of different roles.

Further reading

Bickman, L. and Rog, D.J. (eds) (1998) *Handbook of Applied Social Research Methods*. London: Sage. A well-written and accessible social science methods textbook.

Breakwell, G.M., Hammond, S. and Fife-Schaw, C. (eds) (2000) *Research Methods in Psychology*, 2nd edn. London: Sage. Chapters written by experts in different approaches to research.

Heppner, P.P., Kivlighan Jr, D.M. and Wampold, B.E. (1999) *Research Design in Counseling*, 2nd edn. Pacific Grove, CA: Brooks/Cole. Clearly explains how experimental and quasi-experimental methods derived from the tradition of psychological research can be applied to counselling topics.

Parry, G. and Watts, F.N. (eds) (1996) *Behavioural and Mental Health Research: A Handbook of Skills and Methods*, 2nd edn. London: Psychology Press. The opening chapters in this book provide an excellent introduction to the practicalities of setting up a research study.

Robson, C. (2002) *Real World Research: A Resource for Social Scientists and Practitioner-Researchers*, 2nd edn. Oxford: Blackwell. A widely used and highly recommended general methods textbook.

4   Using Quantitative Methods

Historically, research into counselling and psychotherapy has largely been carried out by people trained in the disciplines of psychology and psychiatry. Within these disciplines or professions, there has existed a powerful adherence to a concept of science represented by practices such as experimentation, objectivity and accurate measurement of variables. Counselling, by contrast, is to a considerable extent a multi-disciplinary activity with practitioners drawn from a range of primary professions such as the arts, education, religion and social work as well as psychology and health care. Counsellors whose original intellectual training emphasised sociological analysis, interpretive approaches to understanding or action research frequently have difficulties in appreciating the contribution which quantitative methods can make to the inquiry process. At the same time, researchers socialised into the institutionally dominant quantitative and statistical model may fail to appreciate the validity of criticisms of their approach made by proponents of other methodological perspectives. The aim of this chapter, therefore, is not only to give an account of the ways in which numbers can be useful for counselling researchers, but also to consider some of the limitations and issues arising from the quantification of human experience.

The nature of measurement in counselling research can be illustrated by imagining a study in which an investigator is interested in the way that the feelings a client has during sessions might change over the course of counselling. For example, the investigator could be attempting to test the hypothesis that clients are more likely to feel anxious in early sessions, because of the unfamiliarity of the situation, and will only be able to express underlying feelings such as anger or grief once the establishment of a good relationship with the counsellor has enabled these initial anxieties to fade into the background. A research study of this kind could produce results that are of relevance to counsellor training, the preparation of clients for counselling, and the construction of models of counselling process. But how might such a study be carried out?

One possibility for the researcher would be to meet with the client after each session for a tape-recorded interview, and ask him or her to talk about what they felt during the session. This research strategy would yield a rich descriptive account or story, probably containing metaphors ('I felt as though I was going to explode') and idiosyncratic references ('I felt just like I did when I was told I had lost my job'). This type of data is not quantitative, but is 'qualitative': experience is encoded through an infinitely flexible language system. However, although qualitative data can be evocative and meaningful, it is difficult and time-consuming to move from the richness of an individual story to a systematic comparison across stories. If the researcher intends to compare the experiences reported by this informant with those elicited from other participants in the research, or wishes to test the hypothesis that feelings change at different stages in counselling, a different approach will almost certainly be required.

The application of quantitative methods makes it much easier to collate data across a number of people. When individual experience is encoded as a number rather than a word, phrase or sentence, a range of operations can be carried out which can facilitate the research process. A simple kind of measurement which could be applied in this study would be to give the client a check-list of feeling words, such as 'worried', 'sad', 'angry' and so on, and ask her or him to tick the ones that applied during the preceding session. This information is readily quanti-fiable, for instance by going through the list and coding 'worried' as '1', 'sad' as '2' and 'angry' as '3'. This kind of measurement is known as *nominal* or categorical, since it involves attaching numbers to named qualities or attributes. A very common kind of nominal measurement in research arises when people are asked to indicate their gender and the researcher codes 'female' as '1' and 'male' as '2'. Nominal measurement represents the most basic variety of quantification. Here, numbers are used as category labels in an arbitrary way; it would make just as much sense to code 'worried' as '3' and 'angry' as '1'. There is no relationship between numerical values in nominal scaling. For example, it would not be possible to argue that a score of 3 was 'more than' a score of 2. Nominal measurement merely allows the researcher to count up the number of times a particular quality or attribute (such as 'worried' or 'male') appears in a particular sample of people.

It should be apparent that there are serious limitations to nominal scaling of information about a psychological phenomenon such as feelings. One serious drawback is that, in the study being discussed, the client might tick 'sad' and also 'worried' because he or she had felt slightly sad at one point and had been deeply worried throughout the whole session. Nominal scaling only codes whether something is there or not, and conceals the intensity or amount of the quality being measured. Another option for the researcher might therefore be to ask the research participant to rank order the list of feeling words in order of which was felt most intensely or most often during the session. The client would be instructed to give '1' to the most powerful feeling, '2' to the next most powerful, continuing through the whole list of words. This kind of measurement is known as *ordinal*, because the numbers reflect a continuum with the largest amount of the quality at one end and the least amount at the other. In ordinal scaling there exists a relationship between numbers, and so more complex operations can be carried out on them. For example, in this study the rank order of feelings reported by one client could be compared, using a *correlation* statistic, with those reported by another client, to give an indication of the level of similarity between the two.

Ordinal measurement is like asking a room full of people to line up with the tallest at one end and the shortest at the other end. A more subtle way of assessing height, however, would be to measure each individual in terms of a standard unit of measurement such as inches or centimetres. The use of standard measurement units is known as *interval* scaling, since the attribute being meas-ured is assessed by units of measurement each of which represents an equal interval on a continuum. Within the field of psychological measurement, interval scaling is often achieved by using a rating scale. For example, a client could be asked to rate how angry he or she feels on a 7-point scale ranging from, say, 'extremely angry' to 'not at all angry'. Alternatively, the client may be asked to indicate the extent to which he or she agrees or disagrees with a statement such as 'during the last counselling session there were times when I felt angry' using a 5-point scale of 'strongly agree' to 'strongly disagree'. There is a special case of interval scaling known as the *ratio* scale, which applies to measurement scales in which the units of measurement are anchored in an absolute zero point. However, ratio scales are not common in social and psychological research.

Much of the time human attributes measured on an interval scale will form a *normal distribution*. The normal distribution is the familiar bell-shaped curve indicative of the fact that, on most human or social phenomena, most people are clustered round the middle of the range, with fewer people at the extremes.

These types of measurement allow a wide range of different forms of statistical analysis, some of which will be described below. Within the realm of statistics used by behavioural researchers, an important distinction is made between *parametric* and *non-parametric* statistics. Parametric statistics are operations that can be carried out on data which has achieved interval scale measurement and which is normally distributed. Non-parametric statistics are operations that can be applied to data that reflects ordinal or nominal levels of measurement. (The concept of the normal distribution has no meaning in relation to ordinal or nominal measures.)

One way of looking at statistics is to see them as a set of tools which can be used to answer questions. The construction of these tools, for example the mathematical assumptions and formulae which underpin them, will not be discussed here. The reader interested in learning more about these matters can consult one of the recommended texts listed at the end of the chapter. The availability of statistics packages on PCs in recent years has meant that it is possible to carry out sophisticated statistical procedures without necessarily knowing much about statistical theory or formulae. The aim in this chapter is to introduce some of the basic concepts of quantitative method, and to examine the ways they have been applied in counselling research.

A note of caution is perhaps appropriate at this point. Viewing statistical procedures as tools may suggest that they are neutral techniques just waiting to be pressed into service by the researcher. At some level this is perhaps true, but it needs to be recognised that statistical techniques not only shape the answers to questions, but can also influence the very questions that are asked in the first place. It could be argued that, too often, the questions asked by counselling researchers have been the ones that could be answered using statistical techniques.

Descriptive statistics

The statistical methods used in behavioural research can be divided into *descriptive* and *inferential* statistics. Descriptive statistics provide a description of the people in the research sample, in terms of the information collected on these people by the researcher. Inferential statistics, by contrast, enable the researcher to assess the confidence with which statements made about the sample being investigated will also be likely to hold true for the population as a whole. Some of the more commonly used descriptive statistics are introduced below.

The *frequency distribution* refers to the number of people who receive each possible score on a variable. This is essentially a tallying of numbers of people recording scores at each point on a scale. Usually, the frequency distribution is presented on a graph or histogram. The same information can be portrayed as a *cumulative frequency* distribution, in which the total number of scores at or below a particular score or interval is recorded. The information contained in a frequency distribution graph can be readily summarised, reducing the need for visual displays. There are two different aspects of the way that scores are distributed over a scale: *central tendency* and *variability*. Central tendency statistics indicate what the sample as a whole is like. The statistic most often cited is the *mean*, symbolised as X^a, which is calculated by taking the average of all scores. However, there are other valuable measures of central tendency. The *mode*, or modal score, refers to the most common score, the one recorded by most people in the sample. The *median* is the value that lies in the middle of the distribution. The median can be used to split a distribution in half, for example where the intention is to compare high- and low-scoring people on a variable.

Variability refers to the amount of spread in the distribution of scores. For example, the scores obtained using a test may fall into the bell-shaped curve of a normal distribution, or they may all cluster closely around the mean, or they may be spread evenly across the range. The *variance* statistic (s^2) indicates the extent to which scores deviate from the group mean. If there is a lot of deviation from the mean (i.e. if scores are spread out right across the range) then the variance will be high. The *standard deviation* statistic (abbreviated as s, s.d. or S.D.) is almost universally given in research reports as a measure of variability. (Standard deviation and variance are essentially the same statistic: standard deviation is simply the square root of the variance.)

The standard deviation statistic is employed to represent units of variability. The statistical convention is to divide the normal distribution curve into sections each of which is one standard deviation wide (see Figure 4.1). These standard deviation units are sometimes known as 'z-scores'. Each of these sections includes a proportion of the subjects in the sample. For example, 68 per cent of the sample lies within one standard deviation above or below the mean. One way of understanding this is to imagine that, roughly speaking, the 'normal' or average members of a sample are contained within this range of score. In therapy research this concept has many uses. For example, if clients entering counselling report scores that are more than two standard deviations above the mean on an anxiety scale, then an index of successful outcome might be that they have moved by the end of counselling to within one standard deviation of the mean. However, the main application of standard deviation statistics in therapy research has been through the concept of *effect size*. This is a concept that is used in studies of the outcome of counselling or psychotherapy. The effect

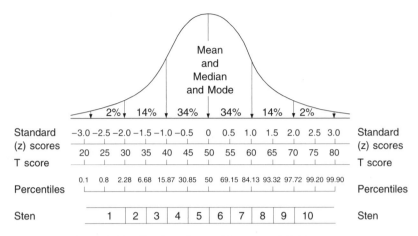

Figure 4.1   The Normal Distribution Curve (Bartram, 1990)

size can be defined as the difference between the means of experimental (treatment) and control (no treatment) groups, divided by the standard deviation of the control group (or the pooled sample of experimental and control groups taken together). An effect size of 1.00 would indicate that the therapeutic intervention being evaluated had been highly successful, because the mean (average) score of the client group had shifted by the amount of one standard deviation in the direction of 'health'.

Another application of the standard deviation and variance statistics in counselling research occurs in examining the question of the negative as well as positive effects of therapy. In many studies of therapy outcome, the mean and standard deviation statistics for a group of clients and comparison/control group are reported pre- and post-therapy. In many studies it can be seen that although the changes in mean scores for the treatment group are in a direction suggestive of good outcome, the variability in their scores as a group has increased, reflecting a wider dispersion between successful and unsuccessful cases than in the control group.

Dividing up the range into standard deviation units or z-scores is only one way of achieving a measure of where an individual score fits in relation to the sample as a whole. In Figure 4.1 it can be seen that the scale can be divided into T-scores, percentiles, standard ten (sten) scores and standard nine (stanine) scores in a similar fashion. These different measurement systems are all attempts to transform actual scores into normal distribution units, to facilitate comparisons between people. For example, a score of 12 on the Beck Depression Inventory and 23 on the MMPI Depression Scale might not mean very much to anyone unfamiliar with these tests. However, if these raw scores can be expressed as z-scores or sten units, then it can readily be seen whether or not the two tests are in agreement.

In many situations it can be helpful to know about extreme scores on a measure, and to achieve this the sample can be described not only in terms of mean and standard deviation statistics but also by giving information about the *range* of scores obtained. This is usually described in terms of minimum and maximum scores.

It should be noted that seldom or never does data fall into a perfectly symmetrical bell-shaped normal distribution curve as depicted in Figure 4.1. In the real world, data is often *skewed* with a tail going to the left (negatively skewed) or to the right of the graph (positively skewed). Some distributions have two peaks, and can be described as *bimodal*. The degree of peakedness or flatness of a distribution is known as its *kurtosis*. However, for most practical statistical purposes these characteristics can be disregraded unless they are of an exaggerated nature, in which case they probably indicate some kind of technical deficiency in the test or measure being employed. For example, if the distribution of responses to a questionnaire item is bipolar, it may mean that the phrasing of that particular question or item is ambiguous, with some of the respondents answering on the basis of one interpretation of the meaning of the question, and the remainder responding to another quite different interpretation of it.

Inferential statistics

The domain of inferential statistics is vast, and no more than a brief introductory sketch can be offered within the constraints of this chapter. For the reader interested in a more comprehensive treatment of this topic, there are several excellent texts listed in the further reading section of this chapter. These texts discuss the application of statistical methods in psychological research in general, rather than focusing specifically on counselling and psychotherapy research. The purpose of inferential statistics is to enable the researcher to test hypotheses. For example, a researcher may hypothesise that clients will report higher levels of satisfaction in sessions where the counsellor diplays a higher proportion of accurate empathy responses. Or the hypothesis may be that group therapy is more effective than individual counselling for students with loneliness problems. In this kind of hypothesis testing, the investigator is anticipating that there will be a predicted relationship between what is known as the *independent variable* (which is manipulated or controlled by the researcher) and the *dependent variable* (which is the response of the subject to the independent variable). So in the first of the examples just mentioned, empathy would be the independent variable, and client satisfaction would be the dependent variable. There is a supposed cause and effect relationship between these two variables. For instance, the researcher could divide the sample into two groups: clients with high-empathy counsellors and those with low-empathy counsellors. The specific research hypothesis in this case is that these two groups would yield different mean scores on a session satisfaction rating scale.

The way that inferential statistics operate is not to test a research hypothesis directly, but to calculate the confidence with which the Null Hypothesis can be rejected. The *Null Hypothesis* (H$_o$) is a statement that the sets of scores that have been obtained for different groups are equal (e.g. that the high- and low-empathy groups are no different in satisfaction). If the scores are *unequal*, then this is evidence to support the research hypothesis (or experimental hypothesis).

The Null Hypothesis is a precise and exact statement: there is *no* difference between the groups. In reality, there will always be some difference in the scores on a test or measure that two sets of people have completed. What needs to be known is whether this difference is due to random or chance factors or whether it is such a substantial difference that it would be unlikely to occur merely through random fluctuations in the sample of people included in each group. The statistical formulae used in inferential statistics essentially give the researcher a means of ascertaining the *probability* (*p*) that a particular result could have been obtained by chance.

The concept of probability refers to the likelihood of occurrence of an event. A high probability would mean that the event was almost certain to happen. A low probability indicates that the event is very unlikely indeed. The convention in mathematics is to report probability on a scale of 0 to 1, with a probability of 0 being equivalent to 'never' and a probability of 1 meaning that the event was certain. A probability of 0.5 would reflect a 50 per cent, or one time in two chance of the event occurring. A probability of 0.01 would suggest a 1 per cent or one time in a hundred chance.

In the type of research being considered here, the question that is being asked is: what is the probability that the differences between the two groups are due to chance? If the statistical calculations carried out to answer this question suggest that there is a high probability that the differences are indeed due merely to chance, then the Null Hypothesis is supported (or, strictly speaking, cannot be rejected) and the research hypothesis is refuted. On the other hand, if the differences are large, the calculation will tell the researcher that there is a low probability that this situation is a chance occurrence. In other words, the lower the probability estimate obtained, the more confidence there can be that the Null Hypothesis can be rejected and the research hypothesis supported.

But, for a probability estimate, how low is low enough? Again, this is another situation where there exist generally accepted conventions. Usually, a probability of less than 0.05 (or one time in 20), would be considered as the threshold for statistical acceptability. If a result is likely to happen more than one time in 20 simply because of random error or chance factors, it is not a very robust or meaningful finding. In research studies, therefore, *statistical significance* (sometimes described as the *alpha* level) values are usually reported in a form such as '*p* < 0.05', which would indicate a probability of *less than* 0.05. Other threshold levels commonly employed are 0.01 and 0.001. Some researchers prefer to report the exact probability value obtained, rather than a 'less than' figure. Setting the probability threshold too high or too low can lead to different types of error. If the threshold is set too low, there is a danger of rejecting the Null Hypothesis even when it is true. This is called a *Type I error*. For example, if a significance threshold of *p* < 0.1 was set, a Type I error would occur once every ten times. If, by contrast, the threshold is too high, then the investigator may make the mistake of rejecting the research hypothesis when it is in fact true. This is called a *Type II error*.

This discussion of inferential statistics has been based on an imaginary example involving the comparison of two groups: high-empathy and low-empathy. The statistical technique that would be used to decide whether to reject the Null Hypothesis would be determined by the level of measurement achieved by the dependent variable of client satisfaction. If, for example, satisfaction was assessed through a nominal or categorical scale such as high/low, then the *chi-square* (χ^2) statistic would be utilised. If the dependent variable was assessed in terms of ordinal scaling, such as ranking the clients in order of expressed satisfaction based on interview data, a non-parametric technique such as the *Mann–Whitney U test* would be applied. Finally, if satisfaction was measured using a scale (e.g. a multi-item questionnaire) that achieved interval scale measurement, then a *t-test* would be employed. The point being made here is that the level of measurement (in combination with the research design) constrains the choice of statistical technique. On the whole, parametric statistics, based on interval-scale measurement, provide the most powerful and flexible tools in research. The remainder of this exploration of inferential statistics will therefore be restricted to an examination of some of the more widely used parametric techniques. The non-parametric equivalents to these techniques are covered by most behavioural statistics textbooks.

The concept of *power* is critical for the use of statistical techniques. Power refers to the likelihood that the test will detect an effect when that effect is actually present. There are many factors that influence the power of a statistical procedure, including: the particular test being used, the alpha or probability level selected, the effect size, and the sample size (Heppner et al., 2002). In general, parametric tests and large sample sizes make powerful statistical analyses possible.

The t-test has already been mentioned as a parametric test for comparing measures collected from two groups of subjects, or the same group assessed on two different occasions. The t-test essentially compares data from the groups on two basic indices: the difference between the mean scores, and the variability within each group. Applying the t-test yields a calculation of *t* for the data that has been collected. If a computer statistics package has been used, the print-out will give the probability of this value of *t* being recorded by chance. However, if the t-test formula has been applied using a calculator, the obtained value of *t* then must be compared to a table of critical values of *t*, which will give a figure for the probability of finding this value given the sample size used in the study. This table of critical values can be found in the Appendix of any statistics textbook. The probability of *t* will depend on whether the research design has stipulated a *one-tailed* or *two-tailed* hypothesis. A one-tailed research hypothesis would make a definite prediction regarding the direction of difference between the two groups (e.g. that one group will have higher scores than the other). A two-tailed hypothesis makes a weaker prediction, that the groups will be different, but does not specify the directionality of the difference.

The t-test is simple to understand and is widely used, but is limited by the fact that it can only be employed to compare two groups. In many research designs there may be three or more groups being compared. The *analysis of variance* (ANOVA), or *F* test, is a version of the t-test that can be applied to studies in which there are two or more comparison groups. If there are only two groups, it produces the same results as a t-test. In studies in which there are several independent variables, analysis of variance can also be used to differentiate between *main effects* (variance in a dependent variable attributable to one independent variable) and *interaction effects* (variance in a dependent variable attributable to two or more independent variables acting in combination).

An example of the use of analysis of variance in a piece of counselling research can be seen in the work of the Sheffield Psychotherapy Project (Shapiro et al., 1990). This research team has carried out a number of studies of the process and outcomes of brief therapy, and in this particular piece of research were looking at the effects of both length of treatment and treatment mode on clients who were depressed white-collar workers. This paper presents preliminary data on 48 clients who were randomly assigned to either prescriptive (cognitive-behavioural) or exploratory (relationship-oriented) therapy, and who received either 8 or 16 sessions. This type of research design is called a '2×2' factor design, since there are four separate groups of subjects: 8 sessions of prescriptive therapy (8P), 8 sessions of exploratory therapy (8E), 16 sessions of prescriptive therapy (16P) and 16 sessions of exploratory therapy (16E). The change scores that were gathered for these clients on a range of standard measures revealed substantial levels of benefit for all four groups. To explore the contribution to outcome of different factors, analysis of variance was used to examine the effects of treatment mode and duration of treatment on each of these change measures. In effect, this statistical test allows the researcher to inquire whether the overall variance in change scores, or spread of scores, recorded on the Beck Depression Inventory (or any of the other outcome measures employed in the study) were associated with mode of treatment, length of treatment or the interaction between the two. The capacity of ANOVA techniques to deal with interaction effects is particularly relevant here. For example, it might be expected on theoretical grounds that prescriptive therapy would be more effective in the context of very focused, 8-session therapy, while exploratory therapy would be more effective in the 16-session condition. In fact, in this study only minor differences in improvement rates due to mode, duration or their interaction were found. This is an interesting result, since it suggests that clients benefit equally from contrasting types of therapy over different lengths of time.

Another statistical test that is widely used in counselling research is the *correlation coefficient*. This is a statistic that shows the strength of relationship between two variables. Although there are a number of different statistical tests that produce correlations, the most commonly used is the *Pearson product-moment* correlation coefficient (r). Strictly speaking, the correlation coefficient should be categorised as a descriptive rather than inferential technique, but its usage in therapy research has encompassed hypothesis-testing as well as description, so it is appropriate to include it in this section of the chapter. The value of a correlation coefficient (r) can range from $+1.00$ to -1.00. A positive (plus sign) correlation means that there is a positive linear relationship between two variables (i.e. higher scores on one variable are associated with higher scores on the other). A negative correlation means that high scores on one variable are associated with low scores on the other: a negative linear relationship. The nearer r is to ±1.00, the stronger the relationship is between the two variables.

Correlation coefficients are employed in a great many counselling studies. For example, the reliability of ratings made by different observers (i.e. the extent to which the two judges agree with each other) is calculated using a type of correlation coefficient (this is discussed in the next chapter). Another use of correlational statistics can be found in a series of studies by Combs (1986) into the personal qualities of effective counsellors. In this research, Combs (1986) assessed the 'perceptual organisation' of groups of trainee counsellors. By 'perceptual organisation', he meant the degree to which these trainees perceived the world from a person-centred perspective. His technique for doing this allowed him to rank order the members of each group, for example in terms of who was most 'open to experience' to who was least. Tutors who knew these trainees well then gave independent assessments on their effectiveness as counsellors. The similarity between the two rankings of the group were then calculated using a correlation statistic. In this set of studies, consistently high correlations were found between person-centred attitudes and counselling effectiveness.

It is important, however, to be aware that to find a high correlation between two factors does *not* mean that one of the variables causes the other. Correlation allows no inference about direction of causality. A high positive correlation between two variables may be accountable in terms of the influence of a third variable on both. In the research by Combs (1986), tutors may have been giving high competence ratings to trainees they saw as similar to them in attitudes and values. The method of assessing person-centred 'perceptual organisation' may have been picking up the extent to which trainees aspired to be similar to their tutors. So, the high correlation between perceptual organisation and effectiveness may be attributable to the impact of an external factor of conformity. Likewise, to return to an example given earlier of a study comparing counsellor empathic responding and client satisfaction, it is quite possible that empathy ratings and satisfaction scores might be highly correlated, but *both* variables could be determined by a factor of client–counsellor personality matching. Counsellors may be able to empathise with clients similar in personality to them. Clients may find counsellors who are the same personality type easier to identify with or use as a behavioural model. Another note of caution in the use of correlational analysis is that this test can only indicate the extent of a *linear* relationship between two variables. It is feasible that in some situations a strong relationship might exist between two factors but that it was curvilinear in nature. A probable example of a curvilinear relationship is the correlation between counsellor self-disclosure and client outcome. On the whole, there does not appear to be any consistent association between these variables. However, it makes sense to suppose that clients find moderate levels of therapist self-disclosure to be helpful, while high levels are overwhelming and a distraction, and very low levels make the therapist appear distant and inhuman.

This discussion of some of the statistical techniques employed in counselling and psychotherapy research is intended to do no more than supply an initial basis for understanding the role of statistics in studies of therapy. There are many more statistical tests than could possibly be covered here, and references to further reading have been given. However, it is vital to be aware that, even though quantitative studies utilising the kinds of statistical tests described here dominate the recent research literature, and are enormously valuable, there remain fundamental issues regarding the appropriateness of these techniques. These concerns will be examined in the final section of this chapter.

Choosing a statistics package

In practice, using statistics involves using a computer. Although it is possible to carry out by hand the calculations necessary for the more straightforward statistical tests, the introduction of personal computers and availability of terminals connected to powerful network systems have meant that it is quicker and more effective to use a statistics software package. There are an increasing number of these packages coming on the market, but the most widely used probably remains the Statistical Package for the Social Sciences (SPSS) system. This product is available in an easy-to-use Windows version and can be accessed through most college and university networks. There is also an ever-expanding range of books written to help users of stats packages not only to choose the appropriate statistical tools for the job, but also to command the computer to carry out the appropriate instructions (see further reading at the end of the chapter).

Issues in the use of statistics in counselling research

Although there is a massive literature on the use of quantitative methods in behavioural research, there remain a number of issues and dilemmas that need careful consideration. These issues include both the misuse of statistics and problems arising from the interpretation of certain types of quantitative data. Dar, Serlin and Omer (1994) have reviewed some of the ways that statistical techniques have been used in psychotherapy research during the 1960s, 1970s and 1980s. One of the issues they addressed was the misinterpretation of the concept of significance level or p value. In the context of Null Hypothesis testing, the researcher should set a p or alpha level (e.g. $p < 0.05$) in advance of the data being gathered and only accept as significant results that fall within that range. However, Dar et al. found that almost half of the sample of 163 studies they examined included discussion of results that failed to achieve the predetermined criterion significance level. Strictly speaking, these non-significant results should be disregarded. Instead, they were described by authors as representing effects that were 'marginal, trends, tendencies, borderline significant, approaching significance, near significant or almost significant' (1994: 77).

Dar et al. (1994) also examined the relationship between alpha level and the number of statistical tests carried out on a data set. An alpha or *p* level of 0.05 implies that the result will be found 1 time in 20 due to chance. Therefore, if more than 20 statistical tests are applied, with a 0.05 threshold, it would be expected that 1 of the 20 tests will produce a significant result, even in the absence of any 'real' difference between groups. When multiple tests are utilised, for example with the analysis of variance (ANOVA) technique and its derivatives, it is necessary to adjust the alpha level so that it represents a more stringent test of significance. It was found, in the Dar et al. (1994) survey, that only 23 per cent of studies included an adjustment of this type. The implication of both of these examples of the misuse of statistical procedure is to inflate the frequency of Type I errors. In other words, the Null Hypothesis is being mistakenly rejected (and significant findings being claimed) in circumstances where no effect has been demonstrated. In their paper, Dar et al. give other examples of misuse of statistics in therapy research, and conclude that 'much of the current use of statistical tests is flawed' (1994: 80). It is important to note, in considering their conclusion, that the research articles they included in their study were all drawn from the *Journal of Consulting and Clinical Psychology*, which is the most prestigious publication in this field. It would seem reasonable to suppose that an analysis of papers in other therapy research journals would reveal an even higher rate of statistical misuse.

A more fundamental criticism of the use of statistical procedures in psychological research is made by Meehl (1967, 1978). The critique offered by Meehl is all the more compelling in the knowledge that he has been a major figure in the development of quantitatively based research within mainstream American academic psychology. His argument rests on the view of the philosopher of science Sir Karl Popper (1959, 1962, 1972) that scientific research makes progress through a cycle of conjectures and refutations. Popper suggested that the role of science is to generate theories that make predictions ('conjectures') about events in the world. However, no theory is ever completely true, and the task of scientists is to find ways to test the limits or truth value of a theory, in other words to 'refute' it. In the 'hard' sciences such as physics and chemistry, the precision of measurement achieved by research instruments and the mathematical rigour with which theories are formulated mean that scientists in these areas of inquiry can make very exact predictions that can then be supported or refuted in a clear-cut manner. Meehl notes that scientists in these disciplines do not employ statistical tests of probability when they check whether a prediction or hypothesis has been verified by the results of an experiment, and asserts that:

> in my modern physics text, I am unable to find one single test of statistical significance. What happens instead is that the physicist has a sufficiently powerful . . . theory that enables him to generate an expected curve for his experimental results. He plots the observed points, looks at the agreement, and comments that 'the results are in reasonably good accord with theory'. (1978: 825)

Meehl also argues that, while the pattern in the natural sciences is for theories to be either supported or refuted and rejected, in social and personality psychology (which he labels 'soft' psychology) there is a tendency for theories to be fashionable for a while and then to fade away rather than be conclusively shown to be wrong. Meehl suggests that there must be something wrong with the way most psychological research is conducted if that research is not able to refute theoretical models in a definitive manner.

For Meehl, the answer to these problems lies in the use of Null Hypothesis testing in psychology. The basis of most statistics used in psychology is to calculate the confidence with which the Null Hypothesis can be rejected. However, as Meehl points out, the Null Hypothesis (that there is no difference between the groups being compared) is, if taken literally, *always* false. For example, in a study comparing self-esteem scores between therapy clients and those allocated to a control group, it is inconceivable that the two groups would be *exactly* equal. There are many factors that could result in one of the groups yielding a higher mean score than the other. If this is so, then 'if you have enough cases and your measures are not totally unreliable, the Null Hypothesis will always be falsified, *regardless of the truth of the substantive theory*' (1978: 822, emphasis in original). Meehl (1967, 1978) suggests that in the physical sciences improvement in instrumentation or experimental accuracy leads to a better chance of refuting a theory. In psychology, by contrast, improving instrumentation and measurement is more likely to lead to support for the theory. This is because more sensitive measures are more likely to pick up any differences existing (for whatever reason) between the two groups.

Moreover, Meehl argues that in psychology any failure to support a theoretical prediction is accounted for by introducing ad hoc explanations for the data in the discussion section of the research report. These ad hoc rationalisations are always available to the psychological researcher because there are so many competing theories available, including common-sense non-scientific ones. He concludes that 'a successful test of a substantive theory in soft psychology provides a feeble corroboration of the theory because the procedure has subjected the theory to a feeble risk' (1978: 822).

Meehl reinforces these points by noting that the areas of psychology that, in his view, have made good progress in developing powerful theories and methods are on the whole those that have eschewed the use of tests of statistical significance. His rejection of this approach to quantitative methodology is uncompromising:

> I believe that the almost universal reliance on merely refuting the null hypothesis as the standard method for corroborating substantive theories in the soft areas is a terrible mistake, is basically unsound, poor scientific strategy, and one of the worst things that ever happened in the history of psychology. (1978: 817)

The arguments put forward by Meehl (1967, 1978) have resulted in vigorous debate (Dar, 1987; Serlin and Lapsley, 1985; Swoyer and Monson, 1975) but have made little appreciable difference to the conduct of research in counselling and psychotherapy, which is still dominated by the Null Hypothesis testing approach.

Conclusions

The aim of this chapter has been to introduce some of the principles involved in using quantitative methods in counselling research. Some of the issues and difficulties associated with this approach have also been rehearsed. Statistical methods represent a powerful tool in therapy research. The main advantages of quantitative methods lie in their ability to:

- deal with large numbers of cases;
- examine complex patterns of interactions between variables;
- verify the presence of cause and effect relationships between variables.

The other advantage of quantitative methods is that, up to now, they have been regarded as having high scientific validity and prestige. This may be changing, as qualitative approaches become more widely accepted. The application of quantitative techniques in particular areas of counselling research is examined in more depth in the next chapter, which deals with questionnaires and other standardised measures, and in Chapter 8, which looks at research into the outcomes of counselling and psychotherapy.

Further reading

Listed below is a range of recommended introductory books on the use of statistics in research.

Argyrous, G. (2000) *Statistics for Social and Health Research*. London: Sage.

Coolidge, F.L. (2000) *Statistics: A Gentle Introduction*. Thousand Oaks, CA: Sage.

Greene, J. and d'Oliveira, M. (1999) *Learning to use Statistical Tests in Psychology*, 2nd edn. Buckingham: Open University Press.

Hinton, P. (1995) *Statistics Explained: A Guide for Social Science Students*. London: Routledge.

Kerr, A.W., Hall, H.K. and Kozub, S.A. (2002) *Doing Statistics with SPSS*. London: Sage.

Salkind, N.J. (2000) *Statistics for People Who (Think They) Hate Statistics*. Thousand Oaks, CA: Sage.

Wright, D.B. (2002) *First Steps in Statistics*. Thousand Oaks, CA: Sage.

5 Tests, Rating Scales and Survey Questionnaires

In counselling research, it is often necessary or desirable to be able to measure key variables as accurately and precisely as possible. Indeed, many important concepts or variables, for example depression, empathy, anxiety, level of adjustment, therapeutic alliance, occur in many different studies. As a result, a number of standardised tests have been developed to measure them. The existence of these tests also reflects the impact on counselling research of the psychometric (measurement of the mind) tradition in psychology (DuBois, 1970). From its earliest years, psychology as a discipline has been concerned with the assessment and appraisal of psychological attributes in individuals. Most of the initial work in this area was not specifically research-oriented, but was driven by practical demands arising from the need to classify or diagnose clients in settings such as mental health care, education and vocational guidance. The work carried out in these applied fields has yielded a robust and widely accepted set of principles and criteria for test design and administration that have subsequently been adopted by researchers. In this chapter, some of the tests employed most widely in counselling research will be examined, and the issues arising from their use will be reviewed.

Principles of test construction

The aim of any psychological test is to measure some individual quality or attribute in as *valid* and *reliable* a fashion as possible. The concept of validity refers to the ability of the test to measure the actual construct it claims to be measuring. The concept of reliability refers to the robustness of the test, its capacity to produce similar results in different situations or when administered by different people or at different times. Strictly speaking, all tests employed in research studies should be backed up by data demonstrating acceptable levels of reliability and validity. For the most widely used tests, this data is available from the publishers of the instrument in the form of a test manual, or is reported in a journal article by the author of the test. If an instrument or test has been created for use in a specific study, reliability and validity information should be provided in the report on the study. However, many tests used in counselling research have been applied in the absence of basic information about reliability and validity, either because no suitable validated test exists, or because the test *appears* to be an appropriate measure of the variable in question. A researcher utilising an instrument that has not been shown to be reliable and valid runs the risk of producing results that are meaningless or lacking in credibility.

The purpose of any test is to provide an accurate estimate of where the subject lies on a dimension or continuum defined at each end by high or low levels of an attribute or quality. For example, there are self-report questionnaires that assess how anxious, or depressed, or stressed a person experiences himself or herself as feeling. The value of the test depends on how well the person constructing the instrument is able to *operationalise* the underlying concept or construct which is being measured. After all, 'anxiety', 'depression' or 'stress' are concepts or ideas. To be able to measure them requires finding procedures or operations that allow their core meanings to be translated into a series of actions. In the measurement of length, for instance, the notion of 'centimetre' can be operationalised through a series of actions carried out with a ruler. Similarly, 'anxiety' can be operationalised through the activity of using a questionnaire or rating scale.

The process of operationalising constructs introduces some fundamental questions about validity. Is it possible to capture all the possible meanings of 'anxiety' in a questionnaire? Even a superficial reading of the literature on anxiety will reveal that there exists a variety of alternative understandings of the nature and expression of anxiety, ranging from the existential concept of 'ontological insecurity' through to physiological indices such as galvanic skin conductance. When constructing a test it is essential, therefore, to define the construct being measured as explicitly as possible. In the field of assessment of anxiety, for example, it can be seen that different instruments reflect slightly different concepts of anxiety. Spielberger et al. (1970) makes a distinction between 'state' and 'trait' anxiety, the Taylor (1953) scale is concerned with 'manifest' anxiety, with items such as 'I frequently notice that my hand shakes when I try to do something new.' By contrast, the Watson and Friend (1969) anxiety scale focuses on social anxiety, with items such as 'I try to avoid social situations which force me to be very sociable.' These scales measure somewhat different aspects of anxiety, and will each produce slightly different results. These differences need to be taken into account when reading research papers. If a researcher reports on the efficacy of a new intervention for anxiety reduction, it is important to look carefully at the measure of anxiety he or she has employed. Does the measure meaningfully capture the type of anxiety experienced by the clients to whom this intervention might be offered?

The construction of a psychological test comprises seven distinct phases:

1   The literature must be reviewed, or an exploratory study carried out, to generate an initial definition of the construct or constructs to be assessed.
2   A large pool of items potentially relevant to this construct is assembled.
3   These items or questions are administered to as large a cross-section of people as possible.
4   These results are examined with a view to reducing the item pool to the smallest possible set of questions consistent with criteria of reliability and validity.
5   The final version of the scale is put together, with careful attention to instructions to respondents, layout, and the order of items.

6   Studies are carried out to evaluate the reliability and validity of the scale.
7   The scale is given to a large sample of the population, and perhaps also to special sub-groups, to generate norms for groups of respondents of different age, gender, occupation, social class and so on.

It can be seen that test construction and validation is a complex and costly business. It is not surprising that many instruments are used that have not undergone this process in full. It is also easy to appreciate the reasons why tests that have passed all these quality control criteria are marketed by educational publishing companies rather than being freely accessible. In most research situations it is preferable to utilise an instrument that has been carefully validated and employed in previous studies. The existence of published journal articles reporting effective use of a scale indicates that the instrument enjoys at least some credibility in the eyes of the research community. Also, these other studies may provide comparative or benchmark data that will allow the results from one investigation to be discussed in the context of findings from other studies.

To examine in more detail the procedures involved in test construction would be beyond the scope of this book. The reader interested in these matters should consult Beech and Harding (1990), Cronbach (1970), Nunnally (1978) and Rust and Golombok (1989).

At the heart of test construction are the concepts of validity and reliability. It is important to recognise that there are a number of different ways of evaluating the validity or reliability of a test (see Box 5.1), some of which are more satisfactory than others. For example, an instrument may possess *face validity* purely on the strength of including items that appear as though they are relevant to the construct being measured. In contrast, *criterion validity* refers to the fact that scores on this test will match scores reported for the same factor achieved from another source, for example judgements made by expert clinicians. Criterion validity clearly provides a much tougher and more convincing form of evidence than does face validity on its own. The reliability index that is most frequently given is that of *internal consistency*, which is reported through the use of a statistic known as Cronbach's *alpha*. The internal consistency of a scale refers to the degree of agreement between items, or the extent to which they all appear to measure the same variable. An alpha score of at least 0.7 is usually considered necessary for a scale to be regarded as reliable enough to be employed in research.

Ultimately, it does not make any sense to carry out quantitative research using a scale that is not valid. To do so would be like building a wardrobe by measuring pieces of wood with a stopwatch. However, it is not at all easy to establish the validity of a test. Each of the forms of validity described in Box 5.1 represents a research study in itself. It is also necessary to note that a test cannot be valid unless it is reliable. For example, when building a wardrobe it would in principle be possible to measure the wood by using a knotted string. Nevertheless, even a string measure would be worthless and misleading if the string stretched each time it was used.

Box 5.1 Types of validity and reliability

Face validity. The test appears to measure what it claims to measure. This can be helpful in gaining acceptance for the test in some groups, but can be a hindrance if it allows respondents to guess what the test is about, and shape their answers to achieve 'impression management'.

Content validity. The items in the test comprehensively reflect the domain of meaning that is intended to be measured. For example, an instrument designed to assess depression will have items relating to all aspects of depression.

Criterion validity. An estimate of whether the instrument differentiates between people in the same way as other types of measures. For example, concurrent criteria for a social anxiety scale might include observations made by nurses. Predictive criteria refer to measures taken at a later time. For example, the predictive validity of a social anxiety scale might be future level of participation in a discussion group.

Construct validity. Scores on the test correlate (or otherwise) with scores on other tests in accordance with theoretical predictions. For example, measures of social and manifest anxiety should correlate more highly with each other (convergent validity) than they do with measures of depression (divergent validity).

Test–retest reliability. An assessment of the extent to which similar scores are recorded on a test administered on two occasions.

Alternate form reliability. The same group of people are given parallel versions of the instrument on different occasions, and their scores are compared.

Internal consistency. A reliability coefficient that estimates the extent to which different items in a test are in agreement with each other.

Inter-rater reliability. The level of agreement between different raters coding or categorising the same set of data.

A feature of test construction that is of great practical relevance to counselling research is that, in general, the more items there are in a test the more reliable and valid it is likely to be. This phenomenon can be understood by returning to the problem of measuring anxiety. An anxiety scale with only one item (e.g. 'Do you worry a lot?') can only invite the respondent to comment on one aspect of anxiety. A scale with 20 items will enable the respondent to reflect on many different

---

Box 5.2   Some alternative response formats for an item on feelings during a counselling session

1   Likert scale
During the counselling session I felt anxious.
  Strongly agree/Agree/Neutral/Disagree/Strongly disagree

2   Bipolar rating scale
During the counselling session I felt:
  Relaxed X- - - - - - - - - - - - - - - - - - -X Tense
  Relaxed X- - -X- - -X- - -X- - -X- - -X Tense

3   Unipolar rating scale
During the counselling session I felt:
  Not anxious X- - - - - - - - - - - - - - - - - -X Anxious
  Not anxious X- - -X- - -X- - -X- - -X- - -X Anxious

4   Anchored rating scale
Put a circle around the statement that best describes your feelings during the counselling session:
  (a) generally anxious
  (b) slightly anxious
  (c) not at all anxious

5   Adjective check list
Place a circle around the words that best describe how you felt during the counselling session:
  Angry   Anxious   Depressed   Happy
  Frustrated   Confused   Light   Tense

---

nuances of their experience of anxiety. It permits the test constructor to explore a whole range of meanings of anxiety, from panic and terror at one end to unease or disquiet at the other. Multiple-item scales also help to prevent any distortion caused by the phrasing of any individual item. A major difficulty arises, however, when a counselling researcher wishes to collect data on several variables. If each variable is assessed through a 20-item scale, in the end the respondent may be required to answer several hundred questions. In these circumstances cooperation may be threatened or the quality of the attention that the respondent gives to each item may be diminished. Another serious consideration in test design and construction concerns the choice of response format. Some of the more widely used response formats are listed in Box 5.2. These response formats have been devised in relation to a hypothetical questionnaire item that aims to explore the feelings a client might experience during a therapy session.

Further information about the principles and procedures of test construction and validation in relation to counselling and psychotherapy studies can be found in Golden et al. (1984), Morley and Snaith (1989), Powell (1989), Sechrest (1984), Watkins and Campbell (2000) and Whiston (2000).

Self-report questionnaires and rating scales

The most widely used instruments in counselling research are self-report ques-tionnaires and rating scales. These 'paper-and-pencil' tests require the person to respond to questions about their experience, behaviour or attitudes. This tech-nique relies on the ability of the person to report on these factors with at least a moderate degree of accuracy, and so it is essential that the instructions to the respondent, and wording of items, are as clear and unambiguous as possible. The primary advantages of self-report methods are that they are relatively easy to administer and interpret, and are generally acceptable to research subjects. As citizens of modern bureaucratic societies, research participants are accustomed to the practice of filling in forms that ask questions about themselves (Shaw and Miles, 1979). The disadvantages of self-report instruments are mainly that they are open to faking or distortion by participants lacking in self-awareness or honesty, are difficult for people with literacy problems to use, and may not measure what they appear to measure (see Kambert, 1999 and McLeod, 2001a for discussion of the limitations of self-report measures in therapy research). Some of the questionnaires used most frequently in counselling research are briefly described below.

The *CORE (Clinical Outcomes Routine Evaluation)* scale is a 34-item self-report questionnaire which measures client distress in terms of four dimensions: well-being, symptoms, functioning and risk (Evans et al., 2000; Mellor-Clark et al., 1999). The questionnaire is easy to understand, and has been found to be acceptable to the majority of clients. Typically, the questionnaire is administered at the beginning and end of therapy, so that change scores can be calculated. Client scores at entry into counselling can be used to examine the profile of clients seen by an agency. There are also assessment and end-of-therapy forms completed by the counsellor, with the result that the CORE system can operate as a comprehensive evaluation package. CORE materials can be copied without charge, and a low-cost software package is available to facilitate data analysis. The CORE questionnaire has been widely adopted by counselling, psychotherapy and clinical psychology service providers in Britain. A great deal of data has been collected on the progress of therapy with clients in a range of settings, enabling 'benchmarking' of standards of effectiveness (Barkham et al., 2001; Mellor-Clark et al., 2001).

The *Outcome Questionnaire (OQ)* is similar to CORE, and is widely used in the USA. The OQ comprises a 45-item scale which provides a measure of overall disturbance, as well as sub-scale scores of subjective distress, interpersonal rela-tions, social role functioning, suicide, substance abuse, and workplace violence. A version of the scale for use with children and adolescents has also been produced. As with CORE, software packages and benchmarking norms are available.

Further information on the OQ can be found in Lambert and Finch (1999), Lambert, Burlingame et al. (1996) and Wells, Burlingame and Lambert (1999).

The *Minnesota Multiphasic Personality Inventory* (*MMPI*) is a 566-item questionnaire developed during the 1930s to generate a personality profile focused on psychiatric or adjustment problems. The ten clinical scales included in the test provide measures of the following variables: hypochondriasis, depression, hysteria, psychopathic deviation, paranoia, psychasthenia, schizophrenia, mania, masculine–feminine interests, and social introversion–extroversion. The MMPI has often been used as a screening device to select subjects for inclusion in a study, and has also been employed in the assessment of change resulting from therapy. Shorter forms of the scale have been devised. Further information about the MMPI is available in Duckworth (1990).

The *Hopkins Symptom Checklist* (*SCL-90*) was initially developed at Johns Hopkins University. The aim of the test is to detect levels of psychiatric symptomatology. The standard 90-item version of the test has nine sub-scales: depression, anxiety, somatisation, obsessive–compulsive, interpersonal sensitivity, hostility, phobic anxiety, paranoid ideation and psychoticism. There also exist shorter versions of the test. The format of the SCL-90 presents the respondent with a list of symptoms, such as 'heart pounding or racing' or 'trembling' (both anxiety items) and the instruction to indicate the severity of these on a four-point scale ranging from 'not at all' to 'extremely'. Derogatis and Melisaratos (1983) offer an expanded discussion of the operation of this test, which is used in a similar fashion to the MMPI in counselling studies, as a screening device and a measure of change.

The *Beck Depression Inventory* (*BDI*) is a short, 21-item scale designed to assess depression (Beck et al., 1961). Each item comprises a set of four or five self-statements of increasing severity (e.g. 'I do not feel sad', 'I feel blue or sad') that can either be read out to the testee or administered as a self-rating questionnaire that the person completes on his or her own. The person selects the statement that best fits the way he or she feels at 'this moment'. The BDI is used in research as a screening and outcome measure. Beck, Steer and Garbin (1988) provide a review of developments in the validation and use of this scale.

Spielberger et al. (1970) devised the *State–Trait Anxiety Inventory* (*STAI*) to assess anxiety both as an enduring personality characteristic or trait, and as a transient condition or state. The scale comprises 40 items, separated into two sections. The first section asks respondents to rate how they *generally* feel (trait anxiety) and the second half instructs them to answer in terms of how they feel now (state anxiety). Items consist of a statement followed by a four-point response scale. The STAI has been used to assess change in anxiety during and as a result of therapy.

Further information on these (and many other) tests utilised by counselling researchers can be found in Bowling (1997, 2001), Bridges and Goldberg (1989), Ferguson and Tyrer (1989), Greenberg and Pinsof (1986), Maruish (1999), Murphy and Tyrer (1989), Thompson (1989a, 1989b) and Watkins and Campbell (2000). At present, there is no single unified handbook or database supplying comprehensive information about research instrumentation in this field.

Observational measures

There are a number of standardised measures used in counselling research that rely on the coding or rating of data by trained external observers, rather than on the self-report of the actual participant (client or counsellor) in therapy. These techniques begin with observational data recorded on tape, for example an audio or video recording of a counselling session. This material is then rated by observers who have no other contact with or knowledge of the client or therapist. When tapes of sessions are used, it is commonplace to select segments of the tape for analysis, rather than whole sessions, to reduce the amount of time needed for the task. An essential characteristic of this type of measure is the construction of a training manual for observers, to ensure that each observer is employing the same definitions of constructs in a systematic manner. It is also necessary to check the performance of observers at regular intervals, to safeguard against 'drift' away from the procedures and criteria specified by the manual (Hill, 1991). The degree of agreement between observers is assessed by calculating an *inter-rater reliability* coefficient (*kappa*) (Cohen, 1960; Shrout and Fleiss, 1979; Tinsley and Weiss, 1975), which to be acceptable would normally be expected to reach 0.7 or above. As with other tests, the instrument cannot be regarded as valid unless it also demonstrates sufficient reliability.

Observational techniques are like other tests in that they offer a way of operationalising constructs or concepts. Compared to questionnaires, however, they are much more complex and demanding to apply. It is as if the decision processes that occur in the mind of the individual replying to a questionnaire item are all being written down in a form that is explicit enough to be understood by members of a team of observers. Another significant difference between observational techniques and questionnaires is that in the former the raw material upon which ratings are made (e.g. the conversation between counsellor and client) needs to be handled. Not only is this time-consuming, but also introduces issues regarding confidentiality and security. Observational instruments may involve the collection of material that is highly sensitive and personal.

Despite these practical difficulties, there are advantages associated with observational techniques. They are, for example, minimally intrusive on the actual therapeutic process – the client is not required to answer questions about his or her experience. They allow variables to be measured that are not readily translatable into questions that would make sense to a client. Also, they provide data from a 'neutral' perspective, rather than information coloured by the distinctive viewpoint of counsellor or client. The main weakness of observational methods is that inevitably they are insensitive to context. Trained observers rating 5-minute segments of therapy tapes will have little or no appreciation of the background to what client and counsellor are saying or doing in these excerpts. It could be argued that it is very difficult for any observer of a counselling session to appreciate the *meaning* of what is happening. Spence (1982) has suggested that the participants in a session possess a 'privileged competence', a special insider knowledge based on actual here-and-now involvement over time in the therapeutic process.

Box 5.3 The Experiencing Scale

Stage 1. Manner of expression impersonal, absence of personal involvement, content abstract, superficial and journalistic. Fluent.

Stage 2. Behavioural or intellectual self-description, no reference to feelings. Usually fluent.

Stage 3. Personal reactions to external events, behavioural descriptions of feelings. Some affect indicators, e.g. laughs, sighs.

Stage 4. Descriptions of feelings and personal experiences with an internal perspective. Subject of discourse is feelings or experiences of events, rather than the events themselves. Focused voice with expressions of affect.

Stage 5. Problems or propositions about feelings and personal experiences. Purposeful elaboration of feelings. Dysfluency – groping, tentative.

Stage 6. Felt sense of an inner referent. A sense of 'more' to be discovered about the identified feelings. Exclamation, alterations of fluency and dysfluency. Present tense or vivid representation of past.

Stage 7. A series of felt senses connecting the referent. Content reveals steady and expanding awareness of immediately present feelings and internal processes. Primarily present tense.

Source: Klein et al. (1986)

An example of an observational instrument that has been widely used in counselling and psychotherapy process research is the *Experiencing Scale* (Klein et al., 1986). This test originally grew out of the research by Rogers, Gendlin and others into the effectiveness of client-centred therapy with schizophrenic clients (Rogers et al., 1967). That set of studies included a number of attempts to identify process variables related to successful outcome. One of the variables most closely associated with success was *depth of client experiencing*. Gendlin and Tomlinson (1967) and Rogers (1958) had proposed that, as clients became more able to trust their therapist, they would move from talking about external events, and attributing responsibility to others, and gradually become more able to express the deeper meanings and feelings arising from the issues they were exploring. The Experiencing Scale was developed as a means of testing this hypothesis.

The current version of the scale consists of a manual (Klein et al., 1969) which is used by trained observers to rate the experiencing levels of client and therapist statements in 2–8-minute segments from recordings or transcripts of individual therapy sessions. Each statement is rated on a 7-point scale of stage of experiencing (see Box 5.3). The procedure yields ratings of the modal (most frequently occurring) and peak experiencing level found in each segment. Considerable evidence has been collected in support of the reliability and validity of the scale and the effectiveness of rater training (Klein et al., 1986). Variants of the scale have been devised to assess experiencing in therapists, non-clients, and groups (Klein et al., 1986).

Several other rating scales have been devised to examine different processes taking place within therapy. For example, the Narrative Process Coding Scheme (Angus and Hardtke, 1994; Angus, Levitt and Hardtke, 1999; Laitila et al., 2001; Levitt and Angus, 1999) enables researchers to code different modes of narrative processing occurring within therapy sessions. The NPCS system uses therapy transcripts as basic data. Another widely used transcript-based coding system is the Assimilation of Problematic Experience Scale (APES), which gives a measure of the client's progress through stages in coming to terms with personal difficulties (Barkham et al., 1996; Honos-Webb et al., 1998, 1999; Stiles, 1991, 2001, 2002; Stiles et al., 1990, 1991, 1992).

Behavioural measures

There may be times in counselling research when it is appropriate or necessary to employ a direct measure of behaviour rather than use a psychological test. Behaviours such as eating, number of hours studying, frequency of visits to shops or engagement in eye contact have all been utilised as dependent measures in studies of therapy outcome. In single-case or 'n = 1' studies (see Chapter 7), procedures for collecting behavioural data will usually be organised to suit the circumstances of the particular case. Nelson (1981) and Kendall and Hollon (1981) are valuable sources of information on behavioural measures. One of the fields of counselling research in which there has been significant use of behavioural measures is workplace counselling, where the impact of counselling in sickness absence and accident rates has provided information that is highly convincing to organisational sponsors of counselling services (McLeod, 2001b).

Survey questionnaires

Another source of quantitative data in many counselling studies is the survey questionnaire. Unlike questionnaire instruments such as the MMPI or BDI which are required to have demonstrable psychometric properties and are used again and again in many pieces of research, survey questionnaires are usually designed for a specific purpose, and are used in only one investigation. It is essential for a good survey questionnaire to possess face and content validity. In other words, it must include questions on all relevant aspects of the topic, and these questions must clearly be seen to provide the information that is required. Typically, survey questionnaires are mailed out to participants, so it is essential that the instructions and covering letter are straightforward and uncomplicated to follow. Some of the other considerations in designing a survey questionnaire are:

1 The layout and presentation of the questionnaire are important. It must look uncluttered and easy to fill in.
2 Begin the questionnaire with factual items (age, gender), to engage the respondent's attention, before moving to more difficult questions that may take longer to anwer.
3 The wording of questions must be direct and unambiguous.
4 Keep the questionnaire as brief as possible.
5 Put a reminder and thank-you at the end to encourage return of the questionnaire.

The issues involved in designing and administering survey questionnaires are discussed fully by de Vaus (1990), Robson (2002) and Sudman and Bradburn (1982). These sources also deal with issues of sampling and compliance, which are crucial in survey research.

There have been several survey investigations of aspects of counsellor attitudes and experience. For example, Macaskill and Macaskill (1992) carried out a survey in which psychotherapists in training were asked about their views on their personal therapy. Morrow-Bradley and Elliott (1986) conducted a survey of research awareness and utilisation in practising therapists. Allman et al. (1992) completed a survey of the attitudes of therapists toward clients reporting mystical experiences. There have been many interesting surveys of therapy clients, for example the research by Liddle (1996, 1997) into the views of gay and lesbian clients regarding the therapy they had received. It is also useful to carry out surveys of public attitudes to counselling, for example the study by West and Reynolds (1995) into attitudes to workplace counselling.

Projective techniques

Projective techniques operate in a quite different way from the other assessment techniques reviewed in this chapter. In a projective test, the participant is asked to respond to a relatively unstructured, ambiguous stimulus in an open-ended way. Typical projective techniques are the Rorschach Inkblot Test, in which the person is invited to report on what they see in each of a set of symmetrical inkblots, and the Thematic Apperception Test (TAT), where the person tells or writes imaginative stories in response to a set of pictures. Another widely used projective test, the sentence completion technique, involves writing endings to incomplete sentence stems. These and other projective instruments are described by Semeonoff (1976). The assumption underlying these techniques is that the person will project his or her characteristic way of thinking and feeling into the way he or she reacts to the open-ended projective task. For example, in a TAT story, the respondent may unconsciously invest the hero or heroine of the story with his or her own personal motives and patterns of behaviour. A person with a strong need for achievement may write stories that all make reference to winning or doing well. Conversely, a person with a strong need for sociability may write stories emphasising relationships and friendships. An important feature of projective techniques is the intention to gain access to fantasy and imagination rather than consciously processed 'socially desirable' responses.

Projective techniques have in the past been widely used within clinical and occupational psychology for such purposes as personality assessment, clinical diagnosis and appraisal of managerial potential. Projective techniques were extensively used in the early research into client-centred therapy carried out by Rogers and his colleagues at the University of Chicago (Rogers and Dymond, 1954). In recent years, however, there has been increasing scepticism over the validity of these instruments. The use of projective techniques can be critised on two grounds. Firstly, the responses that people make to projective stimuli tend to be affected by the situation they are in, their mood at the time of testing, and their relationship with the person administering the test. Secondly, the open-ended and complex nature of the projective response means that it can often be difficult to interpret the meaning or significance of what the person has said or written. Both these factors have led many psychologists to question the reliability of projective techniques. The neglect of projective methods in counselling research can be illustrated by the fact that very few research papers published in recent years report the use of projective instruments.

Despite the recent lack of interest in projective techniques within the counselling research community, there is good reason to suppose that they still have a great deal to offer in some research settings. The value of projective approaches in qualitative research is discussed in Chapter 6. However, even within quantitative studies projective techniques can, if used properly, provide data equal in reliability and validity to any self-report questionnaire. McClelland (1980, 1981) argues that questionnaires evoke only the capacity of a person to respond passively to a stimulus. By contrast, the projective situation forces the person to engage in active, purposeful, problem-solving behaviour. In addition, when a person answers a questionnaire item, he or she is not merely reporting on what they know about their behaviour, but are drawing upon their image, or concept of self. In a projective technique, the person usually has no idea of what the test is about, and answers spontaneously without reference to attitudes and self-images. Both these factors led McClelland (1980) to conclude that, in a projective test situation, the person being tested is displaying patterns of behaviour and feeling that are similar to those they exhibit in actual real-life situations. Evidence gathered by Cornelius (1983) supports this view. For example, in a review of the literature on the assessment of motivation, Cornelius (1983) found higher levels of predictive validity for projective instruments such as the TAT and lower levels for self-report questionnaires.

The implication of the work of McClelland and his colleagues is that projective techniques give access to personality structures and attitudes that are deeper and more fundamental than those highlighted by fixed response self-report questionnaires. It remains to be seen whether, within counselling research, the potential and promise of projective techniques will yet overcome the formidable practical problems involved in their use. In principle, the psychodynamically oriented and phenomenological theoretical basis underpinning projective tests would appear more consistent with much counselling practice than would the trait theory that has guided the construction of many widely used questionnaire instruments. The study by McClelland and Boyatzis (1980), in which projective techniques were used to assess counsellor competencies that were then found to be associated with good client outcomes, offers a small-scale example of what can be accomplished using this methodology.

Conclusions: issues in the use of tests and questionnaires

Standardised tests of the type described in this chapter have made an enormous and valuable contribution to research in counselling. In fact, the majority of counselling research articles published in the major journals have employed these methods. However, despite the pervasiveness and popularity of tests and scales, there remain a number of issues involved in their use, and it is necessary to be aware of these matters when planning research or reading published articles.

One of the compelling features of tests is that their operation is guided by long-established and well-understood quality control criteria arising from the conceptions of validity and reliability developed in applied psychology. However, not all tests deployed in counselling research are backed up by strong reliability and validity data. The tests reviewed earlier in this chapter represent some of the most widely used instruments in the field. Although there is a vast literature on the psychometric properties of the MMPI, Barrett–Lennard Relationship Inventory or the Experiencing Scale, there are many other tests used in research studies that have been only minimally validated. For example, Beutler and Crago listed the change measures used in 150 psychotherapy outcome studies 'selected on the basis of methodological adequacy and scope' (1983: 455). They found that, of a total of 126 different scales utilised, 78 had been used only once. Even well-tried instruments such as the MMPI and STAI had only been used in 24 and 11 studies respectively. Ogles et al. (1990), in a review of 106 studies of agoraphobia published in the 1980s, reported 98 different measures used to assess therapeutic change in this condition. Many of these instruments had been used in only one study.

The presence of so many little-known and little-used tests within the literature suggests that at least some research findings are reliant on measures that lack convincing evidence regarding reliability and validity. Yet, even when well-known tests are chosen, validity problems may occur. Most of the tests in use have been constructed and validated in the USA, and as a result should only be employed in that cultural setting. The meaning of feeling words and other psychological terms in test items may well vary from culture to culture. This source of variance is even more serious when the person completing the test does not have English as a first language.

A fundamental problem in test construction, which has been recognised for many years, is the question of social desirability (Edwards, 1957; Vernon, 1963). For example, when a person responds to a yes/no questionnaire item, his or her answer will be heavily influenced by how socially desirable or acceptable a 'yes' or 'no' might be in this situation. If an item on an 'attitude to work' scale was 'are you a conscientious and careful worker', then most people would consider the socially acceptable answer to be 'yes'. The response given by the person is, therefore, heavily influenced not by any specific attitude to work, but by a more general tendency to want to appear a worthwhile person in the eyes of other people. Another way of looking at this phenomenon is that there exists a pervasive social worthiness/self-esteem theme running through most test items. People taking tests use them, at least in part, to manage the impression others hold of them (Taylor et al., 1976). Even observational scales are influenced by this tendency. An observer rating a tape of a therapy session in terms of therapist empathy is likely to superimpose on the empathy scale judgements a general 'halo' effect of how 'good' or 'impressive' the therapist appears to be (Bachrach, 1976). Careful test constructors go to great lengths to find ways of dealing with the social desirability factor in questionnaire data, for example by including a balance of socially desirable and undesirable item statements or incorporating a lie scale. Nevertheless, the point is that the pervasiveness of this effect is so powerful that it is necessary for researchers developing new tests to be able to demonstrate that they have dealt adequately with it (McLeod, 2001a).

It is clear that not all tests used in counselling research are equally valid. Moreover, the concepts of reliability and validity established in mainstream psychological research may have limitations in the specific context of counselling research. The concept of reliability, for example, refers to the tendency for a scale to produce the same results on different occasions, for different items within the scale to be in broad agreement, or for different viewers of a video to arrive at the same judgement. There are many research situations where this kind of consensus or stability may be necessary. However, there are also questions in the field of counselling and psychotherapy in which sensitivity to change and ability to generate awareness of alternative readings or perspectives are equally important qualities for a research instrument to possess. In outcome research, for example, it is preferable to use a measure such as CORE or OQ, which is sensitive to change, rather than a scale such as MMPI, which assesses personality characteristics that are relatively insensitive to change.

There are problems, too, with the concept of validity. In a classic review of the validity of personality tests, Mischel (1968) found that the correlation between these tests and any form of overt, observable behaviour rarely rose above 0.3. What this means is that, on average, a questionnaire measure of a characteristic such as depression will account for around 10 per cent of the actual differences in depressed behaviour that might be observable in a group of people being assessed. Another way of looking at this result is that, although tests yield data that correspond to actual patterns of behaviour at a statistically significant level (i.e. at a higher level than chance), the picture of the person generated by test data is none the less fuzzy and imprecise. The arguments put forward by Mischel (1968) have triggered off much debate about how best to assess psychological variables in the areas of personal and interpersonal functioning. These arguments cannot be reviewed here. Suffice it to note that the technology of testing is not unproblematic, and that there are many voices in the mainstream of psychological research critical of the basic assumptions and methods of the psychometric tradition.

In recent years there has been increasing interest in administering psychological tests on PC or through the internet. Quite apart from the convenience to the researcher of being able to set up a system for reading questionnaire or rating scale responses straight into a database, there are a number of other advantages to computerised testing. For example, the researcher can record the length of time it took the respondent to answer each question. Errors in data analysis are less likely. New items can readily be added, and the order of items can be randomised or adjusted in the light of answers to previous questions. Rapid feedback of test scores is possible, which has the potential to improve the motivation of participants in a study. There is evidence that in some circumstances people will be more honest with a computer than with a human interviewer (Lucas et al., 1977). It would seem reasonable to suppose that many younger research participants would find it easier and less stressful to answer questions delivered through a computer environment compared with the same questions presented on a paper form. On the whole, scores recorded through computer administered testing are similar to those achieved by traditional methods, although Sampson (1990) argues that 'blanket assumptions of equivalency are unwarranted' since there have been some examples of different norms generated by computerised and non-computerised samples.

The final issue to be reviewed regarding the use of standardised tests concerns access to these instruments. Copyright on most of the widely used scales is typically held by educational publishing companies, who sell test materials and manuals at commercial rates. In the test catalogues produced by these publishers, it can be seen that certain tests will only be sold to people who have attained specified levels of competency in test administration and interpretation. The possession of a degree or postgraduate training in psychology is often regarded as a necessary condition for test user status. In some cases competency and access can only be acquired by attending courses run by the particular company selling the test. These constraints on test availability are intended to maintain standards and safeguard consumers. However, many counsellors or counselling researchers who do not have a background in psychology may find themselves effectively barred from using tests unless they can find a way of collaborating with a psychologist or other registered test user. The CORE system, which was developed with funding from the Mental Health Foundation, is an important exception to this trend. The CORE system has been disseminated on an open access basis, with users permitted to make multiple copies of questionnaires.

Further reading

The most comprehensive overview of the issues involved in using tests and questionnaires in counselling and psychotherapy research is to be found in M.E. Maruish (ed.) (1999) *The Use of Psychological Testing for Treatment Planning and Outcome Assessment*, 2nd edn. Mahwah, NJ: Lawrence Erlbaum.

Basic principles of test design and validity are fully explained in two books:

Watkins Jr, C.E. and Campbell, V.L. (eds) (2000) *Testing and Assessment in Counseling Practice*, 2nd edn. Hillsdale, NJ: Lawrence Erlbaum.
Whiston, S.C. (2000) *Principles and Applications of Assessment in Counseling*. Belmont, CA: Brooks/Cole.

The best sources of information about questionnaires and rating scale measures are the books by Ann Bowling:

Bowling, A. (1997) *Measuring Health: A Review of Quality of Life Measurement Scales*, 2nd edn. Buckingham: Open University Press.
Bowling, A. (2001) *Measuring Disease: A Review of Disease-specific Quality of Life Measurement Scales*, 2nd edn. Buckingham: Open University Press.

The most authoritative source on questionnaire and coding systems for measuring therapy process variables remains L.S. Greenberg and W.M. Pinsof (eds) (1986) *The Psychotherapeutic Process: A Research Handbook*. New York: Guilford Press. It should be noted, however, that a number of important process measures have emerged since the publication of their book.

The classic text on questionnaire design is:

Sudman, S. and Bradburn, N.M. (1982) *Asking Questions: A Practical Guide to Questionnaire Design*. San Francisco, CA: Jossey-Bass.

6 Listening to Stories about Therapy: From Qualitative Research to Human Science

In earlier chapters, there were references to the distinction between qualitative and quantitative approaches to research. The aim of the present chapter is to examine some of the assumptions that underpin qualitative research in counselling, and then to introduce some of the techniques and methods that can be employed in carrying out qualitative studies. The chapter will conclude with an examination of the criteria that can be applied in assessing the validity of qualitative findings.

Qualitative research has often been defined in terms of what it is *not*, i.e. it is research that does not involve the use of measurement or statistical techniques. For example, Miles and Huberman (1994) describe qualitative data as 'words rather than numbers', while Strauss and Corbin (1998) view the qualitative approach as comprising 'any kind of research that produces findings not arrived at by means of statistical procedures or other means of quantification'. The pervasiveness of 'negative definitions' of qualitative methods reflects the fact that, historically, much qualitative research has been explicitly conducted in opposition to, or in defiance of, the dominant positivist paradigm in psychology and social science (see Lincoln and Guba, 1985). However, to appreciate what is involved in qualitative research, it is also necessary to frame a definition that encompasses its main characteristics and goals in a more constructive manner.

Current practice in qualitative research draws upon a number of research traditions, each of which has made a distinctive contribution to the development of this approach to human science: hermeneutics, phenomenology, ethnography, feminist research, narrative analysis, naturalistic research, heuristic research, grounded theory analysis, 'new paradigm' methods and discourse analysis (Denzin and Lincoln, 2000; McLeod, 2001c). The field of qualitative research is methodologically much more fragmented than is the world of quantitative methods. Positivist research, such as experimental psychology, is derived from a philosophical position that regards knowledge as unitary, and therefore attainable through a standardised set of scientific procedures (see Chapter 1). By contrast, most qualitative researchers adopt a philosophical stance that human knowledge is contextualised and local. As a result, different qualitative researchers, influenced by different traditions, have tended to develop fairly idiosyncratic strategies for gathering and analysing data.

Stiles (1993) suggests that qualitative research can most usefully be regarded as a 'natural language' label which is best defined in terms of examples or characteristic features, not all of which are applicable in every case, rather than as a phenomenon that can be strictly circumscribed. From the work of key writers such as Lincoln and Guba (1985), Patton (1990) and Stiles (1993), it is possible to identify a set of interlocking themes, strategies and values characteristic of most qualitative research.

1 *Naturalistic inquiry*: studying real-world phenomena in as unobtrusive a manner as possible, with a sense of openness regarding whatever emerges.
2 *Inductive analysis*: allowing conclusions to arise from a process of immersion in the data, rather than imposing categories or theories decided in advance. A willingness on the part of the researcher to 'bracket-off' his or her assumptions about the phenomena being studied.
3 *An image of an active human subject*: research participants are viewed as purposefully involved in co-creating their social worlds, and are similarly engaged as active co-equals in the research process.
4 *Holistic perspective*: emphasis on the reciprocal inter-relationships between phenomena, rather than attempting to create explanations solely in terms of cause–effect sequences. Keeping the larger picture in mind, rather than reducing experience to discrete variables.
5 *Qualitative data*: gathering mainly linguistically based data that is richly descriptive of the experience of informants. Data as a 'text' rather than an array of numbers.
6 *Cyclical nature of research*: any research study involves a cycle of active data-gathering, reflective interpretation and assessment of the accuracy of findings.
7 *Personal contact and insight*: the researcher is in close contact with the people being studied. The quality of the researcher–informant relationship is of critical importance. The use of the researcher's empathic understanding of informants as a source of data.
8 *Process orientation*: views the phenomenon being investigated as a dynamic system where change is constant and on-going.
9 *Awareness of uniqueness*: a willingness to view each individual case as special and unique. The principle of respecting the particular configuration of individual cases even when developing general conclusions.
10 *Contextual awareness*: findings can only be understood within a social, cultural, historical and environmental context. Part of the task of the researcher is to consider these contextual factors.
11 *Design flexibility*: within a study, methods and procedures are adapted in response to new circumstances and experiences.
12 *Flexible sampling*: the choice of participants in a study is determined by a range of theoretical and practical considerations, not merely by the aim of accumulating a 'representative' sub-set of the general population.
13 *Reflexivity*: the idea that the researcher is his or her primary instrument, and as a result must be aware of the fantasies, expectations and needs that his or her participation introduces to the research process.
14 *Empowerment as a research goal*: an awareness of the social and political implications of research, accompanied by a commitment to using the research process to benefit research participants.

15 *A constructionist approach to knowledge*: taking the point of view that reality is
    socially constructed (Gergen, 1985, 1999). The products of research are not 'facts'
    or 'findings' that reflect an objective reality, but are versions of the life-world that are
    constructed by the researcher (or co-constructed between researcher and
    participants).

Several of these features of qualitative research can also be present in some
quantitative studies. For example, many quantitative researchers would want to
argue that they too are interested in processes, gather linguistically rich descriptive data, sample flexibly and view their research as a cycle of inquiry. Indeed,
many researchers would assert that their ideal would be to create 'pluralist'
research designs that combine those quantitative and qualitative strategies most
appropriate to each specific research problem. (The issues arising from the
adoption of this kind of methodological pluralism are explored in Chapter 11.)
Qualitative research, however, represents a range of approaches each of which
includes in some form *all* of the themes and strategies listed above. The
fundamental goal of qualitative investigation is to uncover and illuminate what
things mean to people. A brief definition of qualitative research might be to view
it as 'a process of systematic inquiry into the meanings which people employ to
make sense of their experience and guide their actions'. The key idea here is that
of *meaning*. The qualitative researcher strives to describe understandings, while
the quantitative researcher attempts to measure variables.

It should be clear by this point that carrying out this kind of research is a
complex and difficult matter. It takes time to establish the kinds of relationships
with informants that will yield high-quality descriptive accounts of their experience. Recording and analysing qualitative data presents many challenges. So,
although doing systematic and rigorous qualitative research can be rewarding, it
makes many demands on the researcher and should not be seen as an easy
option.

Qualitative research in practice

The process of carrying out qualitative research can be divided into two broad
types of activity: gathering data and analysing data. In practice these two
activities will often be carried out as a series of cycles of inquiry, or may even
appear to be happening at the same time. However, for the purpose of the
present discussion, these research operations will be reviewed separately. In the
space available here, it is only possible to outline qualitative research techniques
in an introductory manner. The reader intending to carry out a qualitative study is
recommended to consult other texts that provide more detailed accounts of
qualitative research procedures. Particularly useful are Flick (1998), Kvale (1996),
Lofland (1971), Marshall and Rossman (1999), Miles and Huberman (1994),
Patton (1990), Rennie et al. (1988), Strauss and Corbin (1998) and Yin (1994).

Gathering qualitative data

A wide range of methods has been employed in gathering data in qualitative studies. Each of these methods has its own special advantages and disadvantages. Also, some data-gathering techniques that have been successfully used in qualitative research settings do not appear to have been implemented in counselling research.

Interviewing

Interviewing is a very widely used qualitative data-collection technique. The research interview is a flexible way of gathering research data that is detailed and personal. The presence of the interviewer enables on-going monitoring of the relevance of the information being collected, and enables the researcher to check out his or her understanding of what is being said. One of the principal disadvantages of interviews lies in the amount of time that can be spent in setting them up, conducting the session and then transcribing the tape recording. Some informants (and researchers) find the experience of being recorded intimidating. The quality of information obtained also depends on the level of rapport and trust between interviewer and interviewee.

There are different approaches to structuring qualitative research interviews. Lofland (1971), for instance, describes the process of creating a list of potential questions, arranging them into groups according to different themes to be explored, then working out how to ask these questions most effectively in terms of order of topics, and finally carrying out pilot interviews to tighten up the procedures and check the length of time the interview will consume. This kind of semi-structured interview is highly effective when the researcher feels able to anticipate in advance the areas into which he or she intends to inquire. Good examples of the use of semi-structured interviewing in counselling studies can be seen in the research by Maluccio (1979) into the experiences of clients and counsellors, or the work by Skovholt and Ronnestad (1992) into the personal and career development of psychotherapists.

By contrast, however, in many research situations the qualitative researcher may wish to make as few prior assumptions as possible regarding the topics to be covered. In unstructured or open-ended interviews, the researcher will invite the informant to discuss a broad topic or theme, with the emphasis being on recording the spontaneous, free-flowing meanings that the interviewee is able to articulate. The task of the researcher is to define or delineate the phenomenon to be studied, and then to facilitate the exploration by the participant of what this phenomenon means to him or her. Kvale (1996) has identified a set of key aspects of this type of highly phenomenological research interview. These principles or values are listed in Box 6.1.

The role of the interviewer in qualitative research can be viewed from different perspectives. There is a general assumption that research interviewers need to be

Box 6.1   Aspects of the qualitative research interview

Life-world. The subject of qualitative interviewing is the life-world of the interviewee and his/her relation to it. The purpose is to describe and understand the central themes the person experiences and lives toward. The interview is theme-oriented, not person-oriented.

Meaning. The interview seeks to describe and understand the meaning of central themes in the life-world of the informant. The interviewer registers and interprets what is said as well as how it is said, and must be observant of and able to interpret vocalisation, facial expressions and other bodily gestures.

Qualitative and descriptive. The interview aims at obtaining nuanced descriptions of different aspects of the life-world.

Specificity. Descriptions of specific situations and action sequences are elicited, not general opinions.

Presuppositionless. Rather than coming with ready-made categories and schemes of interpretation, there is an openness to new and unexpected phenomena.

Focused. The interview is neither strictly structured with standardised questions, nor entirely 'non-directive', but is focusd on certain themes.

Ambiguity. The statements of an interviewee may sometimes be ambiguous, reflecting objective contradictions in the world he or she lives in.

Change. During the interview, the informant may come to change his or her descriptions of and meanings about a theme. The process of being interviewed may produce new insight and awareness.

Sensitivity. Different interviewers may produce different material on the same theme, depending on their sensitivity toward, and knowledge of, the topic.

Interpersonal situation. The interview is an interaction between two people.

Positive experience. A qualitative research interview may be a favourable experience for the informant. The interview is a conversation where two people talk about a theme of interest to both parties. A well carried through qualitative interview may be a rare and enriching experience for the interviewee.

Source: Kvale (1996)

skilled in putting people at their ease, using open and closed questions appropriately, listening and reflecting, and monitoring and structuring the flow of the interaction. However, the long tradition of structured, quantitatively oriented research interviewing that is found in opinion sampling, census interviews and market research has contributed to an image of the effective interviewer as someone who is neutral, objective and not personally engaged with the interviewee. This conception of the role of interviewer has come under attack from many qualitative researchers, in particular those who have carried out studies from a feminist perspective (Finch, 1984; Oakley, 1981). These researchers have employed an approach to interviewing that is consistent with the values and philosophy articulated by Kvale (1996). Finch (1984) describes this form of interviewing as one in which 'women talk to another woman in an informal way', where the hierarchical relationship between interviewer and interviewee is reduced as far as possible and the sense of the encounter as a mutual *inter*-view is emphasised. Mies (1983) describes this approach as comprising a 'conscious partiality': the researcher should be willing to be known by, and identify with, the informant. An example of this type of interview study within the field of counselling research is the research by Nicholson (1989) into the experiences of women with post-natal depression.

The research studies carried out by Oakley (1981), Finch (1984) and Nicholson (1989) all involved situations in which the women research participants were happy to talk about particular health and life issues with other women (the interviewers) who could share in these experiences. There are other research situations, however, where differences in power, status and knowledge can make it diffcult to achieve this level of open and mutual participation in a research interview. Mearns and McLeod (1984) have suggested that the principles of person-centred counselling can offer an effective basis for qualitative data gathering. If the interviewer can aim to establish a relationship with the interviewee characterised by high levels of respect, empathy, congruence and acceptance, and a sense of process and becoming, then the informant will be more likely to engage with the research in an authentic and constructive manner.

It is important to recognise that the research interview need not consist merely of sequences of questions and answers. It is possible to use various techniques to facilitate discussion of topics relevant to the aims of the interview, for example showing them pictures, asking them to respond to vignettes (Finch, 1987) or watch a video. Perhaps the most significant development in interview technique in counselling and therapy research to emerge within the past few years has been the employment of Interpersonal Process Recall (IPR) (Barker, 1985) methods to stimulate the ability of the interviewee to remember more about the experience of participating in a therapy session. In IPR 'assisted recall' interviews, the client or therapist is replayed a video or audio recording of the session, with the instruction to stop the tape at regular intervals and report what he or she remembers thinking or feeling at that point in the original session. This use of assisted recall in process research is found in the work of Rennie (1992) and Elliott (1986), described in Chapter 9.

Research interviews with clients or former clients raise a number of distinctive methodological problems. There are ethical issues involved in conducting interviews that have the potential to re-stimulate painful memories or unresolved emotional conflicts. There is also the challenge to the researcher to keep the interview centred on the research task, and to obtain meaningful personal material from the informant without the interview turning into a counselling session. These issues were sensitively dealt with by Brannen and Collard (1982) in their study of the experiences of people seeking counselling help for marital problems. In this study, Brannen and Collard (1982) interviewed 26 wives and 22 husbands representing 28 marriages. These research participants were all people who had recently entered counselling, and were still clients. They found many practitioners reluctant to allow them to approach clients. These counsellors were concerned about the possibility of breaches of confidentiality and afraid that the research interview might damage their relationship with the client, as well as being worried by the prospect that the interview itself might prove emotionally disturbing. As a result, the researchers took great care to collaborate with counsellors in developing appropriately sensitive ways of contacting clients and carrying out interviews. Two researchers were present at each interview, one actually conducting the interview and the other acting as observer.

Brannen and Collard (1982) found that these interviews were deeply moving and involving, for both researcher and informant:

> our respondents were people in crisis, and any question we asked them almost inevitably provoked very painful feelings. Moreover, because they were in crisis they were only too ready to talk to someone who was uninvolved and was not unsympathetic. . . . Such a situation made it extremely important for us to stay with, and to see through, the discharge of our respondents' feelings arising from their efforts to describe their situations. (1982: 23)

They observed that the presence of an observer enabled them to maintain a necessary sense of balance and containment in this highly emotional situation:

> [the observer] seemed to exert some kind of 'holding' balance or safeguard of the emotional boundaries, for both the interviewer and the respondent. It seemed to give courage to the interviewer to pursue areas which he or she might well have avoided as too awkward or sensitive, and to give reassurance that there was someone else to hand if necessary. To the respondents, it seemed to give permission to disclose as freely as they wished, and at the end of the interview they could turn to the second 'silent' researcher in a different vein, having discharged to the first what had been so deeply felt. (1982: 23–4)

It can be seen, then, that interviewing clients can be a difficult and demanding task. Brannen and Collard argue that it is essential that the researcher should avoid being drawn into the role of counsellor, and take particular care to 'handle the respondents and information they impart with respect and integrity' (1982: 26).

One of the drawbacks of carrying out research through individual interviews is the time and expense that is involved in contacting and making arrangements to meet research informants. Also, in the private one-to-one interview, the informant may be strongly influenced by the presence of an authoritative expert other (the interviewer). Some researchers have therefore developed the *focus group* technique (Bloor et al., 2000; Greenbaum, 1998; Krueger and Casey, 2000; Stewart and Shamdasani, 1990), as a means of conducting systematic small group interviews with sets of around seven to twelve people. In these groups, the interviewer acts as a facilitator to draw out the beliefs and attitudes of group members concerning the topic under examination. The group discussion is tape recorded and represents a rich source of qualitative data. In the focus group setting, each member of the group is exposed to an open social situation, one in which the views of the researcher will be a less significant source of influence. The group facilitator or director must, of course, skilfully conduct the session to prevent any members of the group dominating the discussion. Focus groups have been widely used in market research, and in evaluating employee perceptions of organisational change. There do not appear to have been focus group studies on specific counselling-related topics, although the technique is clearly applicable as a method of investigating the views that users of services, or other stakeholders, might hold regarding the work of a counselling agency.

Qualitative open-ended questionnaires

In some qualitative research studies, the researchers may have a list of questions to put to informants, but it may not be practicable or necessary to conduct actual face-to-face interviews. In these circumstances, the *open-ended questionnaire* can be a valuable research tool. A much wider coverage of informants can usually be achieved by using this technique, and short open-ended questionnaires are normally experienced by research participants as straightforward, unintrusive and unthreatening. From the point of view of the researcher, there is the big advantage that qualitative questionnaire data does not need to be transcribed.

However, although open-ended questionnaires are an attractive option for researchers with restricted resources, it is necessary to be aware of their limitations in comparison with interviews. Firstly, it is very difficult for people with literacy problems to complete questionnaires, and they may even react negatively to them. Secondly, the researcher needs to be sure that informants will be able to understand the meaning of questions in a similar manner. For example, a questionnaire that asks social workers to write about 'how counselling conflicts with your other work tasks and roles' could well yield confused and uninterpretable data if, as is likely, different research participants hold different definitions about the meaning of 'counselling'. In a face-to-face interview these meanings can be clarified and agreed, but with questionnaires the informant can only respond to what is on the page. Similarly, simple, unambiguous questions are needed on questionnaires, whereas in interviews it is possible to work with the informant to break complex, multi-faceted issues into their component parts and explore them one at a time.

Questionnaires can sometimes be useful as a technique for gathering sensitive or confidential information, because there is the potential for the informant to write anonymously. On the other hand, it is more difficult to explain confidentiality procedures on a questionnaire top-sheet than it is in person, and there will be less of an opportunity for the respondent to seek clarification on any confidentiality issues that might be of special concern to them.

Despite these limitations, there are many counselling studies that have made good use of open-ended questionnaires. Lietaer (1992), for example, asked clients in client-centred therapy to write at the end of each session about what they found helpful and what they had found hindering to them in that session. Bloch et al. (1979) and Llewelyn et al. (1988) have used written accounts of 'the most helpful event' to explore the perceptions of clients in various forms of individual and group therapy. Bachelor (1988) asked both clients and non-clients to write about their experiences of 'being understood', and used this qualitative material to construct an analysis of 'received empathy'. In all these studies, relatively simple open-ended questionnaires generated data of value for both theory and practice.

Projective techniques

In both interviews and open-ended questionnaires, descriptive material can be supplemented and augmented through the use of *projective techniques*. In all projective techniques, the person is presented with an ambiguous or incomplete stimulus to which he or she can respond in any way they choose. The classic projective techniques, which have in the past been widely used in personality assessment, include the Rorschach inkblot test, where the person is asked to tell what they see in a symmetrical inkblot, the Thematic Apperception Test (TAT), where the person tells or writes a story about a picture, and sentence-completion technique, where the person writes an ending to an incomplete sentence stem. Projective techniques have a long history within psychology and a wide range of such techniques have been invented (Semeonoff, 1976). The fundamental assumption behind the use of this method is that, in making his or her fantasy-based response to the stimulus, the person will 'project' their characteristic way of dealing with situations, and characteristic patterns of feeling, action and motivation. For example, one of the best known TAT pictures is of a boy sitting looking at a violin. Some people respond to this by creating a story of how the boy will one day be a famous musician. Others respond with stories of how the boy will be punished for not practising on the violin. In these simple stories, the respondents are taken to be depicting the kinds of worlds in which they live. The first group might be seen as living in a world in which achievement is expected and rewarded. The second group would appear to see their personal world as a place where failure and attendant punishment is the norm.

Traditionally, projective techniques have been controversial within psychology. Some of these issues and debates are discussed in Chapter 5. Basically, the argument in favour of projective techniques is that the creative use of fantasy and ambiguity enables people to express their deeper feelings about issues. The argument against projective techniques is that it can often be very hard to make sense of what these deeper feelings and impulses might mean, given the radically open-ended nature of the projective task. Despite these problems, however, projective techniques have been successfully employed in social and market research (Branthwaite and Lunn, 1985). Rich qualitative material can be gained from projective questions such as 'if the United Nations was a restaurant, what sort of place would it be, and what sort of food would it serve?', or asking people to write an obituary for a favourite product, describing its strengths and advantages but also its weaknesses and ultimate failings. Nevertheless, despite the fact that projection-based exercises are widely used in counselling and groupwork, there are few examples of the application of this method in counselling research. The potential value of the approach can be seen in the study by West (1992), in which clients who had received Reichian therapy were sent a follow-up questionnaire to investigate their perceptions of process and outcome. Most of the questionnaire items were a combination of open and closed questions, but participants were also asked to offer a metaphor which would 'capture' their therapy experience. Another use of a projective technique is available in the study by Cohen and Taylor (1972) into the experiences of long-term prisoners. It was hard for these men to describe their feelings about being in prison, so Cohen and Taylor (1972) invited them to comment on various fictionalised accounts of prison life.

Participant observation

A strategy for collecting qualitative material that has been employed in a wide range of studies in sociology and anthropology is *participant observation* (Adler and Adler, 1994; Atkinson and Hammersley, 1994; Fetterman, 1998; Fielding, 1993). With this method, the researcher takes part in the lives of the people being studied, and gains as full an appreciation as possible of what different activities, relationships and institutions mean to them. Participant observation requires great skill, patience and persistence on the part of the researcher. Typical problems connected with this method are those of negotiating entry to the field, maintaining relationships with informants, keeping a balance between participation ('going native') and detachment, collecting field notes, and saying goodbye to people who may have become more than mere participants in a research study. Because of these difficulties, and also due to the psychological rather than sociological orientation of most counselling and psychotherapy research, there have been few participant observation studies in this field. Nevertheless, the capacity of this method to generate findings of interest to counsellors is apparent in the impact of the work that has been carried out using participant observation of therapeutic group situations. For example, Holloman

(1974) investigated the process of 'growth' groups from the perspective of an anthropologist, and offered a distinctive interpretation of these groups in terms of ritual. Wilson (1985) carried out a participant observation study of therapeutic processes in a yoga ashram. In both these studies, the researchers were able to gain access to detailed qualitative material that would have been inaccessible or unintelligible using any other approach than lengthy and systematic participant observation. Other examples of participant observation studies of therapy are discussed in McLeod (2001c).

Documentary research

All of the qualitative data-gathering methods reviewed to this point have shared the characteristic of being initiated by the researcher. These techniques can be seen as 'reactive', in that the answers given by research participants will to some extent be a reaction to the personality of the researcher, or to the way the question was asked in the questionnaire or interview. It is therefore very useful to be able to draw upon qualitative material that may have been created spontaneously by research participants completely independently of any research study. The most common data sources of this type are *personal documents* and *official documents* (Allport, 1942). Personal documents include letters, diaries, personal journals, poems and novels written by research participants. There have been a number of client case studies that have included material from the personal diaries of the client (for example, the studies by Evans and Robinson, 1978 and Yalom and Elkin, 1974). Organisational research often makes use of memos, minutes of meetings and organisational archives and correspondence. For example, in their study of the origins and development of the National Marriage Guidance Council, Lewis et al. (1992) consulted a wide variety of such official documents and papers.

Cooperative inquiry groups

An alternative qualitative data-gathering approach is the *human inquiry group*, or the *cooperative inquiry group*. This method represents a synthesis of all other qualitative methods, in the context of a distinctive philosophical stance concerning the aims and purposes of research. The use of cooperative inquiry groups initially evolved from a thorough critique of orthodox, positivist scientific methods (Reason and Rowan, 1981). Many among the network of researchers who contributed to this critique saw themselves as participating in the construction of a 'new paradigm' for human inquiry. The basis for this new approach was the acknowledgement that people are self-determining, and must be regarded as co-participants in research rather than as passive 'subjects' or 'informants'. Research must be carried out in a way that respects the *whole* potential for being human, including feelings and spiritual dimensions of experience as well as cognition and behaviour. Finally, the propositional or theoretical knowledge expressed in research papers and reports 'needs to be rooted in and derived from

Box 6.2 The phases of a cooperative inquiry project

Phase 1. Co-researchers agree on an area for inquiry and identify some initial research propositions. They also agree to a set of procedures for observing and recording their own and other people's experience. This phase is concerned with propositional knowing.

Phase 2. The group applies these ideas and procedures in their everyday life and work. This phase primarily involves practical knowing.

Phase 3. The co-researchers become fully engaged and immersed in the process. Their openness to what is going on for them allows them to bracket off their prior beliefs and preconceptions and so see their experience in a new way. This phase involves mainly experiential knowing.

Phase 4. After an appropriate period engaged in Phases 2 and 3, the co-researchers return to consider their original research propositions and hypotheses in the light of experience. This phase involves a critical return to propositional knowing. New hypotheses and procedures may be identified that lead into another round of the inquiry cycle.

Sources: Reason (1994); Reason and Heron (1986)

the experiential and practical knowledge of the subjects in the inquiry' (Reason and Heron, 1986: 458).

The inquiry group approach to gathering relevant qualitative data is summarised in Box 6.2. It is a strategy that relies strongly on productive, authentic collaboration between members of a group, and the application of a cycle of discovery/divergence and validation/convergence. Reason and Heron write that:

> *Research cycling* means taking an idea several times around the cycle of reflection and action. Primarily, this provides a series of corrective feedback loops; it may also clarify and deepen the ideas being explored. (1986: 467)

An example of one of the ways in which group collaboration and research cycling can operate in this mode of research is the use of the 'Devil's Advocate' in the group. Once some material has been collected and interpreted, a member of the group temporarily takes on the role of radical critic.

In practice, the members of an inquiry group can employ any and all data-gathering techniques: interviewing, keeping diaries, carrying out experiments. The distinctive aspect of the approach is the way that these familiar research techniques are embedded in a collective, cyclical inquiry process. The book by

Reason (1988a) contains a number of examples of the inquiry group method in action. The study by Reason et al. (1992; Reason, 1988b), into the development of a framework through which GPs and practitioners of complementary medicine might collaborate effectively, is a piece of research carried out in this tradition which is potentially of great relevance to counsellors working as members of multi-professional teams. Recent developments in the use of this research model have been reviewed by Reason (1994) and Kemmis and McTaggart (2000).

Personal experience methods

In counselling, the idea that practice involves the systematic 'use of self' is widely accepted. Therapeutic concepts such as countertransference and congruence represent the contribution that self-involvement and purposeful use of personal feelings and experiences can make to the therapeutic process. By contrast, researchers have tended to regard their own personal experience as a potential source of bias, rather than as a source of insight and data. Apart from adherents of the *inquiry group* method described in the previous section, psychological and social researchers have valued objectivity and been suspicious of subjectivity. It is important to note, however, that this was not always the case. In the early years of the development of the discipline of psychology, in the nineteenth century, researchers routinely used themselves as 'subjects' (Danziger, 1990).

In recent times, there have emerged a number of approaches to qualitative research that have sought to restore a place for the personal experience of the researcher. The most widely known of these approaches is the *heuristic inquiry* method developed by Moustakas (1967, 1990a, 1990b, 1994). This form of research requires the total personal immersion of the inquirer in the topic, to the point where a creative 'incubation' brings a new understanding of the phenomenon. The *integral inquiry* approach devised by Braud (1998) and the *intuitive inquiry* model espoused by Anderson (1998) are broadly similar to the heuristic approach, but specifically encourage a focus on transpersonal or spiritual dimensions of personal experience (Braud and Anderson, 1998).

The heuristic, integral and intuitive approaches to research can be viewed as part of a broader approach to knowing that can be characterised as humanistic psychology (Schneider, Bugental and Pierson, 2001). A contrasting approach to the use of personal experience for research purposes can be found in the work of Carolyn Ellis and her colleagues (Ellis and Bochner, 2000; Ellis and Flaherty, 1992; Ellis, Kiesinger and Tillmann-Healy, 1997). Their approach, known as *autoethnography*, is based in a sociological tradition, and combines the use of autobiography and ethnography (participant observation).

At the heart of any of these personal experience methodologies is the positioning of the researcher in relation to the topic of inquiry. What is distinctive about these approaches does not necessarily arise from the ways in which data is collected or analysed, but in the willingness of the researcher to draw upon his or her personal involvement with the study, and to record, take seriously and 'indwell' (Moustakas, 1990a, b) on all aspects of his or her awareness of the phenomenon. Many researchers using personal experience draw upon well-established methods of data collection and analysis:

> Intuitive inquiry (gives) researchers the confidence and incentive to carefully select research approaches and methods, from the many now available, and then creatively blend and synthesize these methods to suit the research project and the talents, skills, and values of the individual researcher. (Anderson, 1998: 90)

However, personal experience research has also generated some novel, inno-vative methods of data collection, such as the use of dreams, art, writing and spiritual practices (see Braud and Anderson, 1998, for examples).

Personal experience research can represent a powerful means of personal development for counsellors. A research project of this type can be as chal-lenging and rewarding as personal therapy, or participating in a training work-shop. It can be difficult, however, to achieve sufficient closure in relation to a study of this kind to arrive at a point of being able to write it up in a way that communicates effectively with others. Part of the difficulty here is that good heuristic or intuitive research requires a willingness to be known, to write honestly and openly about self. Another difficulty arises from the complexity of the writing task itself. Typically, a heuristic study encompasses a mix of personal journey, testimony and analysis. It is no easy matter to construct a report which does justice to these different discourses. A good example of heuristic research in counselling can be found in Etherington's (2000) study of the experiences of male survivors of sexual abuse. This book reflects the sensitivity and intricacy, and also the huge potential impact, of this approach to research. The programme of research by West (1996, 1997, 1998a, 1998b, 1998c, 2001) into the relation-ship between therapy and spiritual experience, similarly reflects the application of a disciplined heuristic approach.

Analysing qualitative data

Analysis and interpretation of qualitative data present considerable challenges to researchers. Typically, the qualitative researcher will gather many thousands of words of transcripts, notes and other written material. This raw data exists in a non-standardised form. For example, a qualitative data set can consist of detailed descriptions of events from some informants, cryptic comments from others, literal accounts and metaphoric allusions, experiential 'stream of consciousness' narratives and distanced explanatory rationalisations. It is probably fair to say that no two researchers approach the task of qualitative data analysis in quite the same way. Writers such as Lofland and Lofland (1984), Yin (1989), Patton (1990) and Miles and Huberman (1994) provide a range of different strategies that can be applied in qualitative data analysis. These strategies depend on the systematic application of five fundamental ideas: *immersion, categorisation,*

Box 6.3   Stages in the analysis of qualitative data

Stage 1: Immersion. The researcher intensively reads or listens to material, assimilating as much of the explicit and implicit meaning as possible.

Stage 2: Categorisation. Systematically working through the data, assigning coding categories or identifying meanings within the various segments/units of the 'text'.

Stage 3: Phenomenological reduction. Questioning or interrogating the meanings or categories that have been developed. Are there any other ways of looking at the data?

Stage 4: Triangulation. Sorting through the categories. Deciding which categories are recurring and central and which are less significant or are invalid or mistaken.

Stage 5: Interpretation. Making sense of the data from a wider perspective. Constructing a model, or using an established theory to explicate the findings of the study.

phenomenological reduction, triangulation and *interpretation.* These research operations represent different stages in the analysis of qualitative information (see Box 6.3). The first step in any qualitative data anlysis is for the researcher to become immersed in the information that he or she has gathered. The main instrument that the researcher possesses is his or her capacity to enter, in an empathic way, the lived experience of the person or group being studied. To gain a sense of the whole of that lived experience, the researcher must temporarily internalise and 'own' as much of the data as possible. Many qualitative researchers will work on coding interviews as soon as they can following an interview, so they do not lose the 'feel' of what the informant has said. Other qualitative researchers will carry around a notebook and jot down analytic themes or ideas whenever they occur to them. It is normal practice to read through field notes or interview transcripts, or listen to tapes, several times before beginning to do analytic work on them.

The process of categorising qualitative material is sometimes called 'coding' or 'classification'. Qualitative data can be viewed as essentially comprising a text or narrative. All qualitative data-collection techniques involve gathering the descriptions, accounts or stories that people create and share in relation to their experience. One of the first tasks of the qualitative researcher is to find ways of breaking down this flow of text into its component meanings. Whether the researcher segments the text into statements, thought units or larger patterns and sequences, it is necessary to assign meanings to these blocks of text in as systematic a manner as possible. The same meaning units may be assigned to as many as ten different categories, reflecting the diverse nuances and horizons of meaning associated with that piece of text. In order to achieve this awareness of alternative meanings, the researcher must develop his or her 'theoretical sensitivity'. Categorisation often goes hand in hand with another qualitative research strategy known as 'phenomenological reduction'. This idea has its roots in phenomenological philosophy and psychology, which are mainly concerned with describing the way phenomena are experienced (Becker, 1992; Osborne, 1990; Spiegelberg, 1960; Valle and Halling, 1989). The aim of a phenomenological investigation is to illuminate the totality of how some event or human action can be perceived and described. To achieve this rich and detailed descriptive account, the phenomenological researcher must suspend or 'bracket-off' his or her assumptions about what is being studied. From a phenomenological position, it is argued that people ordinarily 'take for granted' the experiential world within which they live, they have a 'natural attitude' that accepts that what is perceived is just 'out there' (Holstein and Gubrium, 1994). The researcher using a phenomenological approach, however, is systematically trying to find *new* ways of seeing or understanding the object of inquiry. In practice, it is never possible to put aside all the assumptions that might be held in relation to a phenomenon. The 'essence' of the phenomenon can never be grasped. But the very process of seeking this essence yields an understanding of the various perspectives and horizons of meaning through which the experience of that phenomenon has been constructed. A technique that can be employed to assist in this process is 'imaginative variation'. Here, the researcher does everything possible to find fresh ways of looking at the phenomenon. This involves an intentional disruption of the 'natural attitude'. The outcome of an effective phenomenological exploration of a set of qualitative data is a 'thick' description (Geertz, 1973) of the lifeworld or experiences of the individual or group being studied. This description may be framed as a narrative or story, or it may be organised in terms of a set of categories.

The aim of triangulation is to find agreement about the core meanings or themes in a text. Categorisation and phenomenological reduction are means of generating meanings, and attaching these meanings to the data. Triangulation is the task of finding out which meanings are most valid, accurate or important. It is a process of sifting and sorting meanings. The notion of triangulation comes from map reading, where a navigator will take bearings on different known points and draw a line that intersects on his or her current location. Similarly, the qualitative researcher can look for convergence between the data produced from diverse sources, methods and investigators as a check on the validity of a statement or conclusion. For example, in a study of group therapy using diaries kept by group members, a finding that anger was not expressed in the group until the fifth session would be more credible if it was backed up by diary observations made by all or most of the people in the group. Method triangulation refers to the practice of using different data-gathering techniques in the same study. For example, the experience of a client during a counselling session could be investigated using a combination of interview, open-ended questionnaire and Interpersonal Process Recall techniques. If the conclusions generated by all three methods were in agreement, the researcher could have added confidence in what had been found. Where a research team is used, the triangulation of observations made by different members of the team can be a valuable technique for identifying recurring themes and meanings.

Some qualitative research, for example naturalistic and phenomenological studies, restrict themselves to the production of a descriptive account of what has been studied, and therefore focus mainly on Stages 1 to 3 in Box 6.3. Other researchers find it more useful or appropriate to develop thematic summaries of the data (Stage 4). However, there are some qualitative researchers who seek to examine the theoretical implications of their findings, or even to construct a new theoretical model. This final qualitative approach necessarily involves the use of interpretation.

The act of interpretation involves locating the meaning of an experience or event within the context of a larger set of meanings (Messer et al., 1988; Taylor, 1979). This larger set of meanings would normally be a formal model or theory. It is important to be aware that, as Jones (1975) has noted, all interpretation is 'aspectival'; it is taken from a certain point of view. It is inevitable that there will always exist alternative interpretations, or further interpretations carried out on the initial interpretive framework offered by a researcher. The incompleteness of interpretation has been labelled the 'hermeneutic circle': every interpretation can in turn be interpreted by someone else. Despite the open-textured nature of interpretive activity, it is nevertheless possible to make judgements about the adequacy of any interpretation. Does it accommodate all factual information? Does it ignore important parts of the text or is it comprehensive? Has the writer argued logically from the data to the interpretation? The final criterion for the value of an interpretation is through its use value. Geertz (1973) has this to say:

> theoretical ideas are not created anew in each study . . . they are adapted from other, related studies, and refined in the process, applied to new interpretive problems. If they cease being useful with respect to such problems, they tend to stop being used and are more or less abandoned. If they continue being used, throwing up new understandings, they are further elaborated and go on being used. (1973: 27)

An example of this process of testing interpretations against experience can be given through the writings of the psychoanalyst Bettelheim, who found that what he observed in a concentration camp could not be assimilated into the interpretive schema of psychoanalysis:

> my efforts to understand the concentration camp experience through classical psychoanalysis had broken down, and only then I was willing to accept the need for revising that frame of reference. (Bettelheim, 1960: 31)

This is a dramatic and vivid example of the 'abandonment' of an interpretive scheme. More common, perhaps, is a quiet inner feeling that an interpretation does not work. At a lived, feeling level an interpretation may either be effective in shifting the sense of understanding or it may leave that felt sense unchanged (Gendlin, 1966). The evaluation of interpretations, then, is carried out through a process of appraisal that is both rational (is it supported by the evidence?) and intuitive (does it trigger a feeling of clarity and movement?).

These five stages of qualitative data analysis – immersion, categorisation, phenomenological reduction, triangulation and interpretation – can in practice be operationalised in many different ways, depending on the particular requirements of the research project and the ideological affiliations of the researcher. It is also important to note that, throughout this analytic work, the researcher needs to keep in mind the 'quality control' criteria that are discussed later in this chapter. However, despite the rich diversity of analytic techniques that are used in qualitative research, it is widely accepted that the one methodological approach which has achieved a central position is the *grounded theory* method pioneered by Glaser and Strauss (1967).

Grounded theory

The 'grounded theory' methodology of Glaser and Strauss (1967) provides a set of analytic techniques that can be seen as representing procedures that are consistent with, or have been assimilated into, most other approaches to qualitative research. Recent versions of grounded theory analysis (Charmaz, 2000; Glaser, 1978; Rennie et al., 1988; Strauss and Corbin, 1990, 1997, 1998) describe it as comprising a series of well-articulated analytic steps: coding, categorising, memoing, theoretical sampling, explicating the story line.

The grounded theory approach aims to develop a theory or model of the phenomenon being investigated that is demonstrably faithful to the actual lived experience of the people being studied. It is an inductive approach, beginning with descriptive data and subjecting that material to increasing levels of conceptualisation. An interesting feature of the grounded theory method is that researchers are *not* encouraged to review the literature before embarking on a study, for fear that over-commitment to existing theories and concepts may prevent them from making new discoveries. Strauss and Corbin (1990) write that:

> there is no need to review all of the literature beforehand, as is frequently done by researchers trained in other approaches, because if we are effective in our analysis, then new categories will emerge that neither we, nor anyone else, had thought about previously. We do not want to be so steeped in the literature as to be constrained and even stifled in terms of our creative efforts by our knowledge of it! Since discovery is our purpose, we do not have beforehand knowledge of all the categories relevant to our theory. It is only after a category has emerged as pertinent that we might want to go back to the technical literature to determine if this category is there, and if so what other researchers have said about it. (1990: 50)

So, knowledge of the literature is valuable in so far as it can be used to sensitise the researcher to potential dimensions of meaning. It is an impediment, however, if it gets in the way of discovery.

The first step in a grounded theory analysis is to go through the qualitative data (interview transcripts, field notes, documents) and break it down into meaning units. These units can be very brief (a word or phrase) or can span much longer passages of text. The researcher codes these units by labelling or tagging each of them with as many different meaning words or phrases as possible. This initial trawl through the material will generate a large number of meanings and conceptualisations of segments of the material. It is important to carry out this task with what Strauss and Corbin call an attitude of 'theoretical sensitivity': 'we have to challenge our assumptions, delve beneath our experience, and look beyond the literature if we are to uncover phenomena and arrive at new theoretical formulations' (1990: 76). They suggest a range of techniques for enhancing this kind of phenomenological sensitivity.

The next step in grounded theory analysis is to group these elements of meaning into categories. This involves looking at all the concepts that seem to relate to the same phenomena, and questioning whether they are in fact all examples of one category or can be differentiated into sub-categories. This aspect of grounded theory analysis can be illustrated in the research by Rennie (1990) into the experience of the client during a therapy session. Rennie carried out an IPR recall interview with each client as a means of enabling them to report on what they had thought and felt during a single session (see Chapter 9). Each interview was transcribed and subjected to the coding and categorisation procedures already described. The result of this stage of the research can be seen in Box 6.4, which presents some of the concepts and categories identified by Rennie. It should be noted that, for reasons of space, this Box includes only around one-third of the concepts generated by Rennie (1990).

As the researcher is carrying out the task of categorising the material, he or she will begin to have lots of ideas about how these categories and concepts fit together: tentative hypotheses may emerge about what categories seem to be most important, different words or phrases come to mind that might capture nuances of meaning; possibilities for gathering new data formulate themselves. Strauss and Corbin (1990, 1998) suggest that it is important to separate or 'bracket-off' these ideas so that they do not interfere with the job of assigning concepts to the data. They recommend that grounded theory researchers keep a 'memo' file, in which they record these ideas and hypotheses so that they are not lost but at the same time do not intrude on the detailed descriptive work necessary during the categorisation phase. It is in the memo file that the researcher is beginning to construct an interpretation of the material. The construction of a list of concepts and categories as displayed in Box 6.4 comprises the descriptive phase of grounded theory analysis. The list is the equivalent of a 'thick description' of the data. What follows is further analysis of the material with the aim of constructing a grounded model. This is accomplished through 'axial coding', which involves looking for the linkages and connections between categories of experience. What are the contexts in which certain

Box 6.4   Concepts and categories from a grounded theory study of client experiences of therapy

Main category 1: The client's relationship with personal meaning
(a) The pursuit of personal meaning
     Client scrutinises own processes
     The client's track
     Client narrative/storytelling
     Insight
     Contact with feelings
     Digestion
(b) The avoidance of meaning
     Client's defensiveness
     Playing for effect
     Client's resistance
     Willingness to change
     Lying to the therapist

Main category 2: The client's perception of the relationship with the therapist
(a) 'Nonspecific' relationship factors
     Relationship with the therapist
     Client's perception of the therapeutic task
     Client's dependence–independence
     Client's perception of therapist's evaluation of client
     Therapist's manner
(b) Client's deference
     Concern about therapist's approach
     Fear of criticising therapist
     Client's understanding of therapist's frame of reference
     Meeting perceived therapist's expectations
     Metacommunication

Main category 3: The client's awareness of outcomes
     Impact of therapy
     Impact of inquiry

Source: Rennie (1990)

categories occur? What are the antecedents and consequences of the occurrence of a category? Finally, the researcher is able to identify a core, or central category and brings all the data together to build up a descriptive narrative about the central phenomena of the study. Throughout the analysis, the grounded theory researcher must continually check back to the original data to verify that the themes and story lines that are emerging are in fact consistent with the actual primary experiential material. The whole process can be seen as one in which the data is in a sense systematically dismantled through the act of categorising, then put back together again through the process of theory construction. It is a process that moves from description to interpretation.

It should be clear that a grounded theory analysis will typically yield a complex and multi-faceted picture of the topic being researched. One of the problems that can often arise in this type of research concerns the difficulty of writing up the analysis. There are two general rules that should be observed. First, the material comes alive when the writing concentrates on the active, intentional *processes* in which subjects engage. For example, it is more interesting to read about 'becoming a client' than about a set of categories or themes elicited from people after their first session of therapy. Secondly, it is vital to find a single, clear focus for each report or piece of writing. It is a mistake, in grounded theory work, to attempt to write about everything at once. Instead, in a grounded theory study, the aim is to arrive at a single, 'core' category that captures the essential meaning of the study:

> . . . the central category (sometimes called the core category) represents the main theme of the research . . . it consists of all the products of analysis condensed into a few words that seem to explain 'what this research is all about'. . . . A central category has analytic power. What gives it that power is its ability to pull the other categories together to form an explanatory whole. (Strauss and Corbin, 1998: 146)

Strauss and Corbin (1998: 147) identify a set of criteria for choosing a central or core category, for example:

1. It must be central: that is, all the other categories can be related to it.
2. It must appear frequently in the data.
3. The name or phrase used to describe the central category should be sufficiently abstract that it can . . . lead to the development of a more general theory.

It can be difficult, even for experienced researchers, to arrive at a core or central category that 'explains what the research is all about'. However, the use in grounded theory research of central categories contributes significantly to the coherence and analytic depth of studies that follow this approach.

This strategy of separating out distinct 'aspectival' readings of the data is apparent in the publications following the original account by Rennie (1990) of his study of client experiences during therapy. These subsequent papers have focused on specific themes such as reflexivity (Rennie, 1992), deference (Rennie, 1994a), storytelling (Rennie, 1994b), resistance (Rennie, 1994c) and the experience of metaphor (Angus and Rennie, 1988, 1989).

Although the grounded theory approach provides a framework or template for qualitative data analysis that has been used by many researchers, it is important to acknowledge that there are other ways of working with the products of qualitative inquiry. Huberman and Miles (1994) provide a comprehensive review and source of guidance on these alternative methods.

The use of computers in qualitative analysis

Traditionally, the practicalities of qualitative research have necessitated the compilation of hundreds of pages of written or typed notes, and the creation of a card file to enable the sorting and cross-classification of categories. In recent years, however, the availability of personal computers has meant that qualitative researchers have increasingly written their data straight into computer files and employed specially written software to deal with the tasks of segmenting and classifying data. Fielding and Lee (1991) and Richards and Richards (1994) review the issues involved in the use of computers in qualitative research, and also review the characteristics and features of commercially marketed qualitative software packages such as Ethno, Atlas, Enalysist, the Ethnograph, Hyperqual and Nudist. Some of these packages allow the researcher to work directly from sound files, thus eliminating the need to transcribe all of an interview, while also making it possible to retain the richness of the informant's voice quality. An important advantage of using computers in qualitative research lies in the fact that a section of text does not need to be re-typed every time it is assigned to a new category. The disadvantage is that the researcher can 'lose touch' with the material. For example, when sorting categories into groups or themes it can often be helpful to spread index cards over the floor. This is not possible with computerised records.

Achieving consensus: the use of a research team

One of the most important methodological choices facing anyone beginning a qualitative study is whether to work mainly alone, or to set up a research team. There is a strong tradition within qualitative research of respecting the contribution that can be made by lone researchers. Typically, the data sets that are generated in qualitative interviews or observations are large and complex. To understand fully such a data set may require a supreme act of immersion and concentration on the part of a highly committed individual. The same level of detailed understanding and questioning of the material cannot be achieved by parcelling it into bits and dividing out the task of analysis between members of a team. Some of the most substantial achievements in qualitative research, such as the work of Goffman and Glaser in sociology, or Rennie in therapy research, have derived from the work of individuals who have only 'tested' their analysis on others at a fairly late stage in their work.

An alternative approach is to carry out qualitative research on a team basis. Guidelines for carrying out collective research have been developed by Hill et al. (1996, 1997) and Elliott (2002b). The cooperative inquiry group method, discussed earlier in this chapter, represents another form of collective research. Team-based analysis of qualitative data essentially depends on different members of the group analysing the same material and then comparing what they have found. Hill et al. (1997) describe a method for pooling the analyses of different members, discussing divergent interpretations, and using an external auditor to adjudicate in unresolved instances and to challenge any possible group biases. Elliott (2002b) suggests that the research team divides into two groups who each generate alternative interpretations of the data and then meet to argue their 'case'.

The advantages of team-based research are that it can save time, by dividing up work between people, it can be supportive and enjoyable to be a member of a team, and it can lead to consensus which can claim a certain degree of validity or 'objectivity'. The advantages of working alone are that it may be practically difficult to convene teams, and that a richer and more creative analysis is possible in a situation where different team members do not need to arrive at a compromise judgement. Individual researchers can also point to many ways, other than team consensus, that can be applied in establishing the accuracy or sensitivity of a piece of qualitative research (criteria for evaluating qualitative research are discussed in the following section of this chapter).

It is certainly possible to carry out good qualitative research working alone, or as a team. For anyone embarking on a qualitative study, the choice of an individual or group approach requires careful consideration. In some circumstances, research teams have a training element, with team members comprising students, with the convenor of the team being their research supervisor. In other circumstances, research teams can comprise networks of practitioners who find it supportive and practicable to work together.

Criteria for evaluating the validity of qualitative research

Clearly, the concepts of validity and reliability that have been developed for use in quantitative research (see Chapter 5) cannot be applied in the same way in qualitative studies. A number of different criteria for judging the adequacy or plausibility of qualitative research have been identified (Kirk and Miller, 1986). For example, Lincoln and Guba (1989) have argued that qualitative studies should be judged on the basis of their *trustworthiness*. They further suggest that trustworthiness consists of four components: credibility, transferability, dependability and confirmability. These criteria correspond to the quantitative/positivist concepts of internal and external validity, reliability and objectivity. Other writers in this field have suggested that the distinctive character of qualitative research should be reflected in criteria that do more than merely mirror the positivist tradition. The set of criteria for evaluating qualitative data that are discussed below draws on the review of this topic by Stiles (1993).

1 **Clarity and comprehensiveness of the description of research procedures employed**. In Chapter 2 the well-established format for reporting the aims, methods, results and conclusions of quantitative studies was described. The majority of qualitative studies are too inductive, descriptive or literary to fit easily into this format. Nevertheless, the standard format does require the writer to give a great deal of detail about the way that the study was carried out: how the participants were selected, what happened to them, and how the data was analysed. This procedural detail is often missing from qualitative studies, which can make it difficult or impossible for the reader to determine the plausibility of some of the data. For example, it would be hard to have much faith in a qualitative study in which each interview lasted only 15 minutes, or in which the basis for selection of informants was not explained.

2 **Sufficient contextualisation of the study**. Qualitative research is less interested in defining general scientific laws of universal applicability, and more concerned with developing knowledge that is relevant and useful at particular times and places. It is therefore essential for the qualitative researcher to contextualise the study in its historical, social and cultural location.

3 **Adequacy of conceptualisation of data**. Some qualitative research is explicitly naturalistic (Lincoln and Guba, 1985) or phenomenological (Polkinghorne, 1989) in nature, and will rely on description of experiences and life-worlds rather than on the construction of models or theories. Other qualitative research, however, by contrast, has the aim of developing theory and interpretive frameworks. In this latter type of research, the reader should be able to follow the line of argument and evidence that leads from data to theory. For example, has there been sufficient triangulation to allow the demonstration of links between categories and primary data? From the point of view of grounded theory analysts (Strauss and Corbin, 1990), a key criterion of research quality is the extent to which a theory supplies a complete and coherent account of the data. On the other hand, there are some situations in which the experiential reality that is being researched is so dense and complex that any attempt to create a comprehensive and coherent model would lead to superficiality and falseness. In these instances, it may be necessary to acknowledge the provisional and open-ended nature of the analysis, and to identify any unresolved contradictions and theoretical issues.

4 **Systematic consideration of competing explanations/ interpretations of the data**. Qualitative research is frequently criticised on the grounds that researchers using these methods merely find what they knew already. For a reader of a research paper, any sense that the investigator has done little more than gather information to support his or her pre-existing biases and prejudices will lead to irritation, rejection of the study and a tendency to discount its findings. One of the most effective ways for qualitative researchers to overcome this difficulty is systematically to consider competing or alternative interpretations of the data, and make a reasoned argument for supporting the preferred interpretation over the others.

5 **Credibility of the researcher (reflexivity)**. The main investigative tool in qualitative research is the person of the researcher, and his or her ability to form

relationships with informants that encourage the disclosure and expression of relevant data. However, while in quantitative research the credibility or reliability of a test or observation scheme can be calculated using statistical techniques, it is much harder to evaluate the credibility of a qualitative researcher. An approach that is often employed to enable the consumers of research to assess the role that the researcher has played in a study is for the latter to write a reflexive account that describes the 'internal processes' (Stiles, 1993) or 'progressive subjectivity' (Lincoln and Guba, 1989) associated with conducting the research.

Altheide and Johnson (1994) have identified some of the themes that are often significant in reflexive accounts written by researchers: how contact was made with informants, issues of trust and rapport, how mistakes, misconceptions and surprises were experienced and dealt with. Some of the broader issues arising from the concept of reflexivity in research are discussed by Steier (1991). These are issues that are familiar to counsellors. For example, was the relationship between researcher and informant characterised by positive or negative counter-transference reactions? What was the power balance in the relationship? Was there agreement over goals and tasks? It is much more likely that readers will have confidence in qualitative research in which the writer deals with these issues openly, rather than ignoring them. It is therefore valuable for qualitative researchers to keep a research diary or journal, and to use this document to write their own personal narrative account of the experience of carrying out the study.

6 **Experiential authenticity of the material**. In all qualitative research, a key aim is to achieve a rich, holistic description of the topic being studied. In phenomenological research, the investigator would view such a descriptive account as an end in itself, whereas in hermeneutic or grounded theory studies the description would serve as a basis for interpretation and analysis. The extent to which the descriptive account feels real and authentic is therefore an important criterion in all qualitative research. The classic studies of R.D. Laing into the experiences of people labelled as schizophrenic, or of Goffman into the life-world of the psychiatric patient, have retained their places in the literature for over a quarter of a century because people who read them get a strong sense that what they are writing about accurately reflects the 'way it is'. An essential test of experiential authenticity is the degree to which the research report is received as an accurate description by the actual informants, the people who were (or are) there.

7 **Use of triangulation (including negotiation with informants/ testimonial validity)**. The facticity of the research data can only be established by checking it against other sources of information. The procedure of triangulation is the most widely used check of factual accuracy, and one of the most important criteria that can be applied in qualitative research is the extent and convincingness of the triangulation that has been conducted. Another method for checking both factual precision and interpretive sensitivity is to take drafts or parts of the research report back to informants and ask them to comment on it. This kind of 'negotiation with informants' or 'testimonial validity' can be used to back up the legitimacy of findings. However, in practice it is often a difficult and time-consuming process. Relatively few research informants have

the interest or motivation to read through lengthy research reports. In any case, once a report is written down it may take on an 'official' status, and deter disagreement. Sometimes, research participants can become distressed at seeing things written about them that are dissonant with their conception of self. It is worth viewing the task of negotiating with informants as similar to giving feedback to counselling clients, and to follow the same principles of careful timing, tentativeness and creating conditions of trust and safety.

8 **Catalytic validity**. As Kvale (1983) has suggested, a well-conducted qualitative interview can be a positive, enriching experience for research informants. Stiles identifies 'catalytic validity' as a criterion for judging qualitative research, and defines it as: 'the degree to which the research process reorients, focuses and energises participants' (1993: 611). Implicit in this criterion is the idea that research should empower all those who take part in it. Finch (1984) approaches this question from the opposite position, in arguing that poor research disempowers or exploits those involved in it. In the context of research into women's issues, Finch (1984) observes that:

> there is . . . a very real exploitative potential in the easily established trust between women, which makes women especially vulnerable as subjects of research . . . [research] techniques can be used to great effect to solicit a range of information (some of it very private), which is capable of being used ultimately against the interests of those women who gave it so freely to another woman with whom they found it easy to talk. The prospects for doing that clearly are magnified when (as is so often the case) women interviewers are not themselves the people who will handle and use the data they have created. (1984: 79)

The implication here is that, ideally, any negotiation with informants should include not only their views on the accuracy of the research report but also their account of how taking part in the study has affected their lives. Also, keeping some kind of on-going contact with informants can make it possible to discover whether there are any delayed effects of the research, for example through media publicity once the report or book of the study has been published.

9 **Replication**. The final basis for assessing the value of a piece of qualitative research relates to the extent to which it has been, or could be, replicated. A great deal of qualitative research inevitably depends on the intensive study of single cases, or small numbers of subjects, since it is not possible to do qualitative research well with large samples of people. Nevertheless, it is important for researchers to be able to show that what they have found is not an idiosyncratic result arising from one unique case, but has relevance and applicability to other cases.

Issues in qualitative research in counselling

Although there has been an increasing interest in the application of qualitative methods in counselling research in recent years, there are a number of important issues that have still to be resolved. From a methodological perspective, a key question concerns whether qualitative research represents an approach to inquiry that is fundamentally different from the quantitative/positivist tradition, or whether a 'pragmatic' (Patton, 1990) or 'pluralist' (Howard, 1983) combination of methods is possible. The underlying issue here is whether the root 'images of the person' (Shotter, 1975) implicit in the two approaches are irretrievably opposed to each other, or can be integrated. Rennie (1994e) argues forcibly that qualitative research should be seen as a new kind of distinctive 'human science'.

Another central methodological issue relates to the nature of phenomenological inquiry itself. Some qualitative research is descriptive while other studies take interpretation as their aim. In many qualitative studies, the role of the researcher is a fairly traditional one, emphasising his or her responsibility to collect and analyse according to the rules of scientific method. However, there is also a school of thought in qualitative research, represented by the supporters of feminist and cooperative inquiry methods, that the role of the researcher should be to share responsibility and promote action learning and empowerment. There are many tensions and points of conflict within qualitative research as an enterprise (Denzin and Lincoln, 2000): it is not a unified or unitary approach to knowledge.

A further critical issue that underpins qualitative research concerns the depth of personal exploration and reflexivity that is undertaken by the researcher. In grounded theory research, the investigator traditionally adopts a somewhat detached, objectivist stance. By contrast, in the various heuristic and autoethnographic approaches described earlier in this chapter, the personal experience and positioning of the researcher is of paramount importance. The field of qualitative research is, at the present moment, far from reaching a consensus on this matter. The question of the function of reflexivity, and what constitutes a useful or critical reflexivity, is explored further in McLeod (1999a, 2001c).

From the point of view of the counselling practitioner, the appeal of qualitative research is that it provides the kind of detail and depth of analysis that make its findings relevant to practice. It also represents a powerful discovery-oriented approach to research (Douglass and Moustakas, 1985). However, virtually all of the qualitative therapy research that has been carried out has focused on process rather than outcome. Does this imply that qualitative research is of limited applicability in the sphere of counselling, being restricted to studies of client experience and process? It is of some interest that qualitative techniques have been widely adopted in evaluation research in other areas of social science such as education and management (Patton, 1990). Is there any reason why therapy should be different? To what extent does or should the audience (policy-makers) for outcome research constrain the methods that are utilised? At present, there are few examples of qualitative outcome studies in counselling and psychotherapy – McLeod (2000, 2001b) has reviewed the handful of published studies which are available.

These are all issues that will be examined further in Chapter 11. Their presence is a reflection of the extent to which the counselling and psychotherapy research community is only beginning to forge a relationship with the traditions of qualitative research.

Further reading

Anyone considering undertaking a qualitative research study for the first time is well advised to begin by reading an introductory text such as:

Flick, U. (1998) *An Introduction to Qualitative Research*. London: Sage.
Kvale, S. (1996) *InterViews: An Introduction to Qualitative Research Interviewing*. London: Sage.

The best way to gain a sense of the creativity, excitement and diversity of current developments in qualitative research is to dip into:

Denzin, N.K. and Lincoln, Y.S. (eds) (2000) *Handbook of Qualitative Research*, 2nd edn. Thousand Oaks, CA: Sage.
Miles, M.B. and Huberman, A.M. (eds) (2002) *The Qualitative Researcher's Companion*. Thousand Oaks, CA: Sage.

The application of qualitative methods in counselling and psychotherapy research is reviewed in:

Frommer, J. and Rennie, D.L. (eds) (2001) *Qualitative Psychotherapy Research: Methods and Methodology*. Lengerich, Germany: Pabst.
McLeod, J. (2001) *Qualitative Research in Counselling and Psychotherapy*. London: Sage.

A brief summary of the criteria that might be applied in evaluating the validity of a qualitative study is available in:

Elliott, R., Fischer, C.T. and Rennie, D.L. (1999) 'Evolving guidelines for the publication of qualitative research studies in psychology and related fields', *British Journal of Clinical Psychology*, 38: 215–29.

7 Systematic Inquiry into Individual Cases

The methods and techniques introduced in previous chapters included qualitative and quantitative perspectives, and a variety of measuring instruments and data-gathering approaches. These methods can all be applied to the systematic study of individual cases. Case study research has played an important role in the history of counselling and psychotherapy. Most of the key figures in the development of therapy have published, at early points in their careers, case studies that have exemplified and demonstrated the distinctive nature of their therapeutic approach. The core assumptions and techniques characteristic of psychoanalysis were described by Freud in cases such as Dora (Freud, 1901/1979), the Rat Man (Freud, 1909/1979) and Schreber (Freud, 1910/1970). The founder of behaviourism, J.B. Watson, illustrated the applicability of behavioural concepts to problems of emotional disturbance through his famous study of Little Albert. Carl Rogers (1942a, 1951) included several cases in *Counseling and Psychotherapy* and *Client-Centered Therapy*, the key books that defined the nature of the client-centred approach to counselling. These case studies have been highly effective ways of communicating and teaching the concepts and methods associated with these approaches to counselling. The tradition of using case studies as a teaching tool is also apparent in the collections of cases brought together by Wedding and Corsini (1979), Kutash and Wolf (1986) and Dryden (1987) and in the widespread use of filmed sessions such as the famous 'Gloria' tapes. Also, many training courses require students to present client material in case discussions and case reports which are used for assessment purposes.

However, it is important to emphasise that case studies are not mere teaching tools. Many of the classic case studies cited above have served as starting points for subsequent research. This research has taken the form, within psychoanalytic circles, of the accumulation of additional case studies which either confirm or challenge the conclusions of the initial case report, or the construction, in research into client-centred and behavioural counselling and psychotherapy, of larger-scale, quantitative studies.

The case study method has the potential to contribute knowledge and understanding that is highly relevant to counselling practice. In comparison with large-scale statistical studies, the detailed analysis of individual cases yields information that is immediately applicable to the counselling relationship. Case study methods are also well suited to describing and making sense of processes of change. Finally, case studies are flexible enough to accommodate situations where the researcher may not have, and may not wish to have, any control over the behaviour of the 'subject' of the study, or little control over the amount or type of data being collected.

Nevertheless, despite their many advantages and positive attributes, case study methods have not been widely used within counselling research in recent years. Many writers on research methodology have been critical of the validity of the knowledge produced by this technique, arguing that there are severe problems in such areas as objectivity and generalisability. These critics have been influenced, and horrified, by the kind of case study research produced by Freud and his colleagues. For example, it is known that Freud wrote his notes at the end of a busy day which could involve seeing eight or nine clients. His analysis and interpretation of these notes was made without reference to any other person. There were, as a result, no ways of checking the accuracy of the data gathered by Freud, or the credibility of his interpretations. Indeed, it is not difficult to imagine the existence of various sources of subjective bias in this research process. However, even if the observations and conclusions reached by Freud were true, how generalisable is his model? Would it apply to another client with similar problems?

As discussed in Chapter 1, mainstream counselling and psychotherapy research has been dominated by the traditions of medicine and psychology, which have placed great emphasis on accurate measurement of externally observable, quantifiable behaviour and symptoms, and the application of experimental methods. Researchers trained and employed within this environment have been understandably cautious about using case study methods. Despite this suspicion, a body of work has emerged which has attempted to address the methodological problems inherent in case studies, and has contributed to the development of new approaches to *systematic* case study research. Chassan (1979) made a distinction between *extensive* and *intensive* research designs. The former refers to studies based on comparisons between groups, whereas the latter is concerned with detailed investigation of single, or small numbers of cases. In extensive studies, the researcher analyses variance *between* groups, while in intensive studies he or she analyses variance *within* one case. While much is known about extensive methods in counselling and psychotherapy research, the development of intensive methods is in its infancy. Nevertheless, some researchers have begun to evolve a set of principles and techniques for increasing the validity of case studies, and the ensuing increase in confidence in this approach has been reflected in a marked expansion in the number of case studies being published in major research journals in recent years.

A key stage in the acceptance of case study methods was the publication in 1980 of a series of case studies by Hans Strupp (1980a, 1980b, 1980c, 1980d). Soon afterwards followed a detailed analysis of a single case carried out by Hill, Carter and O'Farrell (1983a). This was the first case study to be published in the *Journal of Counseling Psychology*, together with commentary pieces (Hill et al., 1983b; Howard, 1983; Lambert, 1983). The appearance of the Hill et al. (1983a) paper in a journal that had previously specialised in large-scale, 'extensive' rather than 'intensive' studies represented a breakthrough in legitimacy for this approach. The special section of the *Journal of Consulting and Clinical Psychology* devoted to single-case research in psychotherapy (Jones, 1993) offered a further sign of the increasing recognition given to this method. More recently, the development of the 'assimilation model' of client change has largely relied on testing and elaboration of the model in the context of a series of case studies (e.g. Honos-Webb et al., 1998, 1999).

For many practitioners and researchers in counselling, psychotherapy and clinical psychology, systematic case study research represents the best way of constructing a knowledge base that is relevant to practice. The influential writing of Daniel Fishman (1999, 2000) has argued that the accumulation of much more case-based evidence is a major priority within the field of psychotherapy. The issues involved in developing an appropriate methodology for single-case research in counselling and psychotherapy have been explored by Edwards (1998), Elliott (2001, 2002b) and Schneider (1999).

Case study methods can be employed in relation to a wide range of counselling research issues. Although the most common type of case study consists of research into the process and dynamics of work with an individual client, the case study approach can also be applied to understanding counsellor development, the operation of groups, and the functioning of counselling agencies. There are many different ways of designing and carrying out case study research, depending on the theoretical background, interests and aims of the researcher, the amount of cooperation provided by the subject of the study, and the level of available resources.

Hilliard (1993) has suggested that the different forms of case study research can be categorised in terms of five main types: narrative case studies, single-case experiments, single-case quantitative analyses, research-informed case studies and combined qualitative/quantitative studies.

Qualitative (narrative) case studies

Narrative case studies rely on the use of qualitative techniques to elicit and analyse descriptive accounts. Ultimately, narrative case studies are concerned with making sense of the stories people tell about aspects of their experience. There are a number of different ways of gathering these accounts or stories. Some of the procedures used for gathering this kind of material include recording therapy sessions, stimulated recall of sessions, interviews, diaries or journals, open-ended questionnaires, projective techniques, and observation of meetings. Analysis of this data can be based on the hermeneutic, phenomenological and grounded theory methods described in Chapter 6. A set of narrative case studies that has been widely read is the *Love's Executioner* collection by Irvin Yalom (1989). These case studies are characteristic of the case report written by a counsellor or therapist based on work with one of his or her own clients. Bolgar (1965) reviews the history and use of this type of clinical case study in therapy research. What is being offered in these studies is the therapist's account of what happened, and it is reasonable to suppose that the perspective of the counsellor or therapist differs from that of the client. There is some research evidence to support the idea that counsellors and clients can sometimes diverge greatly in their interpretation of events (Kaschak, 1978; Mintz et al., 1973).

In an attempt to move beyond case studies that depend solely on the counsellor's perspective, researchers have carried out studies that allow the introduction of other sources of information and interpretation on the case. Mearns and Thorne (1988), Dryden and Yankura (1992) and Yalom and Elkin (1974) have each produced case studies that are collaborations between counsellor and client. This strategy is only possible if the inquiry is conducted after the end of all counselling, otherwise the researcher–informant relationship may interfere with the counselling process in ways that are unhelpful and probably unethical. Dryden and Yankura (1992) and Mearns and Thorne (1988) both taped counselling sessions, and reviewed these tapes with the clients some months after the end of counselling. The participants in Yalom and Elkin (1974) kept diaries, and used these to stimulate their memories of the therapy process. However, these studies still represent variants on the 'clinical' case study, because the investigators did not apply systematic methods of qualitative analysis to interpret or check their data.

An example of a more systematic narrative case study is the investigation by Etherington (2000) into the experiences of two male clients who had been sexually abused. This case report draws on a range of analytic strategies drawn from contemporary qualitative research. Other examples of narrative case studies can be found in McLeod and Lynch (2000) and McLeod and Balamoutsou (2000, 2001).

It is important to be aware that there are significant problems and challenges inherent in the use of narrative case studies. To capture the richness and texture of experience over a whole case requires spending a lot of time collecting and analysing detailed information. The authenticity or completeness of this information may depend on the amount of trust between informant and researcher. The analysis of the data relies on the ability of the researcher to hear and understand the meaning of what has been said to him or her. Sometimes the information can be too sensitive to disclose in a research report, or the research subject may be too readily identifiable. The skills necessary to deal with these problems are much the same as the skills needed for effective counselling, and so it could be argued that counsellors are well prepared to employ narrative case study methods well. On the other hand, writing up case material in a form that communicates effectively to an audience represents a significant challenge for many counsellors.

One of the central methodological issues in narrative case study research arises from the realisation that it is always possible to generate *alternative interpretations* of a life or case. The debate over the case of Schreber (Freud, 1910/1979) presents a dramatic example of the radically different interpretations of a case that are possible. Schreber was an eminent German judge who developed paranoid schizophrenia in later life. Freud used the evidence of this case in the construction of his theory of the origins of paranoia in repressed homosexuality.

Much later, Schatzman (1973), drawing on historical work by Niederland (1959), presented an alternative interpretation of the case, viewing the apparent delusions of Schreber as frustrated attempts to communicate about the extreme abuse he had received in early childhood. Another example of alternative interpretation of life history data can be found in the analysis by Runyan (1981a) of 'Why did Van Gogh cut off his ear?' In a review of biographical writing on Van Gogh, Runyan (1981a) found 13 competing, but plausible, psychological explanations for this event in the life of the artist. Runyan (1980) introduces examples of alternative accounts of key episodes in the lives of many other important historical figures. These findings are of great significance for therapy researchers, since the implication is that the more that is known about a life, the less certainty there can be about its meaning or interpretation. The studies of these historical figures show quite clearly how the researcher 'constructs' a reading or version of a life. It is not, as might be supposed by positivist philosophers, that the accumulation of data leads inevitably to a convergence on an agreed truth. The situation is more like that envisaged by 'human science' investigators, in which there is always the possibility that each interpretation is open to re-interpretation in an endless hermeneutic circle. In counselling and therapy case study research much less is known about the person being studied. The therapy researcher gathering data on a case is personally and culturally close to the subject in a way that a psychohistorian can never be. The result of this is, in therapy case studies, to limit the range and scope of alternative interpretations that are generated.

Several commentators have argued that more should be done to address the issue of competing interpretations in psychological case studies. Bromley (1981, 1986) suggests that researchers carrying out case studies should apply a 'quasi-judicial' approach, for example seeking out alternative views on the data, or appointing an 'adversary' to the research team. Murray (1938) used a 'diagnostic council' (McLeod, 1992) of five or six researchers who met to consider different perspectives on a case. DeWaele and Harri (1976) have described a model for research in which two research teams study each case in parallel, coming together at regular intervals to compare findings. Various suggestions have also been put forward concerning how different interpretations should be dealt with once they are constructed. Bromley (1986) takes the view that the field of case study research must create a set of rules and 'case law' that can be applied in deciding the validity of competing explanations of a case. Murray and Morgan (1945) and DeWaele and Harri (1976) propose that competing interpretations can be used in generating hypotheses that guide a further cycle of inquiry and data-gathering. Mearns and McLeod (1984) argue that in some instances alternative interpretations represent different 'realities' that cannot be reconciled, and that these different viewpoints should all be respected in a research report. It is essential for counselling researchers engaged in narrative case study work to be more willing to learn from the experiences of those carrying out similar types of case study in other fields. For example, there have been many case studies of organisations, and there exists a valuable literature on the methodological issues arising from this type of inquiry (Bryman, 1988a; Yin, 1994). Within social psychology and psychoanalysis, there have been psychobiographical or psychohistorical studies of famous people such as Luther, Gandhi, Lincoln, Shakespeare and many others. The methodological dilemmas associated with this field of research have been thoroughly discussed by a number of writers, including Crosby (1979) and Runyan (1981b, 1997). The book by Runyan (1981b) represents an excellent review of this field of study. Life history research has also made an important contribution to disciplines such as sociology, anthropology and cultural studies (Bertaux, 1981). The Narrative Study of Lives series, edited by Lieblich and Josselson (1997) and McAdams, Josselson and Lieblich (2001) provide excellent examples of the type of narrative case study research which has the potential to be highly relevant in the domain of counselling and psychotherapy.

Single-case experiments

The method known as the 'n = 1' or 'single-subject' study represents an application of the case study approach to evaluating therapeutic change in individual cases. Hilliard (1993) uses the term 'single-case experiment' to describe this type of research, since it employs the classic experimental principle of testing a hypothesis. It is a method utilised mainly by practitioner–researchers operating within the behavioural or cognitive-behavioural traditions, although in principle it could be used by counsellors working in any theoretical orientation. The aim of n = 1 studies is to record and assess specific changes in clients attributable to the application of specific interventions. This type of case study is usually based on the administration of a standard test or behavioural assessment on a number of occasions: before, during and after the treatment. The pre-treatment assessments constitute a 'baseline' measure of the target behaviour which it is wished to change. The on-going assessments carried out during treatment display the actual effect of the intervention, while the post-therapy or follow-up assessments give a measure of the stability or permanence of change. This kind of research design is known as 'time-series' analysis, and its simplest form is the 'AB' time series, where A is the pre-treatment baseline and B is the treatment period.

An example of an AB time-series case study is the report by Viens and Hranchuk (1992) on their work with a client with a severe eating disorder. The client was a woman of 35 who presented with a problem of vomiting after eating most types of food. In the past she had been severely obese, and had undergone two surgical operations to remove part of her stomach and abdominal fatty tissue. After these operations her weight dropped considerably, but her pattern of binge eating continued. To maintain her weight, the client began to voluntarily vomit her food. Over time, this vomiting became an involuntary response over which the client had no control. On being accepted for treatment, the client was instructed to self-monitor her behaviour for a period of three weeks. She was required to write down what she ate, how many mouthfuls she took per meal, and how many times she vomited her food during or after each meal. On the basis of this baseline information, a behavioural programme was initiated which

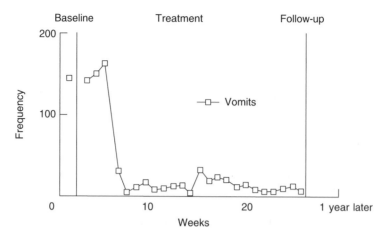

Figure 7.1   An example of data from an n = 1 study (Viens and Hranchuk, 1992)

included continuing to record eating behaviour, beginning a physical activity schedule, regular weighing, practising pacing and relaxation techniques while eating, and reporting progress at weekly therapy sessions. The results of the programme, as reflected in frequency of vomiting, are displayed in Figure 7.1.

The graphical presentation of data in Figure 7.1 is typical of n = 1 studies. The assumption underlying this approach to evaluating treatment is that change will be clinically meaningful and demonstrably visible on a graph. So, although some statistical techniques have been developed for checking the significance of the amounts of change reported in n = 1 cases (see Morley, 1996, for further discussion of these techniques), most case reports rely on graphical data alone. The Viens and Hranchuk (1992) paper also includes a descriptive account of the progress of therapy with this client, and this combination of quantitative and qualitative information can allow a broader consideration of the meaning of the results. For example, Viens and Hranchuk (1992) observed that the increase in vomiting between weeks 13 and 17 coincided with the absence of the therapist, while the sudden improvement around week 3 coincided with the introduction of some adjustments to the behavioural programme.

While Viens and Hranchuk (1992) derived their data from client self-monitoring of behaviour, many other sources of data can be employed in n = 1 studies. Houghton (1991), for example, has published a case study of a cognitive intervention carried out with an Olympic archer who experienced performance-related anxiety in competitive situations. In this case, Houghton (1991) was able to graph the actual tournament scores achieved by the client before and after treatment. This type of objective data can provide highly convincing evidence for the effectiveness of a therapeutic technique. In other clinical situations, however, the distress of the client may mean that it would be inappropriate or unethical to delay treatment by gathering baseline data. McCann (1992) describes the use of the behavioural technique of eye movement desensitisation (EMD) in a case of post-traumatic stress disorder (PTSD). The client in this case was a man who had, eight years previously, survived burn injuries at work which had left him seriously disabled. The client reported that he 'still lived daily with the traumatic experience of being burned', through nightmares, flashbacks, insomnia, startle responses and avoidance behaviour. During one session, the use of eye movement desensitisation enabled the client to release these intrusive memories and images. At one-year follow-up, the PTSD symptoms had not returned. In this case, the effects of the intervention were so immediate and dramatic, and verifiable by the therapist, the client and his nurses, that quantifiable measures were perhaps not necessary. Herbert and Mueser (1992), however, have pointed out that absence of standardised assessments and measures in studies of EMD make it difficult to evaluate its overall effectiveness.

The cases that have been briefly reviewed comprise studies in which it was possible to demonstrate unequivocal behavioural changes attributable to the introduction of an intervention technique. In other cases, the effects of the technique may be less apparent, or more open to dispute. N = 1 researchers have, as a result, devised some important adaptations of this method. The first is the ABAB design, in which there is a baseline period (A), followed by intervention (B), followed by another baseline period produced by withdrawal of the intervention (A), and finally a re-introduction of the intervention (B). This design makes it easier for the researcher to show that change depends on the presence of a particular intervention, rather than merely on the beneficial effects of a good relationship between counsellor and client. For example, in the Viens and Hranchuk (1992) study, it could be argued that the client improved because of the encouragement given by the therapist, rather than as a result of applying the behavioural programme. If the programme had been suspended for a time, and the client had worsened but had then resumed her gains on re-introduction of the package, there would be stronger evidence for a causal link between the behavioural techniques and the outcome. However, the Viens and Hranchuk (1992) study also illustrates the difficulty in using an ABAB design in a counselling setting: the client was quite capable of continuing to self-administer the intervention even if instructed to stop for a while. In practice, most ABAB studies have been carried out in institutional rather than counselling settings (see Heppner et al., 1999; Peck, 1989), with clients who would be less likely to become actively engaged in the process of change.

Some researchers have advocated the use of 'randomised' AB designs, in which an intervention is applied or not in different sessions at random. This approach is described by Heppner et al. (1999). Another variant on the time-series method is known as the 'multiple baseline' study. In this form of n = 1 case study, the impact of an intervention is traced through its application to a series of problems reported by one client.

The n = 1 case study represents a realistic and robust method through which practitioners can critically evaluate the results of their practice and be involved in constructing a body of knowledge that informs clinical work. Unlike the narrative case study, it is not primarily a vehicle for understanding. The strength of this approach lies in its ability to document what 'works', and to provide a source of clinically grounded hypotheses for further research. Among the many excellent sources providing further information on this mode of case study research are Barlow et al. (1984), Barlow and Hersen (1986), Galassi and Gersh (1991), Heppner et al. (1999), Kratochwill et al. (1984), Morley (1996), Peck (1989) and Turpin (2001).

Single-case quantitative studies

Single-case quantitative analysis (Hilliard, 1993) is the term used to describe studies in which the aim is to use quantitative techniques to trace the unfolding over time of variables, but without, as in n = 1 single-case experiments, introducing any experimental manipulation or control of these variables. An example of this type of research is the Hill et al. (1983a) study of process and outcome in a client who received 12 sessions of time-limited insight-oriented psychological counselling. In this study, outcome was assessed by a set of standard measures (Hopkins Symptom Checklist, Tennessee Self-Concept Scale, and ratings of Target Complaints administered before and after treatment and at follow-up, and ratings of satisfaction and outcome on termination and at follow-up). The client and a significant other (her mother) both wrote summaries of their perceptions of the value of the counselling. Process measures included ratings of counsellor and client verbal response modes, anxiety as expressed in client and counsellor speech patterns, activity levels (number of speech acts) of both participants, counsellor intentions, and counsellor and client perceptions of session effectiveness and significant events. Perhaps the most interesting finding to emerge from this study was generated by the comparison of best versus worst sessions. This analysis showed that, for this client, the most valuable counsellor interventions were use of interpretation, specific techniques such as Gestalt dream work, and direct feedback from the counsellor about the immediate impact of her behaviour. Within individual sessions, there was a recurring pattern in which each session began with the client talking in a somewhat descriptive, distanced manner, and only being able to move toward insight and experiencing in response to counsellor interventions, suggesting that this type of deeper insight had not been fully internalised. Finally, the limit of 12 sessions appeared to be insufficient for the client to deal adequately with her presenting issues. Although the client had improved on all outcome measures by the end of therapy, she had significantly relapsed by the time of a seven-month follow-up.

The questions explored in the Hill et al. (1983a) study were further examined by Hill and her colleagues in a series of eight even more detailed cases of time-limited therapy (Hill, 1989), which yielded further confirmation of the importance of specific therapist techniques in a context of an effective working alliance with the client. Other examples of single-case quantitative studies can be found in Horowitz et al. (1993) and Jones et al. (1993).

Research-informed case studies

Some case studies are written as exemplars drawn from extensive studies. Hilliard (1993) describes these as research-informed case studies, since the data and interpretation in the case are given added meaning by their location within a larger study. The best example of research-informed case study practice is the series of cases selected by Strupp (1980a, 1980b, 1980c, 1980d) from the Vanderbilt study (Strupp and Hadley, 1979). The main study had looked at the outcomes and processes of counselling carried out by either highly trained professional therapists and non-professional volunteers. The in-depth case studies were used to explore the processes occurring in cases that had been either successful or unsuccessful. A similar approach has been taken in the Sheffield Psychotherapy project, for example in the case study reported by Parry, Shapiro and Firth (1986), and in other large-scale investigations. As Gendlin (1986) has pointed out, in large-scale comparison group studies, the results typically report group means encompassing a mix of cases across a continuum of success. Gendlin (1986) argues that both practitioners and researchers need to know more about cases in which therapy really works, in order to be able to identify fundamental change processes. Research-informed studies are one way in which this objective can be achieved.

Combined quantitative and qualitative (pluralist) case studies

The final approach to case study method in research into counselling and psychotherapy identified by Hilliard (1993) refers to studies combining quantitative and qualitative techniques of data-gathering and analysis within one study. To some extent, all quantitative case studies apply a version of this approach. It is meaningless to report only behavioural measures or test scores in a case study without also including a narrative account of the client, the treatment and other background factors. However, in these quantitative studies the main findings are clearly based on the measures, with the descriptive qualitative information used to back this up. A stronger form of combined case study would involve giving equal weight to both qualitative and quantitative data. This approach would be essentially a 'pluralist' one (Howard, 1983). The issues associated with methodological pluralism are discussed in Chapter 11, including some examples of therapy research studies that aim to achieve pluralism.

In case study research, the notion of combining qualitative and quantitative data is attractive. It offers the promise of getting closer to the 'whole' of a case in a way that a single-method study could never do. At the moment, however, it could be argued that no counselling or therapy researchers have developed a genuinely combined or pluralist methodology. Nevertheless, the work of Henry Murray and his colleagues in the field of personality research represents a powerful example of rigorous, pluralist case study research. This body of research will be briefly described, in order to allow the identification of some ideas and techniques that could be of value to therapy researchers. The originator of this approach to case study methodology was Henry Murray, whose 1938 book *Explorations in Personality* remains a landmark in the field of personality research. Murray was trained in science and medicine, as well as being influenced by psychoanalysis and Jung's analytic psychology. His aim was to create a method of research that would be:

> the natural child of the deep, significant, metaphorical, provocative and questionable speculations of psycho-analysis and the precise, systematic, statistical, trivial and artificial methods of academic personology. (Murray, 1938: 33–4)

Through collaborative work over a number of years, Murray and his colleagues, who included Robert White and Erik Erikson, derived a set of principles for carrying out systematic case study research. This set of principles, which Murray labelled the 'multiform' method, consisted of the following guidelines.

1   Use as many different sources of information on the subject as possible, for example questionnaires, observations, interviews, projective techniques, autobiography.
2   Use a team of researchers, so that interpretation of the material is less likely to be dominated by bias or counter-transference arising from an individual investigator. This also allows the quality of relationship between the subject and different members of the team to be taken into consideration.
3   Carry out a series of case studies, in which tentative generalisations and conclusions drawn from earlier cases are checked out against later cases.
4   Integrate quantitative and qualitative measures or observations at the level of theory. Members of the research team took both types of data into consideration when deciding whether or not the pattern of findings from a particular subject confirmed some aspect of their theoretical model, or stood in contradiction to the theory and necessitated further development and articulation of the theory.

One of the main assumptions behind this method is that the existence of different sources of information will allow 'triangulation', or convergence of data, to take place. Also, the presence of several researchers allows competing interpretations or 'readings' of the material to be discussed and tested. Murray (1938) developed a process by which the key researchers working on a case would meet as a 'diagnostic council' (McLeod, 1992) to arrive at an agreed formulation of a case. The general approach to case study methodology pioneered by Murray is also reflected in the work of DeWaele and Harri (1976) and Bromley (1981, 1986).

In practice, it is often difficult to gather together a team of researchers all interested in collaborating on the same case. There can also be difficulties in finding research subjects or participants who are willing to spend many hours providing information about themselves. In the context of counselling research, there is the additional problem that gathering such an array of information about an actual therapy case may well interfere with or distort the therapeutic processes being studied.

Qualitative/hermeneutic single-case efficacy studies

The approaches to case study research discussed above have been integrated into a coherent qualitative/hermeneutic single-case methodology by Bohart (2000), Elliott (2001, 2002b) and Partyka et al. (2002). The primary aim of this type of case study is to investigate the effectiveness of therapy through analysis of a series of case studies. The key research questions are:

1   Did the client change?
2   Can causal links be established between therapy process and eventual outcome?
3   How plausible are nontherapy explanations for the change that has been observed?

In any single case, when all three questions are addressed in a rigorous manner, it is possible to determine whether the case represents a good or poor outcome in relation to the application of a specific set of interventions to a client with a specific set of problems. Elliott (2001, 2002b) argues that this approach can provide an alternative to randomised trial as a source of valid evidence about the effectiveness of therapy.

To carry out a single-case efficacy study, it is necessary to assemble a rich case record, for example comprising factual information about the client and therapist, quantitative questionnaire measures, process measures administered on a regular basis, end-of-therapy interviews, therapist process notes, transcripts of sessions, etc. Clearly, the amount of information that is available will depend on practical constraints. However, the key point is that a variety of sources of information are ready to hand, so that interpretations made on the basis of specific client statements or claims can always be checked or corroborated against other statements. Bohart (2000) and Elliott (2001, 2002b) recommend the use of a research team. Once the data set is gathered together, members of the team analyse it in the light of a set of 'plausibility criteria' (see Box 7.1). These criteria operate as a kind of 'case law', by giving explicit rules for arriving at an agreed interpretation of evidence. If possible, the team operates as two sub-groups. One group of researchers seeks to assemble all the information that it can in support of the case that therapy *has* been effective. The other team constructs a case to argue that therapy *has not* benefited the client. The two teams then meet and go through the arguments on each side in turn, until a consensus can be reached.

This methodology is similar both to the approach developed by Henry Murray in the 1930s (described in the previous section), and to the method of consensual qualitative research used by Clara Hill and her associates (Hill et al., 1997). At present, few studies have been carried out using the single-case efficacy design, and the procedures associated with it are not fully codified or tested. However, it seems clear that this approach has the potential to transform counselling and psychotherapy research, by giving practitioners a research tool which is not only compatible with everyday practice, but enhances practice by giving therapists a structured framework in which to reflect on their work.

Box 7.1   Plausibility criteria for analysing case material in relation to therapy outcome

Evidence that the client has changed:
  Clients note themselves that they have changed
  Clients are relatively specific about how they have changed
  They report that others have observed them to change
  They mention problems that didn't change
Evidence that it was therapy that helped:
  Clients themselves reported that therapy helped
  They describe plausible links to therapy experience
  They mention aspects of therapy that didn't help
Evidence that the person did not change:
  Clients note themselves that they did not change
  They are specific about how their life is still the same
  They seem the same in the therapy session
No evidence that it was therapy that helped:
  Clients ascribe changes to events in their life
  They give unabashedly positive testimonials, but provide few details about how therapy helped
  Changes described in the client's life can plausibly account for client's changes, whether client sees it that way or not

Source: Bohart (2002)

Issues in case study research

The types of case study research discussed in this chapter are each associated with distinctive and contrasting aims, sources of data, and applications. Despite these differences, there are some fundamental methodological issues that are relevant to the case study approach as a whole. Whatever kind of case approach is chosen, there remain dilemmas around generalising from single instances, presenting case data in a succinct yet relevant manner, and finding criteria by which to judge the validity of a case study.

Some critics of the case study approach have questioned the extent to which the findings of a single case study can be generalised to other cases. They argue that, even if a case study is capable of yielding a rich descriptive account of one person or group, it is impossible to draw inferences from single cases that can then logically be applied to new cases, or to a broader population. There are, however, several strategies that can be employed to address the issue of generalisability in case studies (Kazdin, 1981; Yin, 1994). First, great caution must be used in reading too much into a single case example. This caution also holds true in large-scale, extensive experimental or survey research. No single experiment or survey provides conclusive evidence taken alone. It is only when a number of studies produce similar results that the scientific community can agree that a robust finding exists. Similarly, the *logic of replication* represents a key strategy in case study research. It is important to emphasise here that the concept of replication implies that each case must be seen as equivalent to a separate experiment or survey. Yin argues that:

> this is far different from a mistaken analogy in the past, which incorrectly considered multiple cases to be similar to the multiple respondents in a survey (or to the multiple subjects within an experiment) – that is, to follow a 'sampling' logic. (1994: 53)

The *logic of sampling* is virtually impossible to achieve in case study research, because of the time and resources required to obtain case data of sufficient quality. The logic of replication, on the other hand, is central to systematic case study research. Ideally, the conceptual model generated in the first case study is tested in the second and subsequent studies. The rationale for selecting these later cases is based on their *theoretical* interest, in other words whether they enable some feature of the emerging model or theory to be confirmed or refuted. The series of case studies carried out by Strupp (1980a, 1980b, 1980c, 1980d) illustrate the use of the theoretically important concepts of success and failure to guide the selection of cases for replication. Yin (1994) gives other examples of this approach. The most ambitious attempt to carry out theoretical replication is the study by Murray (1938), in which a series of 50 cases was used in the development of an influential theory of personality.

Another strategy that allows the case study researcher to bridge the gap between the particular and the general is to regard single cases as exemplars of what is possible. Logically, a single instance or event can be enough to refute a general theory. For example, a theory such as 'all crows are black' will be refuted by a sighting of only one white crow. The notion of falsifiability is pivotal to the philosophy of science constructed by Popper (1959, 1962, 1972) (see Chapter 1). In the world of counselling and psychotherapy, theories are not formulated with the precision of a statement such as 'all crows are black'. Nevertheless, there are many areas of consensus and agreement. Critical case studies can be used to challenge that consensus. The studies of eye movement desensitisation (EMD) discussed earlier in this chapter represent just such a challenge. Before these studies were published, the prevailing view would have been that there was little or nothing that could be done to eliminate the symptoms of chronic PTSD. Certainly, no competent mental health professional would have accepted that symptoms of the severity of those in the case of the client reported by McCann (1992) could have been alleviated in one session. So, even though the studies by McCann (1992) and others may require further replication, they at least give a clear indication of what is *possible*. Further discussion of the logic of case study methods can be found in Fishman (1999) and Elliott (2001, 2002b).

A further critical issue in case study research arises from the *communicability* of case material. One of the most demanding tasks for any case study researcher is to write up the case in a way that conveys what has been found in an interesting and convincing manner. Often, researchers gather more case material than they know how to handle, and produce reports that are lengthy and impenetratable. Yin (1994) suggests that there are six possible structures for a case study report:

1 *Linear–analytic* reports follow the standard format for articles in psychology journals. There is an introduction, literature review, methods section, results and then finally a discussion section. Bromley (1981) offers a valuable discussion of how this model can be adapted to case writing.
2 *Comparative structures* focus on alternative readings or interpretations of the case, before evaluating and discussing these different viewpoints. This approach is evident in the work of Elliott and Shapiro (1992), in which client, counsellor and observer 'versions' of an important therapy event are compared.
3 *Chronological structuring* involves applying some kind of time-series analysis to the case data, or structuring material in terms of stages or phases. This strategy lies at the heart of 'n = 1' single-case experiments, but is also employed in other types of case study (see Jones, 1993). In reviewing his experience with this approach to case writing, Yin (1994) observes that there can be a tendency to give disproportionate attention to early events, such as the early history and background to the case, and give insufficient attention to current status or outcome. He proposes that:

> to avoid this situation, one recommendation, when using a chronological structure, is to *draft* the case study *backwards*. Those chapters or sections that are about the current status of the case should be drafted first, and only after these drafts have been completed should the background to the case study be drafted. Once all the drafts have been completed, the investigator can then return to the normal chronological sequence in composing the final version of the case. (1994: 139)

4 *Theory-building structures.* This approach to composing a case study concentrates on the theoretical implications of the case material. Different sections of the report reveal new elements of the theoretical analysis that is being constructed. Many of the case studies published by Freud were of this type.
5 *Suspense structures* represent an 'inversion' of the standard linear–analytic structure. A 'suspense' study can be likened to a detective novel in which a murder is described on the first page, and the remainder of the narrative comprises the story of 'Who done it?' and 'How done it?' The suspense structure is a valuable device for engaging the interest of the reader, and is also a way of making explicit the significance or importance of the study.
6 *Unsequenced structures* are used when the researcher is presenting case material in thematic sections, and the order of these sections of the report could be changed without affecting their sense. This writing strategy is often adopted in studies of organisations, since it allows complex and interlocking material to be portioned into blocks of writing on themes such as 'leadership', 'external environment', 'organisational culture' and so on. The limitations of this strategy are that it is descriptive, not readily lending itself to interpretive or theory-building analyses, and that any sense of the case as a whole may be lost in the fragmentation of data into separate themes.

The implication of the discussion of case composition stimulated by Yin (1994) is that this type of writing is not just a technical exercise, but involves creativity and artistry. Some researchers trained in the hypothetical–deductive scientific methodologies of psychology and medicine may be uncomfortable with the unfamiliar demands on them associated with this aspect of case study inquiry. Others may find it liberating and exciting.

Another key issue in case study method is the question of *quality* in case study research. What are the criteria for a good case study? Again, Yin (1994) supplies the most useful overview of this topic. Any case study will draw on some combination of qualitative and quantitative methods and will need to do justice to the 'logics of justification' identified with these perspectives (see Chapters 4 and 6). However, Yin (1994) argues that there are additional criteria that become relevant when a case study approach is adopted. These are summarised in Box 7.2. The criteria identified by Yin (1994) are derived from a review of case study research in management, education and sociology. The use of case study methods in therapy research perhaps merits the inclusion of an additional criterion, regarding the need to safeguard the well-being of the research informant or subject. A case study of a social group or organisation can be carried out without requiring any very substantial disclosure of personal information by participants. By contrast, in a therapy case study this sensitive and highly personal material is essential. There is the potential for participants in therapy case studies to be damaged or humiliated in a way that is unlikely in almost any other type of research. The case study may be read by the informant as an

---

Box 7.2   Criteria for a good case study

Significance. A study will have more meaning or impact if it focuses on a case that is unusual, revelatory, or of general public or theoretical interest.

Completeness. The case report should give the reader a sense of understanding the 'whole' of the case. Providing sufficient contextual information convinces the reader that the 'analytic periphery' has been reached. The documentation of the case should demonstrate that all relevant information has been collected.

Consideration of alternative perspectives. The researcher must weigh up the merits and value of alternative interpretations and explanations.

The case study must supply sufficient evidence. The researcher must provide sufficient evidence for the reader to make their own judgement of the case.

Effective writing. It is important for a case study to be written in an engaging manner. Yin (1994) advocates that the investigator communicate his or her enthusiasm to engage, entice and seduce the reader.

Source: Yin (1994)

immensely detailed, authoritative interpretation of his or her life. This is a territory of inquiry in which researchers must move with the utmost care and sensitivity.

Conclusions

There is an increasing acceptance that the case study represents a legitimate approach to research in the field of counselling and psychotherapy. Although case studies have always served as the principal vehicle for knowledge creation and dissemination within the psychodynamic orientation to therapy, and also in behaviour therapy, within the past few years this method has come to be adopted by researchers and practitioner–researchers in other orientations. This new interest in the case study approach has been accompanied by an awareness that there are systematic ways of using this method. If case-based findings are to be seen as valid, credible and robust, they must be the outcome of research procedures that are visible, replicable and consistent. The central features of systematic case study method are:

- use of multiple sources of data;
- different perspectives on the data (e.g. a research team, or an 'adversary');
- studying each case within its social context;
- consideration of competing interpretations of the data;
- data-gathering and analytic procedures that are clear and explicit;
- conclusions backed up by data;
- use of replication.

Case study research produces detailed accounts of individual cases that can be useful for practitioners. It is also a mode of research that enables practitioners to make a contribution to the research literature. At present, the growing acceptance of case study methods in counselling and psychotherapy research has not been matched by any substantial critical debate on the methodological issues and choices that surround it. Nor has the research community fully addressed the question of how best to publish and disseminate case study reports. Therapy research has much to learn from the many examples of good practice in case study research that exist in other disciplines. Taking all these factors together, it would seem reasonable to suggest that counselling and psychotherapy research is about to see a period of innovation and discovery in relation to the utilisation of systematic case study methods.

Further reading

The psychoanalyst Donald Spence has written widely about the shortcomings of traditional clinical case studies. Good examples of his work are:

Spence, D.P. (1989) 'Rhetoric vs. evidence as a source of persuasion: a critique of the case study genre', in M.J. Packer and R.B. Addison (eds), *Entering the Circle: Hermeneutic Investigation in Psychology.* Albany, NY: State University of New York Press.

Spence, D.P. (2001) 'Dangers of anecdotal reports', *Journal of Clinical Psychology*, 57: 37–41.

The essence of the contemporary debate about what needs to be done to carry out plausible, systematic, practice-relevant case studies is summarised in four key papers:

Edwards, D.J.A. (1998) 'Types of case study work: a conceptual framework for case-based research', *Journal of Humanistic Psychology*, 38 (3): 36–70.

Elliott, R. (2002b) 'Hermeneutic single-case efficacy design', *Psychotherapy Research*, 12: 1–23.

Fishman, D.B. (2000, May 3) 'Transcending the efficacy versus effectiveness research debate: proposal for a new, electronic "Journal of Pragmatic Case Studies"', *Prevention & Treatment*, 3, Article 8. http://journals.apa.org/prevention/volume3/pre0030008a.html.

Schneider, K.J. (1999) 'Multiple-case depth research', *Journal of Clinical Psychology*, 55: 1531–40.

8 Does it Work? Evaluating the Outcomes of Counselling

I next saw Marvin one year later: I always schedule patients for a one-year follow-up session – both for their benefit and for my own edification. I also make it a practice to play for the patient a tape recording of part of our initial session. Marvin listened to ten minutes of our initial interview with great interest, smiled at me, and said, 'Who is that jerk, anyway?'

Marvin's quip has a serious side. Having heard the same reaction from many patients, I have come to regard it as a valid marker of change. Marvin, in effect, was saying, 'I'm a different person now. I hardly recognize that Marvin of a year ago. Those things I used to do – refusing to look at my life; trying to control or intimidate others; trying to impress others with my intelligence, my charts, my thoroughness – they're gone. I don't do that any more.'

These are no minor adjustments: they represent basic modifications in person-hood. Yet they are so subtle in character that they generally elude most research-outcome questionnaires (Yalom, 1989: 269).

A significant amount of energy and effort has been devoted to researching the outcomes of counselling and psychotherapy. Does counselling work? This is the big question, the bottom line for therapists and therapy researchers. Some of this research has been motivated by a desire to demonstrate the effectiveness of one brand of therapy as compared to other approaches. Outcome research has also been motivated by a need to be able to legitimise counselling and psychotherapy in the eyes of resource providers such as government departments and health insurance companies. For example, in the 1970s the US government decided that it would only support the use of health interventions that had been shown to be effective in controlled research studies.

Despite a volume of research which by now amounts to a total of several hundred published studies (Roth and Fonagy, 1996; Smith et al., 1980), there are a number of serious methodological problems associated with attempts to assess the effectiveness of counselling or therapy (Kazdin, 1994). The aim of this chapter is to examine the research strategies that have been adopted by those conducting outcome studies, and to explore the issues and dilemmas these researchers have faced. The discussion will focus on 'outcome' defined as the benefits (or otherwise) and changes observable in clients at the completion of a course of treatment. It should be noted that in the literature some writers have studied outcomes or 'effects' in terms of the impact of single sessions or even the impact of single counsellor or therapist statements or interventions. These more limited conceptions of outcome will be reviewed in Chapter 9, which will consider the nature of process research.

The historical development of psychotherapy outcome research

The earliest attempts to evaluate the effectiveness of therapy were carried out in the 1930s, and consisted of follow-up investigations of people who had undergone psychoanalysis. These studies tended to show that around one-third of patients improved a great deal, another one-third were slightly improved, while the rest had either remained the same or deteriorated. These findings were initially viewed as providing positive support for the effectiveness of therapy, but in a highly influential critique of these studies, Eysenck (1952) argued that there was plentiful evidence to suggest that neurotic people who had received no formal psychotherapeutic treatment exhibited similar rates of improvement over time. Eysenck (1952) drew on data gathered by Landis (1938), who had found that at that time around 70 per cent of neurotic patients were discharged from psychiatric hospitals each year in the USA categorised as recovered or improved, and by Denker (1937) who reviewed the records of 500 consecutive disability claims due to psychoneurosis from the files of the Equitable Life Assurance Company. Denker (1937) defined these cases as serious, since the claimants were required to have been away from work for at least three months to be eligible to make a claim. Of these 500 insurance company cases, 72 per cent had recovered within two years, and 90 per cent within five years.

On the basis of these findings, Eysenck (1952) asserted that many people who experience emotional crises undergo a process of 'spontaneous recovery' (sometimes described as 'spontaneous remission'), in which the life problems which were worrying them disappear, or they find their own ways of coping. For Eysenck and other critics of insight/relationship therapy, it was essential for any form of intervention to be able to generate improvement figures significantly higher than those attributable to spontaneous recovery. But, when Eysenck (1952) reviewed the recovery rates reported in the 19 therapy outcome studies available to him, he found recovery rates of 44 per cent for psychoanalysis and 64 per cent for eclectic psychotherapy, using a definition of recovery equivalent to that employed in the Denker (1937) and Landis (1938) studies.

The strong critique by Eysenck (1952, 1960, 1965, 1992) of the evidence concerning the effectiveness of psychodynamic and other insight-oriented forms of therapy had two consequences. One was to stimulate interest in the phenomenon of spontaneous recovery (e.g. Stevenson, 1961). The other was to stimulate therapy researchers to carry out more rigorous and objective studies of the effectiveness of counselling and psychotherapy (Bergin, 1963; Rogers and Dymond, 1954). In particular, many researchers adopted the strategy of including a *control* group in their study, so that the effect of therapy could be contrasted with the naturally occurring change arising in a comparable set of people who were similar in respect of demographic profile and presenting problems, but who did not receive therapy.

A typical outcome study that employs a control group design is the research by Sloane et al. (1975), which investigated the effectiveness of time-limited (average 14 sessions over four months) behavioural and psychodynamic therapy with neurotic clients. In order to estimate the relative effectiveness of therapy in contrast to spontaneous recovery, Sloane et al. (1975) randomly allocated every third applicant for therapy to a waiting list group. However, in acknowledgement of the ethical difficulties involved in denying help to people in need, those on the waiting list were offered plentiful reassurance that they would soon be assigned to a therapist, were given a number to call in a crisis, and were contacted several times during the four-month wait period by a research assistant who checked how they were getting on. The people on the waiting list also experienced an initial assessment interview, in which they were encouraged to talk about their problems to a skilled listener and interviewer. It can be seen, therefore, that those on the waiting list had not received *no* treatment, but had been offered at least a minimal level of support, contact and hope for the future.

The study was carried out in a university psychiatric outpatient clinic. All those seeking therapy were interviewed and assessed, with those considered too disturbed to join the waiting list, or not disturbed enough to need therapy, being excluded from the study and referred elsewhere. Sloane et al. (1975) used three main measures of change: a structured interview to assess levels of social and work maladjustment, ratings by the interviewer and the therapist of the severity of the target complaints reported by the client, and an interview with a close friend or relative. At the end of therapy these measures were repeated. Follow-up interviews were held one year and two years after the initial assessment. A number of other measures, relating to process variables, were also used in this study, but are not relevant to the present discussion of outcome. The therapists in the study were three experienced psychoanalytically oriented therapists and three experienced behaviour therapists. Clients accepted into the study were randomly assigned to a therapist or to the waiting list, and paid for treatment on a sliding scale. The results of this study were that all three groups improved at the end of the four-month period, although the treated clients improved more than those on the waiting list. These gains were maintained at the one-year and two-year follow-up interviews.

The results of this study are consistent with those reported in many other similar studies: people who seek help are likely to gain more from receiving therapy than from a process of spontaneous recovery, and different types of therapy are on the whole equally effective. These conclusions have been supported by the results of a large number of research studies (see reviews by Luborsky et al., 1975; Roth and Fonagy, 1996; Smith et al., 1980).

Nevertheless, a closer look at the Sloane et al. (1975) research illuminates some of the methodological issues that make outcome research so difficult to interpret. For example, the meaning or significance of the experience of being allocated to a control waiting list condition is a crucial feature of this study. It could be argued that the level of contact and support provided for those on the waiting list meant that they had indeed received a form of therapeutic intervention. If this were true, then it would imply that the study was not really comparing therapy against a no-therapy control, but was comparing a specific form of therapy with a brief contact 'non-specific' therapy. In these circumstances any demonstration that the former is more effective than the latter would be important, since the therapy in question would be subjected to a strong test of its effectiveness and power. On the other hand, it is equally plausible to suppose that many of the people assigned to the waiting list experienced this as rejection, and as a result felt angry or worthless. Certainly, almost one in three of the waiting list group declined the offer of therapy made by the research team at the end of the waiting time. This phenomenon could be interpreted as suggesting that the therapy has been subjected to a rather weak test, in that it has been compared to a condition that would cause a lowering of levels of adjustment and a worsening of target complaints.

Another serious issue arising from the design of the Sloane et al. (1975) study concerns the sources of information used to assess change. In this study, change was assessed through ratings made by an expert interviewer, the therapist and a significant other. The views of the client on whether the counselling had been successful were not incorporated in the research design, except in so far as the client was able to tell the interviewer what he or she felt. Another instance of the disregard paid to the views of clients was that clients were not given any choice about the kind of counselling they would receive. They were randomly allocated either to a behaviour therapist or a psychoanalytically oriented therapist. These are quite different forms of therapy, and it is reasonable to suppose that at least some clients might have definite preferences for the kind of approach they would perceive as being most relevant to them. Presumably, giving clients an informed choice about the kind of therapy they were to receive would serve to enhance their positive expectations and motivation and therefore increase the success rate (Brewin and Bradley, 1989).

Finally, there are questions that can be asked about the representativeness of the study. It was carried out in a high-status, well-resourced clinic, with expert, experienced counsellors and carefully screened clients. These factors may not correspond to the reality experienced by many counsellors and their clients in everyday practice. The time limits imposed on the therapists could have been unrepresentative of their normal way of working (Altshuler, 1989). Moreover, only three therapists were used in each group. Were these therapists truly representative of the orientations they espoused? There is evidence that significant differences exist in the success rates of different therapists (Lambert, 1989). It makes sense, therefore, to ask whether the Sloane et al. (1975) study was a test of the efficacy of psychodynamic and behavioural *counselling*, or rather an investigation of the competence of a small group of psychodynamic and behavioural *counsellors*.

This critique of the Sloane et al. (1975) study should be read in the light of the fact that it is generally acknowledged as constituting a thorough and comprehensive piece of research that has been highly regarded and influential among other researchers in this field. The research team in this study gathered a large amount of data on each client over extended periods of time. Careful ethical and professional safeguards were observed. The resources devoted to the study were substantial. Nevertheless, despite all these ingredients, the critic or sceptic looking at it can find many reasons for questioning the validity of its findings. It is important to recognise that this process of critical review is a necessary component of the research process. Very few, if any, pieces of research provide definitive 'proof'. Any research report can be dismantled or critically deconstructed to the point where it almost disappears from view (see, for example, Kline, 1992). The value of this rigorous probing and questioning is to stimulate the invention of new and better research designs and methods. In the context of the Sloane et al. (1975) study, a critical analysis reveals that there is a broad range of intrinsic difficulties in carrying out satisfactory outcome studies. These difficulties are sometimes characterised as 'threats to validity' (Campbell and Stanley, 1963). The *internal* validity of a study refers to the extent to which the researcher has dealt with the existence of alternative or competing hypotheses that would account for the data. The *external* validity of a piece of research refers to the degree to which its findings can be reliably and meaningfully generalised to other situations. Lambert, Masters and Ogles (1991) have compiled a list of internal and external validity threats that commonly appear in counselling and psychotherapy outcome studies. A summary of some of the main validity threats identified by Lambert et al. (1991) is presented in Box 8.1. It can be seen that there are many ways in which the validity of an outcome study can be eroded. Ultimately, these difficulties arise from the application of a laboratory-based experimental design to a real-world applied problem. It is hard to imagine any research situation in which all of these validity threats could be dealt with in a totally satisfactory manner, and so it is necessary to approach reports of outcome studies in an appropriately critical and questioning frame of mind, ready to find a balance between the useful and valid information that has been produced and the areas in which there might be plausible alternative ways of accounting for findings.

Since the Sloane et al. (1975) study was published, the field of counselling and psychotherapy outcome research has been the site of a substantial amount of activity and innovation. A number of strategies have been developed for addressing the kinds of methodological issues and threats to validity raised by this type of investigation. The remaining sections of this chapter describe and discuss these strategies, and seek to provide an overview of contemporary approaches to outcome research.

How best can outcomes be assessed?

The central task for anyone planning and carrying out an outcome study is to find adequate ways of assessing change in clients. Some examples of the wide range of tools and approaches that have been used in studies are summarised below.

> ## Box 8.1 Common validity problems in counselling outcome studies
>
> ### Threats to internal validity
>
> 1 *Statistical regression*. The statistical tendency for extreme high or low scores on a test to revert toward the mean on re-testing.
> 2 *Selection biases*. The method of allocating people to treatment and control groups is not random, but introduces a systematic bias.
> 3 *Differential attrition rates*. More people drop out of one group, thus reducing comparability of groups.
> 4 *External events*. Events other than therapy are responsible for changes in participants (e.g. some members of a waiting-list group may seek therapy elsewhere).
>
> ### Threats to external validity
>
> 1 *Test reactivity*. Taking a test at one time may affect performance on the test at a later date.
> 2 *Reactivity of experimental arrangements*. The fact that they are participating in a study may influence the behaviour of clients and counsellors.
> 3 *Findings restricted to a particular setting*. Results obtained in, for example, a student counselling centre may not be generalisable to other settings.
> 4 *Interaction of history and treatment*. Findings obtained at one point in time may not be generalisable to another time (e.g. enthusiasm effect found in initial studies of new therapies).
> 5 *Pre-test sensitisation*. Clients receiving a battery of tests or lengthy interview before starting therapy may react differently to treatment compared with ordinary clients who do not take a pre-test.
>
> *Source*: Lambert et al. (1991)

Types of outcome study

Client satisfaction studies. A client satisfaction study is a piece of research which evaluates the benefits of counselling by asking clients to complete a short, simple questionnaire once they have finished seeing their counsellor. However, even though this form of evaluation is necessary as a means of enabling clients to register their feelings about a service, it has some quite significant limitations. Clients who complete satisfaction questionnaires tend to give uniformly positive ratings, which do not necessarily relate to the amount of actual benefit they have received. This makes it difficult, or impossible, to use satisfaction data to differentiate between sub-groups of clients who may be gaining more or less from counselling; the satisfaction questionnaire is a blunt instrument. The influential paper by Seligman (1995) illustrates an interesting application of satisfaction research methods, in the form of a client survey carried out by a consumer organisation in the USA. More detailed accounts of the issues involved in assessing client satisfaction can be found in Attkisson and Greenfield (1994), Berger (1983), Lebow (1982) and Webb (1993).

Randomised controlled trials. A randomised trial involves first of all finding a pool of people who are all seeking help and who have a similar problem (e.g. as diagnosed through a psychiatric interview or through their scores on a questionnaire). These clients are then randomly assigned to different 'treatment conditions' (as in the Sloane et al., 1975 study). These conditions may comprise two or three different kinds of therapy, or a therapy compared with a control condition (e.g. remaining on a waiting list for six months) or a comparison with a placebo condition (e.g. being given regular meetings with a helper who does not use actual therapeutic skills or interventions). The client's level of anxiety, depression, phobias or other problems are assessed before therapy, at the end of therapy and then again at a follow-up period. Randomised controlled trials are widely used in medicine, for example in trials of the effectiveness of new drug treatments. In drugs research (but not in counselling and psychotherapy research) it is possible to conduct 'double blind' studies in which neither doctor nor patient knows whether the drug being administered is active or is an inert placebo. In medicine, the randomised controlled trial is regarded as the 'gold standard' in terms of credible research evidence. In a well-conducted RCT, if truly random allocation of clients or patients to treatments is achieved, then any subsequent differences in outcome can only be attributed to the impact of the treatment, rather than to other factors. An RCT is therefore a highly logical and convincing method of evaluation. Many hundreds of randomised trials of the effectiveness of different approaches to counselling and psychotherapy have been carried out (see Garfield and Bergin, 1994; and Roth and Fonagy, 1996, for reviews of this literature). There are, however, some very serious problems associated with the use of randomised trials in counselling and therapy (see Box 8.2).

Naturalistic outcome studies. This kind of study is similar to a client satisfaction study in so far as it involves collecting data on every client who is seen in a clinic or counselling agency. It is similar to an RCT in that before and after measures of change are taken, rather than relying on a one-shot questionnaire completed only at the end of counselling. Naturalistic outcomes are basically built around routine administration of questionnaires or other data collection methods (e.g. target complaint forms) by the staff of counselling agencies. The widespread availability of evaluation tools such as CORE and OQ have made it much easier in recent years for any counselling agencies to participate in naturalistic outcome research. In addition, it is increasingly being appreciated by policy-makers that naturalistic outcome studies have significant advantages in comparison with the 'gold standard' randomised trial. Naturalistic studies cost a lot less to set up (thus allowing a wider range of therapies to be investigated), and provide a picture of therapy as it is practised in real-life conditions, rather than in the somewhat artifical conditions of a 'trial'.

Box 8.2   Issues involved in the use of randomised controlled trails in counselling and psychotherapy outcome research

True randomisation may be hard to achieve. Clients may have preferences regarding the kind of therapy they would like to have, and may resist being randomly allocated to a treatment condition that they do not find credible, or to a waiting list condition. Most clients report a mixed set of problems, and would receive multiple diagnoses (if they were to be diagnosed), thus making it difficult to achieve the kind of clear-cut diagnostic samples that a good RCT requires.

Inadequate sample sizes. The statistical operations which are needed to decide whether an RCT has produced a clear result need reasonably large numbers of clients (i.e. over 20 clients) in each condition. In counselling and psychotherapy research, this can be expensive and impracticable.

Distortion of usual therapeutic practice. To produce the level of methodological control that is necessary in an RCT, counsellors are usually asked to practise according to a manual which specifies a standard mode of treatment that all practitioners in the study are expected to deliver (including the number of sessions). Given that the majority of counsellors and psychotherapists describe themselves as eclectic or integrative in orientation, this requirement greatly limits the 'external validity' of such studies (i.e. the extent to which their results can be generalised to real-world practical settings).

Many types of therapy are not investigated. The complexity of the RCT method means that it is only possible to implement this kind of study in a well-financed, elite establishment. Most RCTs are associated with university medical schools or clinical psychology departments. There are great tranches of everyday counselling practice that have never been evaluated in an RCT: feminist therapy, multicultural counselling, narrative therapy, Transactional Analysis.

N = 1 'single-case' studies. The single-case outcome study is naturalistic in the sense that clients are not randomly allocated to comparison or control groups. This type of study is often described as an 'n = 1' design, where 'n' is the number of 'subjects' in the study. Apart from the difference in number of cases, this type of research differs from other quantitative outcome research in that information on the client is collected not just at the beginning, at the end and at follow-up, but on a much more regular basis. In many n = 1 studies outcome data are collected at each session, or even every day or several times each day. At the heart of the n = 1 study is a graph which charts the change in key problem variables over at least three phases of the therapy: a baseline period before therapy has commenced, the period when therapy is being received, and the period following the end of therapy. The analysis of this data does not usually involve statistics, but relies on visual inspection of the graph. The classic n = 1 case graph will show a high level of problems at baseline, followed by a rapid reduction once treatment has started, remaining at or around the same low level over follow-up. A more detailed discussion of this approach can be found in Chapter 8.

Qualitative outcome studies. Another way of evaluating outcome is to carry out qualitative, open-ended interviews with clients. Perhaps surprisingly, this approach has not been used to any great extent in counselling research, probably due to the domination of quantitative, statistical methods in the outcomes literature. The use of qualitative methods in outcome research is explored in McLeod (2000, 2001c).

Standardised 'self-report' tests/inventories

Tests such as the CORE, the Outcome Questionnaire (OQ), Beck Depression Inventory (BDI), Hopkins Symptom Checklist (SCL-90) and Minnesota Multiphasic Personality Inventory (MMPI) have been widely employed in outcome studies to provide an assessment of personality functioning and adjustment before and after therapy, and at follow-up.

Further information on the design and operation of these techniques can be found in Chapter 5.

Client satisfaction questionnaires

Questionnaires administered at the end of counselling or at follow-up, represent a practicable means of obtaining a global assessment of how the client felt about the counselling he or she received. A typical client satisfaction scale would contain items such as 'How would you rate the quality of service you received?' with a response format of 'excellent–good–fair–poor', or 'If a friend were in need of similar help, would you recommend our programme to him/her?', with response choices of 'no, definitely not', 'no, I don't think so', 'yes, I think so', and 'yes, definitely'. Many such scales also include a section for the client to write in an open-ended way about their counselling experience. The advantages of satisfaction questionnaires is that they are quick and easy for clients to fill in, straightforward for counsellors or reception staff to administer, and readily interpretable. The main disadvantage of the technique is that it can only yield a generalised estimate of satisfaction, rather than tracking change on specific variables such as anxiety or depression. Moreover, there is a strong tendency for people to answer at the extreme positive end of the scale, so it is normal to obtain an average rating of over 4 on a 5-point scale (Berger, 1983). There would appear to be two reasons for this high satisfaction rating. The first is that, on the whole, dissatisfied clients do not bother to complete the form. The second is that, even when counselling has not dealt with the problems of the client, he or she feels grateful and appreciative of the time and attention given by the counsellor. Examples of client satisfaction scales can be found in Larsen et al. (1979) and Hope (1989). The issues involved in using this method are discussed further by Attkinson and Zwick (1982) and Berger (1983), and an example of an outcome study based on this type of data is provided by Sloboda et al. (1993).

Ratings of target symptoms and complaints, and therapeutic goals

Individualised ratings of specific complaints or goals, made by either the client or by an expert clinician who has interviewed the client, have been utilised in several outcome studies. Whereas standardised tests allow assessment of change along a dimension such as social adjustment or anxiety, ratings of target complaints enable appraisal of change in terms of the concrete and specific problems that motivated the client to seek help in the first place. It could be argued, therefore, that target symptom/complaint ratings (also sometimes known as Goal Attainment Scaling) represent a particularly appropriate and sensitive tool for use in counselling outcome studies. In addition, the identification and monitoring of therapeutic goals is likely to be intrinsically helpful for both client and counsellor (Sutton, 1987). In the Sloane et al. (1975) study, the target complaint technique developed by Battle et al. (1966) was employed. This involved ratings made on up to three main symptoms, made before and after therapy by a trained clinical interviewer. The Battle Target Complaints technique involves the use of a visual scale, consisting of 13 boxes arranged in a vertical column and sequentially labelled with phrases such as 'not at all', 'very much' and 'couldn't be worse'. The client, after identifying the target complaint, responds to the question 'in general how much does this problem or complaint bother you?' by ticking a box. With the Personal Questionnaire technique, originally invented by the British clinical psychologist Monte Shapiro (1961), the interviewer helps the client to identify ten items reflecting different areas of functioning (Mulhall, 1976; Phillips, 1986), and then the client does the rating, using a 10-point scale. An example of the use of Personal Questionnaire data in an outcome study can be found in Barkham, Shapiro and Firth-Cozens (1989). Despite the intuitive attraction of target complaint rating as a method for evaluating change, the use of this technique is not unproblematic. The issues identified by a client in pre-interview counselling may change radically during counselling, as new material emerges (Sorensen et al., 1985). Also, it is often difficult for interviewers to establish therapeutic goals that are equivalent in severity across different clients in a study (Cytrnbaum et al., 1979). Despite these difficulties, ratings of target complaints and goals represent an important research tool, because they are highly sensitive to the specific personal difficulties experienced by each client. The trend in recent years has been to develop methods of allowing clients to identify their own therapeutic goals or presenting problems, rather than to use an interviewer. Simple formats that allow clients to do this have been developed by Paterson (1996) and Deane et al. (1997). An alternative approach, developed by Cheyne and Kinn (2001a, 2001b), has been to train the counsellor to administer a specially designed 'quality of life' tool within actual counselling sessions. This strategy of integrating the research task in a therapy session has been found to provide a useful vehicle for some clients to express their needs and concerns to their therapist.

Behavioural measures

Measures such as college grades, number of cigarettes smoked in a day, or number of trips out of the home, have been widely used in studies of outcome of behavioural counselling. The kind of self-monitoring required in a task such as keeping a diary of food intake may well make a positive contribution to therapy, as well as yielding research data. For counsellors and therapists influenced by behavioural or cognitive-behavioural perspectives, these measures give a much more convincing and sensitive estimate of real client change than would movement in scores on a standard depression or adjustment inventory.

Other behavioural measures that can be employed in counselling agencies as part of their evaluation are the drop-out and completion rates of clients. If, for example, 75 per cent of clients who make an appointment with a student counselling service do not return after the first session, there is probably something wrong. On the other hand, if 75 per cent are still seeing a counsellor after two years, there is probably something else wrong. In some situations direct observation of client behaviour may be undertaken by staff or key workers, or by family members. The use of behavioural measures in both clinical work and research is explored by Nelson (1981), and is discussed more fully in Chapter 7.

Structured interviews by expert clinicians

Such interviews have been utilised in some outcome studies as a means of obtaining an 'objective' measure of change from an independent source. For example, the Psychiatric Status Schedule (PSS) (Spitzer et al., 1970) was used in the Strupp and Hadley (1979) study into the role of non-specific factors in counselling. The PSS, which consists of questions designed to elicit information on 17 symptom scales, was administered before counselling, at termination and at follow-up. Another similar instrument is the Structured and Scaled Interview to Assess Maladjustment (SSIAM) (Gurland et al., 1972) used in the Sloane et al. (1975) study. These techniques are time-consuming, with each interview requiring up to an hour of client and clinician time, involve careful training of interviewers, and are open to distortion arising from the interaction between client and interviewer. There is also some evidence (Auerbach, 1983) that such instruments are relatively insensitive to change, in comparison with data arising from other sources such as self-report questionnaires. Auerbach (1983) provides a comprehensive review of the issues associated with this change assessment strategy.

Ratings by significant others

A few studies have deployed ratings by family members or colleagues of clients to supply information about therapeutic change (Davidson and Davidson, 1983). The attraction of data contributed by significant others is that these people will have known the client in a variety of situations over a long period of time, and may therefore possess a more complete picture of his or her behaviour, thoughts and feelings. There are, however, serious difficulties and obstacles inherent in this approach. It would not be ethical, for example, to put pressure on a client, or offer inducements, to obtain research data from a significant other. When a friend, family member or colleague does cooperate with a study, it may be impossible to control their level of motivation and interest in the task, or how much information they actually have about the client.

Ratings by therapists

Typically, the therapist or counsellor will either make the same ratings as an independent expert judge, or will rate change on a separate scale. In some cases, the therapist completes a scale parallel to a questionnaire filled in by the client. Considerable attention has been devoted to assessing the correspondence between client and counsellor evaluations of counselling, with the evidence appearing to suggest that, on the whole, counsellors and therapists are more cautious in their evaluations of change than are clients. It is as if the counsellor can always sense other therapeutic work that might be done. Issues in the use of therapist ratings are discussed by Newman (1983).

Cost–benefit analyses

In this kind of assessment of change, the criteria chosen are those relevant to the needs or interests of a third party paying for the counselling. The views of clients, counsellors, significant others or expert clinicians are not taken into account except in so far as these sources of worth have a payoff for the third party. Examples of cost–benefit analyses include monitoring productivity or days off sick in users of an employee counselling scheme, reduction in student drop-out arising from the appointment of a student counsellor, or calculating subsequent drug use or clinic visits by patients seen by clients of a counsellor in a GP practice. It is important to make a distinction between cost–benefit and cost-effectiveness studies. The aim of the former is to estimate the economic savings that are associated with a given amount of expenditure on an intervention. For example, finding out whether the salary and support costs of a college counsellor are balanced by the savings in fees from students who would otherwise have dropped out. The latter, cost-effectiveness studies, aim to discover the economic benefits accruing from different types of intervention. For example, investment in time-limited counselling might be more effective than investment in open-ended psychodynamic counselling for a GP looking to cut the drugs bill. These studies are difficult to carry out, with relatively few economic studies having been published to date. However, the increasing pressures on publicly funded services are inevitably leading to a significant expansion in this type of research. Useful general papers on this approach are McGrath and Lowson (1986), Mallett (1991), Mangen (1988), Parry (1992) and Ross (1989). An excellent guide on how to carry out different types of economic analysis of counselling has been published by Tolley and Rowland (1995). The edited collection of articles assembled by Miller and Magruder (1999) brings together a wide variety of different types of economic research into psychotherapy. The studies by Friedli et al. (2000) into the cost-effectivenss of counselling in primary care, and by Guthrie et al. (1999) into the savings in NHS costs resulting from offering brief psychotherapy to high utilisers of psychiatric services, are good, readable examples of economic research. McLeod (2001b) has summarised the existing research into the cost-effectiveness of workplace counselling.

A significant feature of this area of research is the challenge it presents to the predominant client-centred value base espoused by the counselling and psychotherapy community. It remains to be seen whether the effect of evaluating therapy in terms of the economic interests of the client's employer or educational institution (e.g. students staying at college, employees working harder) will, in the long term, cause conflict between counsellors and their employers.

Comparing sources of evidence about the effectiveness of therapy

The existence of such a wide variety of techniques and perspectives for assessing the effectiveness of counselling and psychotherapy can make it difficult to select measures for use in any specific study. In most research, practical factors and resource limitations mean that the researcher must choose a relatively narrow set of assessment tools. From the earliest research by Rogers and colleagues (Rogers and Dymond, 1954), it has been recognised that different participants (client, counsellor, outside observer) tend to evaluate therapy differently. Strupp and Hadley (1977) have suggested that there are three main 'stakeholders' or interest groups that each possess different criteria and standards for change: the client, society and mental health professionals. To be demonstrably effective, a form of therapy must be acceptable to all three constituencies. These considerations have lead Waskow and Parloff (1975) to argue that it would be helpful to establish a core battery of standardised measures that reflected all these different perspectives. Up to now, however, little progress seems to have been achieved in arriving at any such consensus. Different research groups continue to develop their own measures in response to their own local circumstances and theoretical preferences. While this state of affairs may be tolerable for well-funded research group teams able to find their way around the maze of instrumentation on offer, it has almost certainly been an obstacle to individual practitioners or small agencies seeking to introduce systematic evaluations of their work. Although the growing use in Britain of the CORE system, and in North America of the

Outcome Questionnaire (OQ), can be seen as an important step in the direction of a widely-adopted 'pantheoretical' outcome measure, it is clear that these questionnaires remain grounded in a version of the client's perspective on therapy – a version mediated through the questions and categories of therapists.

Issues in the design of outcome studies

There are some fundamental methodological issues that must be confronted by any researcher wishing to study counselling outcomes. Four of these issues will be discussed here: the role of the control group, the use of appropriate quantitative analyses, strategies for handling clients who drop out of treatment, and standardisation of treatment delivery.

The use of control groups

The importance of control groups in outcome research is demonstrated by the fate of the early studies of the effectiveness of psychoanalysis. In these studies, clients were merely followed up after the end of therapy. This kind of data can only provide weak evidence of the effectiveness of any form of intervention if, as Eysenck (1952) and others would assert, people with similar problems and needs were equally likely to improve in the absence of professional therapeutic help. It is necessary to acknowledge, however, that although post-counselling interviews or satisfaction questionnaires provide only weak evidence of effectiveness, *they are better than nothing*. The vast majority of counsellors and counselling agencies do not carry out any systematic evaluation of client satisfaction, and carefully collected retrospective post-counselling data will yield findings that can make a difference to practice. Hunt (1985) and Sloboda et al. (1993) are good examples of outcome studies of this kind.

In more ambitious studies that utilise control groups, the researcher must make a choice of the type of control or comparison condition that is appropriate for his or her purposes. The different types of control group designs used in counselling and psychotherapy outcome studies are summarised in Box 8.3. Each of these control group formats has its distinctive advantages and disadvantages. DiMascio et al. (1979), for example, wished to study the effects of psychotherapy with acutely depressed clients, but were concerned about the ethical implications of denying help to research participants allocated to a control condition. They therefore established an elaborate arrangement they described as *non-scheduled treatment control*, in which control group clients were told that many people spontaneously recovered from depression, that they could enter therapy whenever they wished, and that they would be regularly re-assessed by an independent clinical evaluator to see if they needed immediate treatment. Under these very carefully planned conditions, only 33 per cent of the control clients remained in the control group at the end of the planned 16-week waiting period. Although

Box 8.3 Types of control group used in counselling and psychotherapy outcome studies

Waiting list. Clients are randomly allocated to a waiting list and receive no treatment or contact while on the list.

Minimal contact. Clients randomly allocated to a waiting list are contacted regularly and given reassurance. Clients in need are removed from the study and given treatment if necessary.

Non-scheduled treatment. Clients randomly allocated to a waiting list are invited to begin treatment whenever they feel they need it. They are regularly re-assessed and are automatically removed from the list if in need of treatment.

Placebo controls. Clients randomly allocated to a control group are given an active placebo experience (e.g. reading instructional literature) that induces positive expectations for change.

Own controls comparison. All clients have to wait for a period of time. Change during counselling is compared with baseline measure obtained before counselling.

Non-client comparison group. Change over time is assessed in a group of people who report psychological problems but who are not seeking help.

Normative comparison. Change in clients is defined as movement from extreme symptomatic scores to 'normal' range on a standardised measure with reliable norms (i.e. use of criteria of reliable and clinically significant change).

this design involved some sacrifice of scientific rigour, it was highly respectful and caring in terms of responding ethically to the needs of clients.

Prioleau, Murdock and Brody (1983) argue that any control condition that involves just passive waiting for therapy to commence does not offer an appropriate comparison in counselling and psychotherapy outcome studies. They assert that:

> wait-list controls may lead to outcomes that are more negative than would have occurred merely through the passage of time. Individuals who seek therapeutic services and who are placed in a wait-list may be disappointed. In addition, such individuals may be experiencing an unintended reverse placebo effect. In being told they are being placed on a wait list, they are in effect told that they should not expect to improve. . . . (1983: 276)

Prioleau et al. (1983) suggest that only placebo controls, in which clients genuinely believe they are receiving treatment that will help them, and in which the treatment does not comprise any other 'active ingredients' apart from this belief, can operate as true controls in testing the effectiveness of therapy. Their point is that the work of Frank (1973) and others on the effect of 'non-specific' factors, such as the induction of positive expectations for change, would imply that there already exists a strong placebo or expectation factor in all forms of therapy. The task of the researcher, in the eyes of Prioleau et al. (1983), is to ascertain whether there is anything *more* to therapy than simply this expectation effect, or whether counselling and psychotherapy are little more than sophisticated and complex emotional placebos.

In their paper, Prioleau et al. (1983) draw on the image of the chemically inert pill employed in double-blind drug trials, as supplying a vision of an ideal placebo condition. However, although in pharmacology a pill can contain an active drug or contain sugar and yet be equally plausible to the patient, it is much harder in counselling to devise an equivalent to this pill. There is a deep cultural awareness of what happens in counselling, and it is not easy to accept that group play reading or group discussion of general topics (examples of placebo conditions reported in studies reviewed by Prioleau et al., 1983) are experienced by people as placebos in the same way that a pill might be in a drug trial.

Basham (1986) makes a strong attack on the validity of research designs that employ no-treatment control groups. He argues, along the same lines as Prioleau et al. (1983), that people allocated to a waiting list are not simply waiting. There is, for Basham, a powerful set of 'demand artifacts' generated by being allocated to a no-treatment group. He suggests that people who volunteer to participate in therapy research have 'clear expectations that treatment will be helpful' (1986: 89), and there is no way of concealing from these people that they are being denied such treatment. Basham refers to the extensive literature on the pervasive role of demand characteristics in psychological research in general (e.g. Rosenthal and Rubin, 1978) to back up his assertion that hidden demand artifacts can significantly distort experimental findings. The answer to this dilemma, for Basham, is to carry out *comparison group* rather than control group studies. In a comparative study, all research participants receive therapy straight away. Comparative studies can be used to answer questions such as 'which works best?' and 'how do they differ?' rather than the absolute question 'does it work?'.

The research into the comparative effectiveness of non-professional counsellors (Hattie et al., 1984) offers an example of the value of the comparison group strategy. Most of the studies reviewed by Hattie et al. (1984) were comparison group designs which showed that non-professionals were equally as effective as highly trained professional counsellors. Basham (1986) suggests that this use of a comparison group has resulted in more compelling evidence than if no-treatment control groups had been employed. It would be only moderately interesting to discover that non-professional volunteers were more effective than no treatment. It is *very* interesting to discover that these volunteers produce outcomes that are the equal of those reported by professionals.

The argument put forward by Basham (1986) in favour of comparison group designs in outcome studies needs to be set against the case made by Kazdin (1986) against such studies. He suggests that there are four serious limitations to comparison group designs. Firstly, this approach emphasises the treatment as an independent variable while minimising the relevance of other important variables such as therapist or client characteristics. Secondly, treatments may be entered into comparison studies prematurely, before enough is known about the client groups for whom they are applicable. Thirdly, there are so many alternative techniques that it would be impossible to test them all against each other. Finally, and most important of all, the comparison group studies that have been carried out typically find little or no difference between therapies (Smith et al., 1980) and so fail to answer the key question of which is better.

A completely different approach to demonstrating change in outcome studies involves using well-validated standardised scales, and arguing that the therapy being evaluated can be shown to be effective if the test scores recorded by clients move from the symptomatic range before therapy into the normal, asymptomatic range following treatment. An example of this type of study is the Barkham and Shapiro (1990) investigation of the outcome of very brief (three-session) therapy with moderately depressed white-collar workers. In this study, the criterion for success was that, over the course of treatment, a client would improve at least one standard deviation below the mean of scores obtained in pre-therapy administration of the test (in this case the Beck Depression Inventory or BDI). This strategy for assessing therapeutic outcome supplies an elegant way of dispensing with the conventional control or waiting list group. Being able to show that clients move from 'distressed' to 'normal' is a powerful demonstration of the effectiveness of a form of counselling or psychotherapy. The counter-argument to this approach, made by many writers from Eysenck (1952) onwards, is that, over time, the majority of untreated depressed people would likewise move from 'distressed' to 'normal', without the intervention of a professional counsellor. The force behind the 'normative control' approach lies in the abundant evidence that tests such as the BDI are highly reliable, so that, on average, groups of people get the same scores on different occasions. It may well be, however, that the general or average stability of scores on tests such as the BDI conceal wide variations over time on the part of individuals, with some people gaining lower scores on a re-test, and others gaining higher scores. The phenomenon of spontaneous recovery would appear to suggest that, at least on measures of emotional disturbance and adjustment, troubled people do get better anyway.

Doing without control groups: the use of clinical significance as a criterion for change

The use of normative controls in outcome studies is associated with a debate that has been going on among therapy researchers over the most appropriate statistical techniques to employ in assessing change scores. In most outcome studies, for example in the Sloane et al. (1975) study reviewed earlier, change is assessed by comparing the average or mean score of a group of clients on measures taken before therapy with scores on the same measures administered at the end of therapy. The difference between the two group means is subjected to a statistical test to determine whether the change is attributable to chance, and if the test allows the researcher to reject the Null Hypothesis (that there would be *no* difference between the two means) then the outcome is reported as, say, significant at '$p < 0.01$' (see Chapter 4). This would denote that the probablity (*P*) of the result occurring by chance was less than 1 in 100. In most studies, a statistical adjustment is made to the post-therapy scores to compensate for the baseline amount of change found in the control group (see, for example, Strupp and Hadley, 1979).

The majority of outcome studies have employed this approach to evaluating change (Smith et al., 1980). Nevertheless, a number of researchers have been critical of this use of statistical techniques. Jacobson, Follette and Revenstorf (1984) have identified two main problems with it. Firstly, group statistical comparisons 'are based on the average improvement score for all clients and thus provide no information on the effects of therapy for individual clients in that sample' (1984: 337). Secondly, 'the "significance test" itself imposes a criterion for determining a treatment effect which often has little clinical relevance' (1984: 337). It is this second objection, arising from the way statistical tests are applied in outcome studies, that is pertinent to the present discussion. If large enough samples of clients are used, marginal differences in scores before and after therapy may produce a statistically significant result, even though the post-therapy scores may indicate that most of the clients remain disturbed or mal-adjusted. Jacobson et al. (1984) suggest that research that is clinically meaningful must be based on change measures that reflect the extent to which clients have eliminated their presenting problem, improved their everyday functioning or changed in a manner recognisable to significant others. In other words, the change must be 'practically important' (1984: 338) not merely statistically significant.

Jacobson and Revenstorf (1988), Jacobson et al. (1984) and Tingey et al. (1996) have suggested some alternative methods for assessing change, based on estimating whether a client has moved out of the dysfunctional and into the range of scores that exhibit healthy functioning. They advocate that studies should report outcome findings in the form of percentages of clients who have improved in this way, rather than in terms of statistical differences in group means. These researchers advocate the use of two key criteria for evaluating change: *clinically significant change* (the client moves out of the 'problem' or 'clinical' population and into the 'normal' range), and *reliable change* (the magnitude of the change is large enough to exceed any measurement error that might be associated with the particular assessment instrument that has been used).

There remain, however, several difficult issues associated with the use of these criteria. In some situations it may be difficult to identify an appropriate normative group. In other situations, movement into the 'normal' range of functioning may be too stringent a criterion to apply. An example that Jacobson et al. (1984) give is that of research into the rehabilitation of hospitalised schizophrenic people. They point out that, for these clients, a realistic index of success may be a reduction in the rate of re-hospitalisation, as opposed to any goal that only registered success in terms of achieving an adjustment score reflecting membership of the well-functioning population.

The calculation of clinically significant and reliable change indices can be a complex undertaking. Lambert and Hill (1994) and Ogles et al. (2001) provide clear accounts of the ideas underlying the concepts of clinical and reliable change. In recent years, the adoption of clinical significance as a criterion for change has revolutionised the field of outcome research. If well-validated measures are employed in a study, such as CORE or the BDI, it is possible to know with some confidence the proportion of clients who would clinically improve in the absence of therapy (by looking, for instance, at the change figures for control groups in previous studies). It is therefore possible to carry out an outcome study without using a control or comparison group: if the percentage of clients who report clinical and reliable change is high enough, the therapy can be accepted as effective. It also becomes possible to estimate whether an individual client has changed significantly or not by the end of therapy. These possibilities open up outcome research by allowing researchers to do convincing and robust studies that are 'naturalistic', in reflecting everyday practice, rather than always creating the somewhat artificial conditions demanded by randomised controlled trials.

Attrition rates

Another dilemma associated with the design of outcome studies is the question of whether to include in the analysis, in some way or another, data relating to clients who have terminated therapy before the planned end of the course of treatment. Attrition clients will not usually make themselves available to participate in follow-up interviews or testing, and so it may seem reasonable to exclude them completely from the analysis of results. On the other hand, it can be assumed that most clients who terminate unilaterally have done so because they are dissatisfied with the treatment they have received, and so should be counted as 'failure' cases. Shapiro (1977) has suggested that one factor in the discrepancy in success rates found between studies of behaviour therapy and those of insight-oriented therapies might be that most of the former exclude early terminators, while most of the latter have counted them as poor outcome cases. Howard, Krause and Orlinsky (1986) suggest a number of strategies for dealing with the attrition issue.

Treatment fidelity: the use of manuals

One of the recurring concerns for those planning and carrying out studies into the effectiveness of different approaches to therapy has been the problem of how to control differences in technique and effectiveness between the various therapists participating in the study. There is considerable evidence that different practitioners claiming to be working within the same orientation may demonstrate quite marked contrasts in actual behaviour. For example, in a comprehensive study of encounter group leaders, Lieberman, Yalom and Miles (1973) found that facilitators supposedly running similar groups differed from each other on a number of dimensions of leader behaviour. There is also evidence that there can be substantial differences between even experienced and well-trained therapists in the outcomes they achieve with clients (Lambert, 1989). These factors create significant methodological difficulties for researchers seeking to evaluate the effectiveness of forms of therapy, since the implication is that outcomes will be more attributable to therapist variance than to actual treatment mode. This is a very serious problem, since typically – as in the Sloane et al. (1975) study – there will only be a small number of therapists contributing to a study. If, say, one of a group of three or four therapists delivering a treatment modality is markedly more (or less) effective than the others, then any difference in outcome between that modality and a comparison approach can almost certainly be accounted for in terms of this factor.

The solution to this problem that has been adopted in virtually all large-scale outcome studies in recent years has been to strive to standardise the performance of therapists by training them intensively in the approach being studied by using a treatment manual, and then assessing their adherence to that manual by sampling segments of sessions to ascertain whether their in-session behaviour accords sufficiently closely to the model. Manual-guided training and research has been applied in studies of time-limited dynamic psychotherapy (Strupp and Binder, 1984), supportive-expressive psychoanalytically oriented psychotherapy (Luborsky, 1984), cognitive therapy for depression (Beck et al., 1979), and several other approaches (Van Hasselt and Hersen, 1996). Reviews of developments in the use of manuals in research are available in Binder (1993), Lambert and Ogles (1988), Luborsky and DeRubeis (1984) and Moras (1993).

On the whole, reports on the use of manualised treatment in research studies seem to suggest that this technique represents a practical and effective means of enhancing therapist competence and reducing differences between therapists. On the face of it, the increasing use of manuals would appear to indicate a growing divergence between the highly controlled and monitored world of the outcome study and the rather more messy real-life environments in which most counselling and psychotherapy is practised. It also sits uncomfortably with the finding that the majority of practitioners describe themselves as eclectic or integrationist rather than espousing a single theoretical orientation (Garfield and Kurtz, 1974). In so far as this is the case, manual-based studies can be viewed as an illustration of the tension in counselling research between relevance and rigour. On the other hand, several writers have observed that their experience with manuals has convinced them that this technique has a lot to offer in terms of its applicability to counsellor training in general (Dobson and Shaw, 1993; Luborsky, 1993; Moras, 1993; Weiss and Marmar, 1993). So it may well be that, in the future, manualised training will become a standard element of good practice rather than being restricted solely to the research domain. However, it should be noted that, so far, these manuals have been applied to the function of training practitioners who are already moderately experienced, rather than to the task of initial training. Also, there have been suggestions that therapists trained through manual instruction may acquire a relatively superficial grasp of the approach being taught, learning to employ techniques rather than internalising the theory and philosophy of the model at a deeper level (Lambert and Ogles, 1988). Research into the experiences of therapists who have used treatment manuals (Addis and Krasnow, 2000) has found a range of opinion: some therapists believe that treatment manuals help them to respond to clients in a systematic manner, while others view manuals as stifling their individual creativity.

What makes the difference: the therapy or the therapist?

Many hundreds of psychotherapy outcome studies have been carried out, in which different models of therapy have been compared with each other, or with the effects of no treatment or a waiting time. The overwhelming evidence from these studies is that there is very little difference in effectiveness between different approaches to therapy. This conclusion has been called the 'equivalence paradox' (how can very different types of therapy yield equivalent outcomes?) and the 'Dodo Bird verdict' (from *Alice in Wonderland*, where, at the end of a race, the Dodo Bird announced that 'everyone has won and all must have prizes'). By contrast, there have been relatively few studies in which the effectiveness of *therapists* rather than *therapies* has been compared. In all of these studies it has been found that some therapists are significantly more effective than others (Blatt et al., 1996; Crits-Christoph et al., 1991; Elkin, 1999; Lambert, 1989; Luborsky et al., 1997; McLellan et al., 1988). The difference in effectiveness between individual therapists does not appear to be associated with levels of training or experience. The research into 'therapist effects' raises important questions about the therapy outcome literature as a whole: have researchers been asking the wrong questions?

The relevance of outcome studies for practice

The aim of most outcome studies has been to establish the efficacy of the particular approach to therapy under scrutiny. The results of these studies are communicated through journals almost as fixed modules of 'fact' concerning the type of therapy under examination, so that after a time the finding becomes one in a series of reference sources used to reinforce statements regarding the effectiveness of that type of therapy in cases of a particular type of disorder. This research strategy ignores the dynamic relationship between research and practice. In many other fields of human service work, evaluation research is carried out with the explicit aim of improving current service delivery. As Patton (1990:

12) has written, 'the purpose of applied research and evaluation is to inform action . . . [it] is judged by its usefulness in making human actions and interventions more effective'.

For the most part, the relationship between therapy outcome studies and practice has been implicit, indirect and diffuse. A good example of the potential benefits of integrating research into practice can be seen in the history of the programme of studies into client-centred counselling directed by Carl Rogers between 1945 and 1962, first at the University of Chicago and then at the University of Wisconsin. All of the key staff involved in this set of studies were both therapists and researchers. There was an active interplay between research and clinical work, with hunches and hypotheses from the latter being tested out in studies, and the theoretical model emerging from the studies being used to shape actual work with clients. The impression that is gained is that, through the interaction of research and practice, the very nature of client-centred counselling and psychotherapy changed and developed (McLeod, 2002b). Client-centred counsellors in the late 1960s were doing different things from those in the early 1940s.

A more explicit approach to employing feedback from outcome data to improve practice can be seen in Sloboda et al. (1993). This study has been designed to evaluate the effectiveness of time-limited counselling provided for employees of a social services department. Clients who use the employee counselling service are invited to complete a questionnaire that includes items about their general satisfaction with the counselling, their feelings about the counsellor and the limit on number of sessions, and their perception of specific aspects of the agency such as accessibility and quality of environment. The client is also asked whether he or she will give approval for their counsellor to see the questionnaire. The research team are therefore able to supply the counsellors in the agency not only with regular feedback on their overall effectiveness, but also with information about outcomes with individual clients. The evidence suggests that the counsellors involved in this project are able to use this data productively to direct the development of their practice. In contrast to most counselling settings, where it is rare for counsellors to find out what their clients really felt and thought about their therapy, these counsellors received regular client feedback.

The use of information technology has made possible a number of innovatory projects involving the use of feedback from outcome questionnaires. These projects, in the USA and Germany, have involved asking clients to complete questionnaires at regular intervals, and then returning the analysed results to counsellors, their supervisors or case managers within a short space of time (Kordy et al., 2001; Lambert, Hansen and Finch, 2001; Lueger, 1998; Lueger et al., 2001). Typically, the feedback focuses on identifying cases in which the client has not improved in line with an 'expected treatment response' (Lueger et al., 2001) or 'expected recovery curve' (Lambert, Hansen and Finch, 2001). In one study, the impact on counsellors of receiving feedback data of this kind was assessed (Lambert, Hansen and Finch, 2001; Lambert et al., 2001). In this large-scale study, more than 600 clients completed the Outcome Questionnaire (see Chapter 6) on a weekly basis, as a 'tracking' measure. In half of the cases, counsellors did not receive feedback. In the other half, feedback was communicated to counsellors through a simple and vivid colour scale:

White feedback: 'The client is functioning in the normal range. Consider termination.'

Green feedback: 'The rate of change the client is making is in the adequate range. No change in the treatment plan is recommended.'

Yellow feedback: 'The rate of change the client is making is less than adequate. Recommendations: consider altering the treatment plan by intensifying treatment, shifting intervention strategies, and monitoring progress especially carefully. This client may end up with no significant benefit from therapy.'

Red feedback: 'The client is not making the expected level of progress. Chances are he/she may drop out of treatment prematurely or have a negative treatment outcome. Steps should be taken to carefully review this case and decide upon a new course of action such as referral for medication or intensification of treatment. The treatment plan should be reconsidered. Consideration should also be given to presenting this client at a case conference. The client's readiness for change may need to be re-assessed.' (Lambert et al., 2001: 55–6)

The results of this study showed that about 1 in 10 clients was flagged up in the yellow or red categories. Where feedback was provided to counsellors on 'off-track' clients, therapists adjusted their approach, specifically by offering these clients more sessions. Compared to the 'off-track' clients in the no-feedback group, many more of the feedback clients ended up benefiting from therapy, and fewer dropped out prematurely. It was also found that the number of sessions offered to white/green clients in the feedback condition was on average less than in the no-feedback branch of the study. The counsellors reported that, on the whole, they valued this kind of feedback, and about half of the time actually discussed the feedback with their clients. The overall outcome of the experiment, therefore, was to enhance clinical outcomes while at the same time reducing costs by reducing the overall number of sessions that were used, despite offering nearly twice as many sessions to some of the needier clients. For some counsellors and clients, the idea of this level of surveillance might be threatening. On the other hand, from the perspective of Lambert et al. (2001: 65), 'given independent information on patient progress, therapists and patients tend to be efficient'.

The role of systematic reviews: evidence-based practice

Outcome research in counselling and psychotherapy can have important political implications. Policy-makers in health and other fields use outcome evidence to guide their decisions on which types of intervention they should support or allow.

This issue has become expressed in recent years in the debate over 'evidence-based' or 'empirically validated' treatment. Professional associations and government bodies in North America and Europe have sought to restrict therapeutic training and practice only to those approaches which are 'evidence-based' or 'empirically validated' (the phrase used in North America) in terms of findings derived from quantitative, randomised controlled trials. There are several important ethical and methodological questions linked to this debate:

- Are 'controlled', quantitative studies the best or only way to evaluate the effectiveness of therapy?
- How adequately do controlled trials reflect everyday therapeutic practice?
- Does the lack of positive research evidence mean that an approach to therapy is invalid, or merely that those who practise it do not have access to the resources necessary to carry out rigorous research?
- Should clients be given a choice in which kind of therapist they see, regardless of the research evidence?
- How important, in the context of this debate, is the research evidence which suggests that the quality of relationship between client and therapist is a better predictor of good outcome than is the type of therapy being offered?

Good sources of further reading around this critical issue are the book edited by Rowland and Goss (2000), and a Special Issue of *Psychotherapy Research* (Elliott, 1998; Henry, 1998).

Decisions over evidence-based practice rely on a technique known as 'meta-analysis'. In a situation where there are several studies on the effectiveness of a type of therapy, but each employs different outcome measures, it is not a straightforward matter to 'add up' the findings of all the different investigations that have been carried out. To overcome this problem, research reviewers calculate the *Effect Size* of each intervention in each study, and work out the overall Effect Size of that type of intervention across all the studies that have been carried out). The Effect Size is a statistical estimate of the overall amount of change reported in a sample. Reviewers also evaluate the methodological rigour of each study, and give a higher weighting to the most robust studies. A number of projects have been set up to produce systematic reviews of interventions in health and other areas of care. One of the most important projects has been the Cochrane Review series (named after a famous medical researcher, Sir Archie Cochrane). An influential Cochrane Review has been published of the effectiveness of counselling in primary health care (Bower et al., 2002).

In a social and political climate in which all forms of medical, nursing and social care are required to be 'evidence-based', it is surely reasonable that counselling and psychotherapy should be fully accountable. But the decisions that are taken will affect both therapists' livelihoods and clients' choices, and represent a crucial test of the trustworthiness and value of the research which has been carried out. Some research carried out by Lester Luborsky and colleagues (Luborsky et al., 1999) raises questions about the interpretation of existing research into the effectiveness of therapy. Luborsky et al. (1999) reviewed 29 studies in which the relative effectiveness of two forms of therapy was compared. They then carried out a painstaking analysis of what was known about the therapeutic allegiances of the researchers who conducted the studies. They found a significant positive relationship between allegiance and outcome. For example, in a study carried out by a psychodynamic researcher, comparing cognitive-behavioural and psycho-dynamic therapy, it would be virtually certain that the results would favour the psychodynamic approach. In a study carried out by a researcher positively oriented towards cognitive-behavioural methods, CBT would be likely to emerge as the most effective therapy. Luborsky et al. (1999) argue that researcher allegiances can seriously distort the findings of outcome studies. They make a number of suggestions for eliminating this possible source of bias.

Beyond outcome studies: evaluating the quality of service delivery

The studies discussed in this chapter have focused on outcome research which attempts to assess the effectiveness of counselling and psychotherapy in terms of – mainly – differences in scores on standardised measures of anxiety, depression and other symptom dimensions, administered before and after treatment. The consistent finding to emerge from these studies is that therapy is highly effective. It is important, however, to be aware of the limitations of existing knowledge about the effectiveness of therapy. As Luborsky et al. (1999) have pointed out, there is a worrying tendency for researchers, even in highly controlled studies, to find what they want to find. It is also necessary to acknowledge that the majority of studies have been carried out in somewhat unrepresentative conditions, for example research clinics and special projects; there are relatively few studies of the effectiveness of therapy under ordinary, everyday clinical conditions (Shadish et al., 1997). Beyond these issues, it is possible to ask whether therapy researchers are asking the most appropriate questions in terms of being able to determine the overall social benefits resulting from the provision of counselling and psychotherapy. Barkham and Mellor-Clark (2000) have argued that it is not sufficient to concentrate solely on individual change. They propose that a broader 'quality evaluation' perspective should be adopted, which addresses such aims as:

- demonstrating the appropriateness of service structures;
- enhancing accessibility of service provision;
- monitoring the acceptability of service procedures;
- ensuring equity to all potential service recipients;
- improving the efficiency of service delivery.

For example, a counselling agency may report excellent outcome results for those clients who complete therapy, but be inaccessible to some members of the community (e.g., those not on a bus route), unacceptable to others (who may hold specific cultural expectations) and inefficient (in that many clients miss sessions, thus wasting valuable therapist time). Is such a counselling agency offering an effective service?

Conclusions

Counselling is a complex, multi-faceted activity, and it is not a simple matter to evaluate whether it 'works'. It is important to recognise, moreover, that the very act of asking whether it 'works' is embedded in a particular way of seeing. Orlinsky (1989) has proposed that there exist four 'images of psychotherapy' that have guided the conduct of research. Counselling and psychotherapy have been seen as *treatment* for psychiatrically diagnosable disorders. Therapy has been seen as an *educational* process of re-learning. It has been seen as *reform*, a subtle form of social control, and finally as *redemption*, a ritual that gives 'a sense of purpose and justification' (1989: 419) to those who participate in it. For Orlinsky, each of these images or metaphors can be of value in shaping and informing outcome research. Nevertheless, he acknowledges that the image of therapy as 'treatment' represents a dominant 'official' view that is rarely challenged by researchers.

The pervasive sense of therapy as treatment of illness emerges again in what Stiles and Shapiro (1989) have called the 'abuse of the drug metaphor' in research. They argue that researchers have carried out research as if counselling or psychotherapy was a drug being given to a patient. The classic paper by Howard et al. (1986) into the 'dose–effect' relationship (i.e. more sessions of therapy is equivalent to a stronger 'dose') is but one example of the influence of this metaphor. Another example lies in the adoption of treatment manuals, as a means of 'purifying' the 'drug'. Stiles and Shapiro distinguish several reasons for the ubiquity of this image of therapy:

> with no consensus about which theory is best . . . research conducted within one framework is regarded as outlandish from another viewpoint. The drug metaphor has served as a conceptual lowest common denominator – a simple model that proponents of all schools (and journal reviewers of diverse orientations) can use . . . The drug metaphor may also have psychological appeal independent of its explanatory power. Its attributional bias toward the therapist as change agent may serve the profession's need to see itself as potent. Finally, the example of medicine is a socially powerful, economically compelling one for psychotherapy. (1989: 537)

There are strong factors reinforcing the priority and status given to research based on a 'medical' image, despite the many ways in which counselling and psychotherapy are clearly not best viewed as forms of medical treatment. Relatively few clients can plausibly be seen as 'ill'. Therapy is not a medical technology that can be administered in a neutral fashion but might be viewed as a conversation or learning experience that depends for its effectiveness on the quality of relationship between participants.

Outcome researchers are pulled in two directions. To attract funding for their research they are required to show that their work is scientifically respectable within the canons of the experimental, applied medical research tradition. To demonstrate the relevance of their findings to practitioners they need to acknowledge the non-scientific educational, reformist or redemptionist dimensions of therapy. The discomfort of many key members of the research community has been expressed around the margins of the literature for many years (e.g. Bergin and Strupp, 1972).

An important consequence of the preoccupation of the research community with drug-trial research designs has been to engender an attitude that research is not worth doing unless it is done 'properly', on a large scale, with big samples, control groups and manuals. Horowitz (1982) has pointed out that the cost–benefit ratio associated with comparison group studies is low. Very large sums of money are spent for relatively small pay-offs in terms of increases in knowledge. Horowitz (1982) urges researchers to be more willing to conduct theoretically informed case studies and correlational studies, rather than allow themselves to become over-absorbed in methodological sophistication and elegance.

A high proportion of published research is generated by the activities of a relatively small number of research centres. In the field of outcome research, the studies that have emerged from these elite groups have consistently confirmed that therapy is more helpful than not receiving therapy, and that no one form of counselling or therapy is appreciably more effective than any other. However, the social and organisational context of these studies must be taken into account. To engage in a large-scale comparative study with careful screening, testing and follow-up of clients demands the cooperation of a well resourced and administered clinic. It would seem reasonable to suggest that, for the most part, outcome studies have been carried out in the 'best' counselling and therapy agencies. It might be sensible to re-direct some of this effort toward the needs of less well-resourced clinics and agencies, particularly if outcomes can be fed back into practice in a form that allows practitioners to use research data to enhance their work with clients. Finally, despite the emphasis in outcome studies on assessing the effectiveness of *therapies*, there is a case to be made that equal attention should be given to assessing the effectiveness of *therapists* (Blatt et al., 1996; Crits-Christoph et al., 1991) and the influence of the organisational environment within which they work (McLeod and Machin, 1998).

Further reading

Two excellent books on general issues and methods in outcome research are:

Cone, J.D. (2001) *Evaluating Outcomes: Empirical Tools for Effective Practice*. Washington, DC: American Psychological Association.

Mace, C., Moorey, S. and Roberts, B. (eds) (2001) *Evidence in the Psychological Therapies: A Critical Guide for Practitioners*. London: Brunner-Routledge.

The single best reference source for any question relating to psychotherapy outcome research remains:

Bergin, A.E. and Garfield, S.L. (eds) (1994) *Handbook of Psychotherapy and Behavior Change*, 4th edn. Chichester: Wiley.

Informative and comprehensive coverage of the debate around evidence-based practice, and its implications for counselling and psychotherapy outcome research, can be found in:

Rowland, N. and Goss, S. (eds) (2000) *Evidence-based Counselling and Psychological Therapies: Research and Applications*. London: Routledge.

For an alternative perspective, which examines the shortcomings of psychotherapy outcome research, see:

Dineen, T. (1999) *Manufacturing Victims: What the Psychology Industry is Doing to People*. London: Constable.

9 Exploring the Interior of Therapy: Method and Strategy in Process Research

One participant in my study was astonished to realise that, on hearing the tape replay of her therapy session, her therapist had actually only basically repeated what she had said. She had not experienced it this way at all. She had experienced it as advice because that was what she had been looking for. (Rennie, 2001: 84)

The previous chapter reviewed some of the extensive literature on research into the effectiveness of counselling and psychotherapy. In the 1980s, it began to become apparent to most members of the counselling and psychotherapy research community that therapy was, on the whole, effective and beneficial. The focus of much research then started to move in the direction of seeking to identify the processes within the therapy hour that were associated with good client progress. Outcome research appeared to suggest that not all clients improved to an equal extent. Some clients even deteriorated during therapy. What were the processes occurring in the therapeutic relationship that led to satisfactory outcomes? What were the processes that resulted in the worsening of client problems? Over the last 20 years, the search has intensified for ways of gaining an understanding of what went on in the interior of therapy. This research activity has generated a range of new approaches and techniques for investigating process issues.

There are a number of substantial difficulties facing any researcher intending to carry out a process study. First, it is necessary to arrive at a working definition or understanding of process. The counselling and psychotherapy literature contains many diverse ideas about the nature of process (see Elliott, 1991; McLeod, 2003). For some writers, a process is a general condition that exists in a therapeutic relationship, for example an emotional climate of acceptance and warmth. For other writers a process consists of a sequence of behaviours or actions engaged in by either the counsellor, the client, or both together. Some researchers have viewed process in terms of aspects of the experience of either the client or the counsellor. Yet others have adopted a definition of process that encompasses contractual aspects of therapy such as the frequency, length or number of sessions. Another set of problems for the process researcher arises from the challenge of gathering valid and relevant data on what takes place during a therapy session. However process is understood or defined, there is general agreement that it comprises a highly complex and elusive set of phenomena, as can be seen from the excerpt from Rennie (2001) quoted above. It is difficult to observe or measure these phenomena. Finally, there are issues arising from the requirement to collect this information ethically. In comparison with outcome research, where in principle all the research data can be gathered outside of sessions, in process studies it may be necessary to intrude into the on-going flow of the therapeutic work between client and counsellor. With this intrusion comes the danger of harming the client.

The purpose of this chapter is to review the various research strategies that have been employed in therapy process research. This discussion of the methods used in process studies will be followed by an exploration of some of the fundamental methodological issues associated with the use of these techniques.

Gaining access to the interior of therapy: tools and methods

Researchers have pressed into service a wide range of methods of gathering information about what happens during therapy sessions. Much of the early research into this topic was based on open-ended *client accounts* of their experiences during therapy. Rogers (1951) contains a chapter on 'the relation-ship as experienced by the client' which draws on diaries kept by clients. Axline (1950), Fitts (1965) and Lipkin (1948) invited clients to write descriptions of their experiences. Other researchers have elicited open-ended accounts of process from clients through in-depth interviews (Brannen and Collard, 1982; Maluccio, 1979; Mayer and Timms, 1970; Timms and Blampied, 1985). All of these account-gathering studies have invited clients (and in some instances counsellors) to describe the whole of their experience in therapy. Bachelor (1988) gathered more focused, briefer, descriptions from clients of specific episodes of 'feeling understood'. Lietaer (1992) used open-ended questionnaires to compile client accounts of what they found helpful and hindering in counselling. Berzon et al. (1963) and Bloch et al. (1979) used an open-ended questionnaire to elicit from participants their descriptions of the 'most important event' in group therapy. Llewelyn et al. (1988) adopted a similar approach in asking clients in individual therapy to write about 'helpful aspects' of sessions. Martin and Stelmazonek (1988) invited clients to recall the most memorable images or events from sessions.

The distinctive characteristic of the account-gathering approach for investi-gating process is that it yields rich descriptive data that are clearly authentic and stimulating. On the other hand, the stories that clients and counsellors tell about their experiences of therapeutic process are complex and multi-layered. It can therefore be difficult to make sense of this material, and to organise it in terms of themes and processes. Another limitation of this kind of account-gathering is that informants undoubtedly forget at least some of what happened during sessions, and may to some extent offer the researcher a reconstruction of the process, based on what they now believe must have happened, rather than a direct description. In addition, what emerges from the interview must always be regarded as, at least to some extent, a 'co-construction' which draws on both informant and interviewer perceptions of the topic.

A research strategy that overcomes many of the problems of the accounts technique is observation of therapy sessions. For research purposes, observation means recording on either video or audio tape. The earliest recordings (in fact on acetate discs) of therapy sessions were made by Frank Robinson and Carl Rogers at Ohio State University in the 1940s (see Hill and Corbett, 1993; Rogers, 1942). In this research, transcripts were made of client and counsellor statements, and various methods were developed for categorising these verbal events. In more recent times, transcripts have been supplemented by coding done by trained raters who either watch or listen to the actual tape, thus preventing loss of crucial information about such non-verbal dimensions as voice quality, posture and gaze. There is now available a wide range of tools for carrying out ratings of process variables based on session tapes. Some of the most widely used of these instruments are listed in Box 9.1. The application of this approach involves constructing a coding manual, training raters and monitoring inter-rater reliability. Hill (1991) provides an excellent review of the practical issues involved in this type of investigation. Another perspective on the analysis of session tapes has been taken by Mahrer, Nadler et al. (1986), who advocate the use of a team of expert clinicians as observers, each offering his or her 'reading' of the process material.

The main advantage of observation as a means of gathering information about process is that it enables the researcher to glean standardised, quantitative data.

Box 9.1   Questionnaire-based therapy process measures

Working Alliance Inventory (WAI). Client and counsellor forms. Scales: working alliance factors of goals, tasks and bond. (Horvath and Greenberg, 1986, 1989)

Barrett-Lennard Relationship Inventory (BLRI). Client and counsellor forms. Scales: level of regard, congruence, empathic understanding, unconditionality of regard. (Barrett-Lennard, 1986)

Therapy Session Report. Client and counsellor forms. Scales include: topic and concerns in session, affective quality of session, relatedness, goal attainment, evaluation of session. (Orlinsky and Howard, 1975, 1986)

Session Evaluation Questionnaire (SEQ). Client and counsellor forms. Scales: depth, smoothness, positivity, arousal. (Stiles, 1980; Stiles and Snow, 1984)

Also, observational data on tape can be readily used to analyse *sequences* of behaviour. It is clear from the tape what behaviour is preceded, or followed, by other behaviour. The primary weakness of observational material is that it gives insufficient access to the internal processes occurring in either client or counsellor.

A method that retains the advantages of structure and quantification associated with coding of observational data, while nevertheless including the actual experiences of clients or their therapists involves the use of *questionnaires* or *rating scales*. There are a number of questionnaires assessing process variables that clients or counsellors can complete at the end of sessions, or periodically throughout a course of treatment. Some of these process instruments are described in Box 9.2. These scales can be completed in a few minutes, and are convenient for both researcher and research participant. However, it is important to note that these tools can only give access to process factors operating over a whole session (or several sessions), and are not applicable for the study of discrete episodes or events within single sessions.

A limitation of all the process research strategies reviewed so far is that none of them readily allows access to the flow of covert processes taking place in the exchange between client and counsellor. It could be argued that, for all their value, account-gathering, observations and questionnaires can never deliver anything better than a fuzzy picture of therapeutic process. The development of a means of obtaining a sharper and clearer image of the interior of therapy has relied mainly on the application and adaptation of a technique known as *Interpersonal Process Recall* (IPR). Kagan and his colleagues evolved IPR in the 1960s primarily as an approach to training counselling skills (Barker, 1985; Kagan, 1980, 1984; Kagan et al., 1963). At the heart of the IPR method is the recall interview. An audio or video tape is made of a counselling session. Soon after the end of the session, a recall interview is carried out with one of the therapy participants (client or counsellor) in which they are invited to respond to a structured set of questions about what they were experiencing at different points on the tape. The recording is played back to the participant, who will usually be in charge of the stop–go controls of the tape. Whenever the person decides that something significant is happening on the tape, he or she pauses the playback and explores what he or she was thinking and feeling at that point during the original session. The assumption is that if the recall interview is carried out within a few hours of the therapy session, it will be possible by this method to re-stimulate the actual experience the person had during the session. In the context of training, the purpose of the exercise is to help the trainee counsellor to be more aware of the richness and diversity of his or her reactions to the client, and to become more skilled and confident in drawing on these reactions during therapeutic work. The distinctive merits of the IPR method are that it slows down the process of interaction, thus allowing informants to unfold more of their experience and awareness than they would normally be capable of disclosing, and that the skill and presence of the interviewer enables the informant to feel safe enough to be open in acknowledging all facets of the process.

It can readily be seen that IPR represents a unique and invaluable tool for process research. Elliott has suggested that this method:

Box 9.2   Observational measures of therapy process

Accurate Empathy Scale. A 9-point scale, applied by trained observers to tape segments. Similar scales for non-possessive warmth and genuineness. (Truax and Carkhuff, 1967)

Working Alliance Inventory (WAI). Observer form. Scales: working alliance factors of goals, tasks and bond. (Horvath and Greenberg, 1986, 1989)

Experiencing Scale (EXP). Seven-point scale, applied by trained observers to 2–8-minute tape segments, transcripts or written materials. Measures depth of experiencing in client, counsellor or group. (Klein et al., 1986)

Client and Therapist Vocal Quality. Coding made by trained observers. Each client/therapist statement is coded. Four categories of vocal pattern: focused, externalising, limited, emotional. (Rice, 1992; Rice and Kerr, 1986)

Client Perceptual Processing. Trained judges rate seven categories of perceptual processing, using both transcript and audiotape. (Toukmanian, 1986, 1992)

Verbal Response Modes. Trained judges rate 14 categories of verbal behaviour, using transcripts of whole sessions. (Hill, 1986)

Vanderbilt Psychotherapy Process Scale (VPPS). Eighty Likert-scaled items used by trained raters. Scales: patient exploration, therapist exploration, patient psychic distress, patient participation, patient hostility, patient dependency, therapist warmth and friendliness, and negative therapist attitude. (Suh et al., 1986)

Narrative Process Coding Scheme (NPCS). Trained judges code therapy transcripts in terms of topic shifts, and internal, external and reflexive modes of narrative processing. (Angus et al., 1999)

allows the researcher to gather information on the moment-to-moment perceptions, intentions and reactions of clients and therapists during therapy sessions – subjective impressions which are missing from even the best transcriptions or recordings. (1986: 505)

The application of IPR in research situations allows the investigator to gather fine-grained descriptions or moment-by-moment ratings of critical episodes within the therapy hour. Elliott et al. (1982), for example, have used this technique to examine the perceived helpfulness of different kinds of therapist interventions. Angus and Rennie (1988, 1989) have employed the method to explore the meaning for clients of metaphors that emerge during therapy. Hill (1989) has utilised IPR as part of a battery of techniques included in a series of intensive case studies.

The main disadvantage of IPR methodology is that it can be highly time-consuming and demanding for both researchers and informants. To address this problem, Elliott has devised a form of IPR known as *Brief Structured Recall* (Elliott and Shapiro, 1988), in which the informant selects only one or two events for intensive analysis (e.g. the most helpful event), rather than working through the whole tape. Another difficulty with IPR studies is that it is not possible to know whether the informant is in fact recalling what actually happened, or is to a greater or lesser extent imposing a retrospective gloss on what is being shown or heard on the tape. Normally, participants are given careful instructions to engage in the former rather than the latter type of activity.

A final approach to gathering data about process has been on-line live *self-monitoring*. For example, in a study of empathy, Barkham and Shapiro (1986) asked clients to press a concealed button whenever they felt that the counsellor was understanding them well. The ouput from the button was fed into a computer record. This technique has the strength of providing direct recording of process factors at the time they are occurring. On the other hand, it is likely that many counsellors and clients would find this approach unacceptably intrusive. Certainly, this type of technique has not been widely used in process research. It can be seen, then, that there are a number of strategies for investigating processes in therapy sessions. Each of these strategies has something to offer, but all have their limitations. As in other areas of therapy research, the diversity of approaches and instruments gives the impression of fragmentation and incoherence. In the field of process research, such coherence as exists has centred upon a number of thematic programmes of research.

Facilitative conditions: the client-centred research programme

The single most important programme of research into therapeutic process has been the series of studies of aspects of client-centred counselling and psycho-therapy carried out by Rogers and his colleagues. This series of studies is significant for two reasons. Firstly, it pioneered many research methods that have subsequently been widely adopted. Secondly, it used research to test and develop theory in a systematic manner. The major research publications from this programme were Rogers and Dymond (1954) and Rogers et al. (1967). Summaries of the aims and scope of this body of work can be found in Barrett-Lennard (1979), Lietaer (1990) and McLeod (2002b). Box 9.3 summarises the stages in the evolution of research into client-centred counselling and therapy. The client-centred programme has spanned a much greater length of time than the other

Box 9.3 Stages in the development of research into client-centred therapy

1 Talk by Rogers at the University of Minnesota in December 1940 on 'newer concepts of psychotherapy', later to appear as Chapter 2 of *Counseling and Psychotherapy* (1942).

2 1940–45. Early research studies at the University of Ohio, mainly based on coding and analysis of transcripts of therapy sessions.

3 1945–57. Research group at the University of Chicago Counseling Center constructs a distinctive client-centred research model. Methods include: Q-sort, TAT, Rorschach, questionnaires, case studies. Research explores links between process (e.g. congruence between client self and ideal self as assessed by Q-sort) and outcomes. Publication in 1957 of 'necessary and sufficient conditions' paper.

4 1957–65. Research group at University of Wisconsin carry out large-scale project on process and outcomes of client-centred therapy with hospitalised schizophrenic patients. New methods include rating scales to assess process variables such as empathy, acceptance, congruence and experiencing.

5 1965–1980. No strong institutional base for client-centred research. Continuing research on core conditions (e.g. Barrett-Lennard, 1986) and experiencing (e.g. Klein et al., 1986). Research mainly into client-centred and person-centred concepts rather than therapy.

6 Resurgence of research into person-centred and experiential therapy (Cain and Seeman, 2002; Elliott, 2002a; Greenberg, Watson and Lietaer, 1998) using a range of qualitative, quantitative and case study methodologies.

sets of studies in therapy process that will be discussed later in this chapter, and so it can be used to exemplify some of the general issues that concern researchers interested in process themes. The first phase of the programme was mainly concerned with describing process variables such as 'non-directiveness' and 'self-acceptance' in terms of client and counsellor behaviours and actions. The second phase, centred on the Rogers and Dymond (1954) book, explored the relationship between process and outcome, and continued to develop new techniques, such as the Q-sort, that could be used for this purpose. These first two phases depict a path that has been followed by most subsequent process researchers. The next phase in the client-centred programme represents a stage of development that has been achieved by few other process researchers. In 1957 Rogers integrated the findings from the work done up to that point into an explicit theoretical model that made powerful predictions about the links between process and outcome. This model postulated certain 'necessary and sufficient conditions' (subsequently labelled 'core conditions') for positive personality change in clients. Rogers wrote that:

For constructive personality change to occur, it is necessary that these conditions exist and continue to exist over time:

1 Two persons are in psychological contact.
2 The first, whom we shall term the client, is in a state of incongruence, being vulnerable and anxious.
3 The second person, whom we shall term the therapist, is congruent or integrated in the relationship.
4 The therapist experiences unconditional positive regard for the client.
5 The therapist experiences an empathic understanding of the client's internal frame of reference, and endeavours to communicate this to the client. The communication to the client of the therapist's empathic understanding and unconditional positive regard is to a minimal extent achieved.

No other conditions are necessary. If these six conditions exist, and continue over a period of time, this is sufficient. The process of constructive personality change will follow. (1957: 95)

This theory acted as a catalyst for a substantial number of studies designed to test its predictions. However, there turned out to be major methodological difficulties involved in assembling a combination of clients, therapists and research instruments appropriate to testing the theory. For example, the instruments designed to assess levels of therapist empathy and acceptance revealed that most therapists exhibited only moderate levels of these qualities. A more satisfactory test of the theory would have been to have compared groups of therapists that were either high or low in facilitative conditions, but this was not possible for practical and ethical reasons. Several studies assessed the conditions, but not from the perspective of the client. Other researchers found that observers rating therapy tapes on the conditions found it hard to differentiate between congruence, empathy and acceptance, but appeared to be basing their ratings on their image of a 'good therapist'. The result of all this has been that the theory has been neither unequivocally supported nor rejected, even after several major research projects devoted to it (Cramer, 1992). Watson (1984), for example, comes to the conclusion that the research has not been rigorous enough to test the theory properly, so no judgement can be made on whether it is true or not. Patterson (1984), while acknowledging these methodological problems, nevertheless argues that the trend of results has been in favour of the facilitative conditions model.

The debate over the status of the facilitative conditions model has largely died away. Practitioners within the person-centred approach continue to find the theory useful in guiding their work with clients. However, despite some lingering attempts to carry out the definitive study that will prove it right or wrong (Cramer, 1990), researchers have on the whole moved on to other concerns. The main ideas of the facilitative conditions model have been assimilated into the *therapeutic alliance* theory developed by Bordin (1979) and Horvath and Greenberg (1986). Some of the main concepts of the facilitative conditions model, such as empathy (Barrett-Lennard, 1981; Bohart and Greenberg, 1997) and congruence (Grafanaki, 2001; Greenberg and Geller, 2001) have begun to be dismantled and re-defined.

The story of the client-centred research programme, and particularly the research into facilitative conditions, illustrates some fundamental issues about process research. It is relatively easy to describe process phenomena that appear to make a significant contribution to outcome and are acknowledged by clinicians as interesting and worthy of research. It is harder, but possible, to devise instruments for measuring these phenomena. However, it is extremely difficult to construct a theory that will allow the interactions between these phenomena to be understood. Finally, even if such a theory is constructed, it is almost impossible to test it adequately. In the field of process research as a whole, it can be seen that much emphasis has been placed on the observation and description of process variables, with corresponding lack of emphasis on the development of relevant theory.

Helpfulness of therapeutic communication studies

Following on from at least one of the major lines of inquiry opened up by the client-centred research programme, a number of investigators have developed methods of examining the types of communication that therapists use with clients. Behind this research is an assumption that some types of communication, or therapist intention, may lead to good outcomes while other types may in fact hinder clients. The approach that has been taken in these studies has been to develop a list or taxonomy of relevant therapist behaviour, and then, using a modified recall interview, to ask the client to rate the helpfulness of therapists' responses contained within segments of each session. An alternative approach has been to carry out ratings on segments of therapy tapes, without involving the actual therapy participants (Stiles, 1986). In a review of the literature in this area, Elliott et al. (1987) have identified more than 20 different systems for classifying counsellor behaviour or response modes. The response modes that appear in most of these systems are: questioning, advising, giving information, minimal responding, reflecting, interpretation, self-disclosure, reassurance, confrontation and acknowledgement. The validity of these categories is supported through demonstration that therapists using different approaches exhibit different profiles of verbal behaviour (Hill, 1986).

One problem with this approach is that research evidence suggests that the relationship between counsellor response mode and outcome is not high. For example, Hill et al. (1988) explored the effect of counsellor response modes on outcome as assessed through standard measures of change in client experiencing level, and client perceptions of helpfulness, and found that only 1 per cent of the variance in immediate outcome was attributable to the type of response the therapist had made. This result may indicate a limitation of the response mode technique: it assesses only the presence or absence of a mode, and not the skilfulness with which it is delivered. Hill and O'Grady (1985), Hill et al. (1988) and Martin et al. (1989) would argue that it is more appropriate to assess therapist *intentions* rather than their behaviour or response mode. Hill and O'Grady (1985) developed a list of 19 therapist intentions: set limits, get information, give information, support, focus, clarify, convey hope, cathart (*sic*), identify maladaptive cognitions, give feedback on behaviour, encourage self-control, work with feelings, encourage insight, promote change, reinforce change, overcome resistance, challenge, resolve problems in the therapeutic relationship, and deal with therapist needs.

An approach that similarly sets out to explore the intentional, purposive quality of the therapist role is the research by Mahrer and others (Mahrer et al., 1984; Mahrer, Sterner et al., 1986) into *microstrategies*. Mahrer, Sterner et al. (1986) found that therapists from different traditions displayed distinctive, recurring patterns of purposeful activity in relation to clients. Although the 35-category set of microstrategies employed in this research overlaps with the categories generated by Hill, Elliott and others, it has the added feature of exploring sequences of such behaviours. For example, in the Mahrer, Sterner et al. (1986) study, it was shown that, although both Rogers and Ellis engaged in interpretation, for Rogers interpretive responses were preceded by reflection, while for Ellis interpretation followed challenging. Research into counsellor response modes, intentions and strategies has an immediate relevance to anyone involved in counsellor training. Indeed, both Hill (1986) and Stiles (1986) describe their initial interest in this area of research as growing out of their own experiences in training and their later work as trainers. It would be unrealistic to expect high correlations between specific intentions or response modes and outcome, given the complexity of factors involved in the therapy process. Nevertheless, as Hill (1989) has shown, when individual cases are explored in depth, therapist behaviours clearly play a role in outcome with specific clients.

Events, tasks and good moments

The research carried out within the client-centred programme, and the studies of therapist responses and intentions, has been in the form of correlational studies. These pieces of research have examined the relationship between global (whole session or segments sampled from a whole session) measures of a process variable such as empathy or interpretation and associated ratings of helpfulness or satisfaction. A number of researchers have criticised this approach on the grounds that there is more value, on practical as well as theoretical grounds, in studying the microprocesses that occur within specific change *events*. For example, Elliott and Shapiro write that:

> significant therapy events are portions of therapy sessions (generally 4–8 minutes in length) in which clients experience a meaningful degree of help or change. . . . We see significant events as windows into the process of change in psychotherapy . . . instead of taking random samples from therapy sessions, we look where the 'action' is most likley to be . . . significant events represent important general therapeutic factors but in more concentrated form. (1992: 164)

These researchers have developed a style of process research that has been labelled the 'events paradigm'.

Some of the most influential events research has been produced by the research team led by Robert Elliott (1986). The basis for their work has been the application of IPR methods to the *Comprehensive Process Analysis* (CPA) of helpful events. The aim of CPA is to develop an understanding of significant events in a way that takes account of the *context* within which the event takes place (e.g. the therapeutic alliance, the general coping style of the client), the important features of the *event* itself (e.g. counsellor response mode and client reaction), and the *impact* of the event in terms of outcomes such as insight or decreased anxiety. Elliott (1984) has described his approach as a 'discovery-oriented' method, a way of enlisting therapists and clients as 'guides' to the 'uncharted territory' of change events in counselling and psychotherapy. For Elliott (1984), the fundamental research question is: 'What would we find out if we asked clients and therapists to point to significant moments of psychological change in psychotherapy?' His assumption is that if researchers can supply participants in therapy with the means of describing in close detail what goes on before, during and after these change events, then powerful models can be generated that can be applied to make therapy more effective.

In the studies carried out by the Elliott team, a video recording is made of a therapy session. Following the session, the client participates in a modified version of IPR, known as *Brief Structured Recall*, which involves identifying the most helpful event in the sessions, tracking through the tape to find the event, and then engaging in a CPA interview, which consists of answering a number of questions about the meaning and impact of that event as that section of the tape is being re-played. Subsequently, the therapist is played the identified event, and participates in a similar CPA inquiry interview. At some time following the client and therapist interviews, which need to be carried out immediately after the therapy session, a group of observers carry out a parallel CPA exploration of the event. The actual CPA inquiry always begins with an *expansion* of the event. In this phase, the client, therapist or observers 'spell out' their sense of the implicit meanings or what is said 'between the lines'. Having established this expanded version of the event, the research participants answer questions (quantitative and qualitative) concerning context, event structure and impact. Finally, the client and therapists are re-played the identified event later, to enable delayed or undisclosed feelings about the event to be included in the data.

Having amassed this material, which is all carefully transcribed, the research team then collates the data into client, therapist and observer *versions* of the event. The similarities and differences between these versions are identified, and the areas of greatest discrepancy analysed in further detail. The outcome of this process is the construction of a *consensus version* of the event. Elliott and Shapiro describe the data analysis as an 'iterative, cyclical process' (1992: 173) involving considerable dialogue between the members of the research group. Detailed accounts of this methodology are available in Elliott (1984, 1986) and Elliott and Shapiro (1992). The products of this approach can be seen in Elliott (1983a, 1983b) and Elliott and Shapiro (1992).

Greenberg (1984b, 1992) and Rice (1992; Rice and Saperia, 1984) have approached the investigation of change events from the point of view of *task analysis*. Rice and Saperia (1984) suggest that:

> successful psychotherapy can be viewed as involving the resolution of a series of affective tasks. . . . One of the things that distinguishes the experienced therapist from the beginner is the ability to recognize certain kinds of client statements as 'markers' signifying that there is an affective task that needs to be worked on and that the client is ready to work with it. Experienced therapists also have some general, often implicit, guidelines, derived from theory and extensive clinical observation, for working with different kinds of affective tasks. (1984: 29)

A distinctive feature of task analysis studies has been a rigorous focusing on the experience of the *client*: 'the client is the one in whom change takes place; the therapist's job is to facilitate the process of client change' (Rice and Greenberg, 1984b: 23). The assumptions that drive task analysis research are that the identification of task sequences associated with successfully working through different types of 'stuck' or problematic feeling states will be of great practical value as well as being instrumental in the creation of new theory.

The research strategy used in task analysis studies has been to begin with a therapist-defined 'recurring event' that appears to be productive in terms of its potential as a vehicle for client change and development. The implicit cognitive map that the therapist uses to make sense of this type of event is elicited from him or her by the investigator. A particularly important element in this 'map' will be the 'markers', in terms of patterns of client behaviour and expressed feeling, that indicate the beginning of an event. Other elements that are identified at this point are the intentions and operations carried out by the therapist during such an event, the resulting client process, and the indicators of the final resolution of the event. These elements constitute an initial, therapist-defined model of the task. The next stage in task analysis is to verify the existence of this event by asking clients, who have to complete post-session questionnaires.

Having identified a recurring event that appears worthy of further intensive investigation, the researcher now goes on to construct a *performance diagram* of the sequence of client tasks that comprise the event. Greenberg (1992) describes this step as a 'rational analysis' or 'thought experiment', in which the researcher tries out in imagination various task sequences before arriving at one that appears to provide an appropriate framework for understanding the actual task performance of the client. The researcher then finds ways of measuring as many aspects of the performance diagram as possible through standard techniques and scales. This diagram is then applied to the intensive analysis of a series of actual events, thereby expanding and making corrections to that model. This intensive analysis is based around an IPR recall interview focusing on the event, supplemented by any appropriate test and rating data. As the model becomes more explicit, hypotheses can be derived from it and tested against the data. The final stage of the task analysis process is to gather data relating successful task completion to outcome measures.

The task analysis approach to process research can be likened to carrying out a multi-stage research programme, encompassing rational analysis, model-building, verification and evaluation, on a single type of recurring therapeutic event. This research strategy has resulted in the publication of a manual of process-experiential therapy (Greenberg et al., 1993) which includes guidelines for working with clients in relation to six key therapeutic tasks:

1 Systematic evocative unfolding at a marker of a problematic reaction point.
2 Experiential focusing for an unclear felt sense.
3 Two-chair dialogue at a self-evaluative split.
4 Two-chair enactment for self-interruptive split.
5 Empty-chair work to resolve emotional 'unfinished business'.
6 Empathic affirmation at a marker of intense vulnerability.

The work of Greenberg, Rice and Elliott (1993) demonstrates how process research can contribute to the construction of an effective, research-informed approach to therapy. Their research programme also illustrates one of the ways in which the original Rogerian 'conditions' of empathy, acceptance and congruence has influenced a later generation of researchers: for Greenberg and his colleagues, the 'core conditions' are viewed as essential elements within longer task sequences.

A third approach to the investigation of significant events in therapy has been pioneered by Mahrer (Mahrer and Nadler, 1986; Mahrer, Nadler et al., 1986; Mahrer et al., 1987). The aim of this research programme has been to identify the therapist operations that contribute to the creation of 'good moments' in therapy. Mahrer and Nadler propose that 'it is axiomatic that there are identifiable moments when clients manifest good therapeutic process, good movement, improvement, progress or change' (1986: 10). Using this broad definition of the 'good moment' in psychotherapy sessions, Mahrer and Nadler (1986) carried out an extensive review of the theoretical and research literature, and arrived at a set of 12 categories of observable change points (providing meaningful information about self, exploring feelings, emergence of previously warded-off material, expression of insight and understanding, communicating expressively, manifesting a good working relationship with the therapist, expressing strong feelings toward the therapist, expressing strong feelings in extra-therapy contexts, manifesting a qualitatively altered personality state, undergoing new extra-therapy behaviours, reporting changes in target behaviour, expressing a general state of well-being). They then constructed a coding manual and instructions so that judges could reliably define these moments in audio tapes and transcripts of therapy sessions. A distinctive feature of the research strategy adopted by Mahrer and his colleagues has been the explicit use of a group of expert therapists as observers of process (Mahrer, Nadler et al., 1986), on the basis that only clinically sophisticated judges would be able to understand the significance of good moments.

The procedure followed by this research group can be illustrated by the study by Mahrer, Nadler, Gervaize and Markow (1986). The research team began by selecting an audio tape (contributed by a practitioner from an on-going case) of an hour of therapy that appeared to represent a 'good' session. Each of the 11 members of the research group took four categories, and initially coded *every* client statement that qualified as meeting the definition of one of their categories.

Following this, all 11 judges reviewed these provisional codings, and examples that were agreed by 70 per cent (eight members) of the team were accepted and retained. Then, the judges reviewed the data yet again, and classified some of the statements as examples of 'very good' moments. This data provided a picture of the type of 'good moment' prevalent in this therapy dyad. In order to generate some hypotheses concerning what the therapist and client did to bring about these good moments, each of the judges independently generated a set of hypotheses that might account for each cluster of moments. The research team discussed these hypotheses and arrived at a consensus account.

The work of Elliott, Greenberg, Rice and Mahrer represent different approaches to investigating the incidence, form and sequencing of helpful events in therapy sessions. These researchers may have contrasting ideas of how best to identify and make sense of an 'event' but all are engaged in trying to understand, with as much depth and detail as possible, the micro-processes that are the primary vehicles of therapeutic change.

Client experience studies

An important strand of process research has been the interest in the way that clients experience therapy. It is clear that clients differ, to some degree, from both their therapists and from external observers in terms of how they perceive the processes and outcomes of counselling (Kaschak, 1978). It seems reasonable to assume that the more accurately and sensitively a counsellor understands how his or her client is feeling or perceiving the world, the more effectively he or she will be able to engage in meaningful therapeutic work with that client. The main aim of client experience studies has been to create a picture of what the therapy is like from the point of view of the client. It is therefore important to distinguish between client experience studies and other types of research (e.g. many outcome studies) in which clients are asked to answer questionnaires on the basis of their experience, but where the goal of the study is to assimilate that experience into a measure of, for example, empathy or satisfaction, rather than describe the experience as such.

The earliest studies of the experiences of clients in therapy were carried out using questionnaire methods. For example, Strupp, Wallach and Wogan (1964) used a long questionnaire, which included closed as well as open-ended questions, to gather retrospective accounts of their experience from psychotherapy clients. In more recent times, two questionnaires have been widely employed in client experience research. The *Therapy Session Report* (Orlinsky and Howard, 1975, 1986) is a questionnaire designed to be completed by either counsellor or client, and is intended to take no longer than 15 minutes to complete. Normally, this questionnaire would be administered immediately after the end of a session. The instrument takes the form of a debriefing interview, beginning with the question 'how do you feel about the session?', and moving to items concerned with content, feelings expressed, relationship with the counsellor, progress, motivation and benefit. Therapy Session Reports have been employed in a large number of studies, encompassing over 1500 clients in all. The other paper and pencil instrument that has been devised to study the experience of the client is the *Session Evaluation Questionnaire* (SEQ) (Stiles, 1980; Stiles and Snow, 1984). This tool consists of a rating scale, in which clients are asked to respond on a 7-point scale to 24 bi-polar adjectives descriptive of the session and how they feel at the end of the session. (An example of an item would be: 'Right now I feel: bad . . . good'.) The SEQ produces an assessment of client experience in a session in terms of four dimensions: depth, smoothness, positivity and arousal.

Several researchers have used in-depth semi-structured interviews to explore the experiences of clients, for example Brannen and Collard (1982), Howe (1989), Maluccio (1979), Mayer and Timms (1970) and Timms and Blampied (1985). Although this strategy allows the researcher to collect rich, detailed and authentic accounts of experience, there are two main problems associated with it. First, it can be difficult to maintain the boundary between research and therapy in this kind of interview situation. The approach taken by Brannen and Collard (1982) to address this issue is examined in Chapter 6. Secondly, an immense amount of complex interview material is inevitably produced when clients are asked to describe their experience as a whole, rather than being forced by a questionnaire to focus on discrete elements of that experience. It is, therefore, a substantial and laborious task to analyse this sort of data and present it in an effective manner. The book by Maluccio (1979) is generally considered to provide a particularly impressive example of a thematic analysis of client experience material derived from interviews.

The programme of research carried out by Rennie (1990) and his associates exemplifies a rigorous and systematic use of IPR interviews to explore the client experience of individual sessions of therapy. In this research, the client reviews the whole of the tape of a therapy hour, giving as comprehensive an account as possible of what he or she was thinking and feeling during that session. The transcript of this recall interview is then subjected to a *grounded theory* analysis (Rennie et al., 1988). This technique, described in more detail in Chapter 6, involves breaking up the text into separate 'meaning units' which are categorised in terms of meanings that are grounded as closely as possible in the experiences of the informant. The researcher then reviews this set of categories in order to conceptualise more abstract, higher-level categories and eventually to construct a model or theory of the phenomenon that is firmly 'grounded' in actual experience. The findings of this research programme have emerged as a series of papers on fundamental themes in the experience of being a client: reflexivity (Rennie, 1992) and deference (Rennie, 1994a). Angus and Rennie (1988, 1989) have applied this approach to investigating the ways in which clients experience the use of metaphor in therapy. A comprehensive review and discussion of these and other grounded theory studies of the client's experience of counselling and psychotherapy can be found in Rennie (2002).

The investigation of the experience of the client is a complex matter. The research strategies described in this section have generated different types of data and have examined different units of experience (single sessions vs. whole treatment). The literature arising from this research, and associated methodo-logical issues, has been reviewed by Elliott and James (1989) and McLeod (1990).

Studies of process from a psychodynamic perspective

Some of the most powerful and clinically relevant ideas about therapy process have been developed within the psychoanalytic or psychodynamic tradition. The therapeutic processes originally identified by Freud and his colleagues included transference, counter-transference, interpretation, free association and resis-tance. However, the study of these processes presents unique methodological problems for researchers. From the point of view of psychodynamic theory it is impossible to understand and observe phenomena associated with, say, trans-ference, without having had many years of clinical training. Some psycho-dynamic therapists would even argue that only the actual therapist who is actually there with the client can really know whether transference is occurring. Psycho-dynamic commentators would also suggest that the operation of defence mech-anisms makes the client an unreliable source of information about process. The point is that, to carry out credible research into psychodynamic concepts and processes, it is necessary to find ways of gathering data that are consistent with the underlying psychodynamic theory. Interviewing clients, using minimally trained raters or employing IPR techniques are simply not appropriate in this field of counselling research.

Researchers carrying out studies of psychodynamic processes have generally used expert clinicians to make sophisticated judgements about therapy tran-scripts. For example, in their research on transference reactions, Luborsky, Crits-Christoph and Mellon (1986) developed an instrument known as the *Core Conflictual Relationship Theme Method* (CCRT). In this technique, transcripts of therapy sessions are obtained, and narrative episodes describing relationships with significant others are extracted by trained judges. These relationship episode segments are then passed on to another group of judges, who have the task of identifying the three components of a CCRT within each narrative. These are: (a) the main wishes, needs or impulses that the client exhibits toward the other person in the story; (b) the responses of the other person; and (c) the responses of the self. An example of such a relationship narrative told to a therapist by a client might be: (a) I want to be free of an unwanted visitor, but (b) he wouldn't understand, he would be insulted, and (c) I feel hassled, resentful, compelled to suffer his presence (from Luborsky et al., 1986: 42). What the research team are attempting to do is to a reduce these everyday life narratives told by clients to their core meanings. So, if the example given was taken out of the specific context of the unwanted visitor, it might be formulated as: (a) I wish to be free of obligations; but (b) other people do not respond; so (c) I comply. Using this technique, Luborsky et al. (1986) have been able to show strong similarities in the core relationship themes that clients produce about significant others, about their relationship with the therapist, and in response to an invitation to share a memory of an early interaction with a parent figure. In other words, it would appear that people unconsciously create patterns and themes in their relationships, based on early childhood experience, that they then project on to all new people they meet, including their therapist. This is strong evidence in support of the Freudian concept of transference.

Sampson and Weiss (1986), Curtis et al. (1988) and their colleagues at the Mount Zion Medical Center in San Francisco have been working on another aspect of process from a psychodynamic perspective. Their view is that in childhood people can develop frightening and constricting 'pathogenic beliefs' that interfere with their ability to enjoy life. In adulthood, the individual has a strong desire to change these beliefs. If such a person enters therapy, the safe relationship with the therapist offers an opportunity to test out these beliefs and learn how to change them:

> the patient enters therapy with certain unconscious and conscious goals and with the primary purpose of solving problems and achieving these goals. The obstacles to achieving these goals are the patient's pathogenic beliefs which suggest that the pursuit of these goals *will endanger oneself and/or someone else*. One of the patient's primary efforts in therapy is to disconfirm pathogenic beliefs by testing them in the relationship with the therapist. The therapist's function, according to this theory, is to help the patient understand the nature and ramifications of his or her unconscious pathogenic beliefs by interpretation and by allowing the patient to test them in the therapeutic relationship. (Curtis et al., 1988: 257, emphasis added)

The key to this process is the unconscious 'plan' that the client brings to the therapeutic situation. The research carried out by the Mount Zion group has looked at how to arrive at a definition or formulation of this 'plan', and then examine the extent that successful psychodynamic therapists deal effectively with the demands and challenges that the plan imposes on them. Each case plan formulation is arrived at by a team of three to five experienced therapists who work with transcripts of an intake interview and the first two therapy sessions. They seek to achieve agreement on four elements of the client's plan: goals, obstructions, tests and insights. An example of a plan formulation is given in Box 9.4. In subsequent sessions, which are also transcribed, the researchers rate the extent to which interpretations made by the therapist are compatible with the plan formulation, and look at the relationship between the ratio of plan-compatible/incompatible interpretations and good or poor outcomes (Silberschatz et al., 1986, 1989).

Another influential line of psychodynamically oriented process research has explored the ways in which Bowlby's theory of attachment can be used to understand the dynamics of the relationship between client and therapist. Several research studies (Eames and Roth, 2000; Hardy et al., 1999; Kivlighan et al., 1998; Rubino et al., 2000; Tyrrell et al., 1999) have provided convincing evidence for the role of both client and therapist attachment style in shaping the

Box 9.4   The formulation of a client's unconscious 'plan'

Goals

To work toward ending her relationship with partner

To feel less responsible for her mother and exert more control over this relationship

To allow herself sexual gratification in a relationship with a man

To develop a meaningful and mutually satisfying relationship with a man

Obstructions

She believes that she is capable of seriously harming others if she does not carefully tend to them

She believes that she is being disloyal to and thus hurtful of her mother if she expresses sexual pleasure in a satisfying relationship

She believes that she would be disloyal and abandoning of her mother if she developed new relationships

She believes that she is responsible for the difficulties of those less fortunate than herself

Insights

To become aware of the degree to which she has complied with her mother's expectation that she assume a caretaking, self-renunciating role

To become aware that she inhibits herself from developing and enjoying relationships with others because she feels guilty allowing herself more than her mother has

To become aware that her professional isolation represents an identification with her mother

To become aware that she has felt angry and resentful toward her father for not shielding her from her mother's influence

Tests

She will disagree with the therapist to see if he is critical of her or is hurt or upset by her defiance

She will act as if the pursuit of a goal is a selfish or otherwise undesirable action to test whether the therapist wants her to hold herself back

She will boast about an accomplishment to see if the therapist is bothered by her self-assurance and success

She will exaggerate her occupational strivings (e.g appear 'ruthless') to see if the therapist approves of her legitimate professional aspirations

Source: Curtis et al. (1988)

process of therapy. Much of this research has made use of the *Adult Attachment Interview* (AAI), a standardised method for assessing patterns of attachment (Hesse, 1999; Main, 1991). The AAI consists of a 15-item clinical interview, which normally takes around two hours to complete. The questions asked in the interview are intended to 'surprise the unconscious': the person will find himself or herself saying things, or contradicting themselves, in ways that are beyond their conscious control. For participants, the interview is similar to a therapy session, in that they are invited to talk openly, and at length, about childhood experiences and memories which may be quite painful. Analysis of the interview does not depend on the content of what the person says, but is largely derived from the style or manner in which the person tells the story of his or her early life. Detailed protocols have been prepared for reliably analysing AAI material. As with CCR and plan analysis, the AAI represents a research tool which is designed to access unconscious processes.

The research into CCRT, plan formulation and attachment style represent some of the most significant recent attempts to study psychodynamic processes. Studies into these and other aspects of psychodynamic theory are reviewed in Henry et al. (1994) and Miller et al. (1993).

Other process studies

The studies already covered in this chapter have been selected to give a sense of the diversity of research into process factors in counselling and psychotherapy. For reasons of space and clarity, many other interesting and significant avenues of process research have been omitted. Among the many other process issues that have been investigated are studies of the therapeutic alliance (Horvath and Greenberg, 1986), therapist errors (Sachs, 1983), 'things not said' in sessions (Wright et al., 1985), the use of language (Russell, 1989), the impact of non-verbal behaviour (Wiener et al., 1989), the experience of cultural difference (Thompson and Jenal, 1994; Tuckwell, 2001), the operation of transition objects (Arthern and Sussman, 1999), and the significance of psychoperistalsis (Sussman, 2001).

Process–outcome research

A central theme in process research, that can be traced back to the earliest studies carried out by the client-centred research group, has been the aim of identifying process variables that make a difference to outcome. Indeed, the ultimate purpose of process research is to make a contribution toward the increased effectiveness of counselling and psychotherapy. In a recent review of the process–outcome literature, Orlinsky, Grawe and Parks (1994) collated the results of more than 2000 studies. The main conclusions of this review are summarised in Box 9.5. The authors suggest that:

the quality of the patient's participation in therapy stands out as the most important determinant of outcome. The therapeutic bond, especially as perceived by the patient, is importantly involved in mediating the process–outcome link. The therapist's contribution toward helping the patient achieve a favourable outcome is made mainly through empathic, affirmative, collaborative and self-congruent engagement with the patient, and the skilful application of potent interventions such as experiential confrontation, interpretation and paradoxical intention. These consistent process–outcome relations, based on literally hundreds of empirical findings, can be considered *facts* established by 40-plus years of research. (Orlinsky et al., 1994: 361)

It is intriguing to contrast this review with the aims of the original process studies carried out by Carl Rogers and his colleagues. These 'facts' bear a striking resemblance to the facilitative conditions theory, but at the same time point clearly to three aspects of process missing from that equation: the type of

---

Box 9.5 Relationship between process variables and therapeutic outcome

Process variables consistently associated with outcome

Goal consensus
Client role preparation
Client suitability
Therapist skill
Focus on life problems and
   core personal relationships
Experiential confrontation
Interpretation
Paradoxical intention
Client cooperation
Positive client affect
Therapeutic alliance
Client openness
Client expressiveness
Therapist affirmation of client
Reciprocal affirmation
Positive in-session impact
Longer treatment duration

Process variables not consistently associated with outcome

Scheduling (weekly vs other)
Time-limited vs unlimited
Fees
Focusing on here-and-now
Therapist support
Therapist self-disclosure
Reflection/clarification
Client negative affect
Client self-exploration

Source: Orlinsky et al. (1994)

---

contract between therapist and client, the active participation of the client, and the active use of interventions by the therapist.

Conclusions: issues in the study of therapy process

This discussion of counselling and psychotherapy process research has examined a number of research strategies. There are two underlying issues that run through the body of work considered in this chapter. These issues concern the methodological choices relating to *unit of analysis* and *observer perspective*.

Studies of therapy process have employed quite different units of analysis: the whole of treatment, single sessions, significant (5–10 minutes) segments of sessions (events), and micro-segments (e.g. therapist or client statements) (Elliott, 1991). It is clear that there is no one 'right' unit of analysis. Researchers adopting different unit lengths have all produced valuable results. However, the selection of unit of analysis has important implications for the type of data that can be gathered. For example, it is futile to expect to find sequences of client task performance in retrospective interviews after treatment has ended. On the other hand, Mintz and Luborsky (1971) and Bachrach et al. (1981) have argued that it can be very hard to understand the meaning of short segments from a therapy tape in the absence of what has been happening in the rest of the session. Increasing the focus on micro-sequences inevitably results in loss of information about context (Friedlander et al., 1988).

A second fundamental issue in process research concerns the choice of observer perspective. Spence (1982) has made the case that the actual participants in the therapy dyad, the counsellor and client, possess a 'privileged competence', an intimate knowledge of the process that no one else can ever fully appreciate. Spence (1986) goes further in suggesting that any attempt on the part of the therapist or client to explain his or her experience of the process to a third party will inevitably result in a 'smoothing' of that experience. The earliest process studies, carried out by Rogers and Dymond (1954) came to the conclusion that therapists, clients and outside observers had quite different perspectives on process and outcome. Although these perspectives overlap and are in agreement on many occasions, there are also significant areas of disagreement. Process researchers have attempted to resolve these issues of perspective in a number of ways. The use of IPR methods, for example, can be seen as a determined effort to retrieve as much as possible of the privileged data that Spence (1982) would suggest was inevitably smoothed away immediately the therapy hour finishes. Some researchers, such as Elliott (1986), have taken up the challenge of integrating client, counsellor and observer perspectives in a single version. Others, such as Rennie (1990), have constructed a rationale for concentrating solely on the experience of the client.

The field of counselling and psychotherapy process research represents an area of investigation which has seen a substantial amount of innovation. It is no easy matter to disentangle the complex interactions which take place between clients and counsellors. At this point, there exists a large number of research studies which provide important insights into the process of therapy. What is perhaps required now is further attention to how best to integrate these studies into a general theoretical framework, and how to make use of them in training and practice.

Further reading

A primary resource for information on methods used in process research is:

Greenberg, L.S. and Pinsof, W.M. (eds) (1986) *The Psychotherapeutic Process: A Research Handbook*. New York: Guilford Press.

An invaluable exploration of the practicalities of process research can be found in:

Hill, C.E. (1991) 'Almost everything you ever wanted to know about how to do process research on counseling and psychotherapy but didn't know who to ask', in C.E. Watkins and L.J. Schneider (eds), *Research in Counseling*. Hillsdale, NJ: Lawrence Erlbaum.

An interesting collection of examples of process research is:

Toukmanian, S.G. and Rennie, D.L. (eds) (1992) *Psychotherapy Process Research: Paradigmatic and Narrative Approaches*. London: Sage.

Excellent reviews of different areas of process research are:

Agnew-Davies, R. (1999) 'Learning from research into the counselling relationship', in C. Feltham (ed.), *Understanding the Counselling Relationship*. London: Sage.
Rennie, D.L. (2002) 'Experiencing psychotherapy: grounded theory studies', in D.J. Cain and J. Seeman (eds), *Humanistic Psychotherapies: Handbook of Research and Practice*. Washington, DC: American Psychological Association.
Sachse, R. and Elliott, R. (2002) 'Process–outcome research on humanistic therapy variables', in D.J. Cain and J. Seeman (eds), *Humanistic Psychotherapies: Handbook of Research and Practice*. Washington, DC: American Psychological Association.

10   An Ethical Framework for Research Practice

It is necessary to give careful consideration to ethical issues at all stages of the research process: planning, implementation and dissemination of results. Research in counselling is bound by a general set of ethical guidelines applicable to all types of investigation of human subjects, but also generates unique dilemmas and problems distinctive to the nature of the counselling process. The aims of this chapter are to review the main ethical issues that arise in counselling research, and to explore the adequacy of different approaches to resolving them.

The literature on research ethics is derived from the much larger field of moral philosophy. It is not possible to do more here than identify some of the major themes of philosophical discourse on morals and values. In much of the discussion of ethical dimensions of applied disciplines such as medicine, education and counselling, writers have tended to focus on the implications of a small set of basic ethical principles (Beauchamp and Childress, 1979; Kitchener, 1984). These are: *beneficence* (acting to enhance client well-being), *nonmaleficence* (avoiding doing harm to clients), *autonomy* (respecting the right of the person to take responsibility for himself or herself), and *fidelity* (treating everyone in a fair and just manner). Taken separately, each of these moral principles can be seen to embody values with which most people would agree. However, in practice many everyday situations can occur in which choices must be made between two or more ethical principles. For example, in research into the effectiveness or outcome of counselling, it may be decided that the benefits of an approach can only be demonstrated by randomly allocating half of the potential clients to a control group who must wait six months before receiving treatment. The general aim of the study is beneficent (to gain knowledge about what will help people), but random allocation of clients to treatment and control groups violates their autonomy, and the people in the waiting list group may suffer as a result of being denied help (a violation of the injunction to avoid maleficence). The researcher carrying out such a study must find ways of carefully balancing such conflicting ethical rules. This example illustrates three fundamental points about the relationship between ethics and research design in counselling.

1   *It is impossible to design ethically neutral research.* All research necessitates making value decisions which may be in conflict with the beliefs and values of some other people. For instance, in the context of outcome research, some people might argue that it is *never* justifiable to deny assistance to people in need.
2   *Ethical decisions always have some bearing on the quality of results obtained in a study.* For example, in an outcome study the way that people are allocated to a

waiting list may induce expectations and fantasies that influence their scores on assessment questionnaires and interviews.

3 *The ethical issues that arise through the conduct of the research are the same as those that occur in the context of counselling practice.* As Wing points out: 'every (ethical) problem that arises in research – whether it involves the balance of good against harm, a decision to undertake a laboratory procedure or to give or withhold a treatment – also arises in everyday clinical work' (1991: 432).

There is a wide range of ethical issues associated with counselling research. Some of the more frequent dilemmas are:

- studying experimental or innovative treatments that may cause harm to clients;
- excluding people from therapy unless they take part in a research study;
- compromising the confidentiality of the client–counsellor relationship by making recordings of sessions that may subsequently be heard by several members of a research team;
- research interviews or questionnaires triggering off painful material for clients;
- counsellors in research studies feeling self-conscious or anxious and as a result not functioning at their best for clients;
- using archival information about clients (e.g. case records) without their consent;
- unconsciously manipulating therapy process or content to produce results that conform to a research hypothesis;
- the possibility of coercion arising from asking a current client to take part in a research study conducted by their therapist.

A common theme across this set of issues concerns the abuse of power on the part of researchers. Ideally, client and counsellor engage in an alliance which is primarily in the interests of the client. The participation of researchers in this relationship introduces a new source of power and control, and a new and different set of interests. Strategies for dealing with these issues fall into three main categories: appropriate research design, ensuring informed consent and maintaining confidentiality.

Appropriate research design

In planning a piece of research, it is important to consider the ethical and moral implications of all aspects of the study. Most research carried out in institutional settings such as hospitals, schools, social services departments and prisons is scrutinised by a local Ethics Committee which has the task of safeguarding the well-being of its clients. Wing (1991) has estimated that around 5 per cent of the proposals received by these committees include research procedures that could be seriously harmful to clients. Research carried out in voluntary agencies is usually vetted by a management committee, and any research carried out by a practitioner on his or her own clients should always be thought through in consultation with a supervisor. The value of these external monitors lies in the fact that the person carrying out a research study may be highly committed and passionate about the project and therefore less open to seeing potential problems. The crucial question to ask in assessing the ethical acceptability of a study is, 'What will this experience be like from the point of view of the research participant or informant?' It is necessary for the researcher to imagine himself or herself in the role of the participant, and creatively to think through how he or she would react to the demands of the study, and how they might think or feel if they knew about what was being done with the data. Appropriate research design then takes account of this information.

Different types of ethical dilemma arise from different types of research. In much qualitative research, for example, the researcher is interested in gathering thorough and detailed accounts of the experiences the person might have had. The process of gaining access to this type of material involves developing a close relationship with the informant, and encouraging him or her to write or talk openly and honestly about themselves. What emerges for the informant may be painful and distressing, and it is the responsibility of the researcher to do everything possible to ensure the well-being of the person. For example, in an interview study of the experiences of people who were receiving marital counselling, Brannen and Collard (1982) were concerned about the potentially distressing nature of the topic for their informants. Brannen and Collard took great care to plan and conduct the interviews in an appropriate manner (see Chapter 6 for more detail on how they achieved this). The careful planning undertaken by these researchers to maintain emotional safety for research participants was not only ethical, but also contributed to the quality of data they gathered. Informants who feel safe are more likely to share more of themselves. Researchers who know that they have made rigorous plans for dealing with interviewee distress are more able to concentrate on the interview. Stanton and New (1988) have reviewed a range of strategies that can be used to ensure the safety of research participants who may be depressed or suicidal.

In counselling and psychotherapy process research, the well-being of the client can be threatened by intrusion of the research into the actual therapy session itself. In the review of process studies in Chapter 9, it could be seen that many researchers attempted to overcome this problem by asking clients and counsellors to complete research questionnaires and scales only after the end of a session. However, with research techniques such as Interpersonal Process Recall (IPR), the client is invited to re-experience the session through watching or listening to a tape. One researcher using this method (Rennie, 1994d) was concerned about the impact this might have on research participants, and carried out a follow-up study of people who had taken part in his studies. He found that in only one from 16 cases was there even the slightest indication that the recall interview had been harmful for the participant. Many of the other people who had taken part in the research reported that they had found it useful and enlightening.

Research into the effectiveness or outcomes of counselling presents a number of planning dilemmas arising from ethical issues. Such research almost always requires careful selection of clients. Even when no-treatment, placebo or waiting-list control groups are not used, it may be necessary to screen applicants for therapy to find those who fulfil criteria stipulated by the research hypothesis. For example, Strupp and Hadley (1979), in a study of the relative effectiveness of professional and non-professional therapists with socially anxious and depressed male college students, selected students who conformed to a particular MMPI personality profile. Unable to find enough clients with the appropriate profile, they advertised for clients, thus potentially exposing themselves to the hazards of counselling people who had not initially defined themselves as requiring it. Applicants not used in research may be referred to another agency or even refused therapy. Because of practical and resource constraints in doing outcome research, the majority of outcome studies restrict the length of treatment offered to clients. Some clients may feel under pressure to participate in research, in the belief, mistaken or otherwise, that they would not otherwise receive therapy.

The most pressing ethical issue in outcome research arises from the imposition on the counselling situation of the degree of control necessary to enable the use of quasi-experimental research designs. For example, in many outcome studies the effectiveness of counselling is compared to the amount of change that occurs in an equivalent or matched sample of people who do not receive counselling. It is difficult to argue that it is fair or beneficent to allocate clients to receiving treatment which is non-existent or believed to be less effective or even bogus (as in a placebo condition). In a study by Anderson and Strupp (1996), clients participating in a large-scale randomised trial of therapy were interviewed about their experience of being in a research study. Some of them reported that they had been aware that they had been allocated to a 'control' condition, and were angry at receiving what they perceived to be 'second best'.

It is reasonable to conclude that any research design will generate ethical dilemmas. The implication is not that research should be abandoned, but that every effort should be made to examine the effect that a study will have on all of the people who participate in it (Firth et al., 1986). Although the research literature contains many examples of solutions to ethical problems, it would certainly be valuable if more researchers were to write about their experience of these issues, thus allowing a wider awareness of good practice.

Informed consent

One of the most frequently used strategies for dealing with ethical dilemmas is to rely on the fact that participants have been fully informed about research procedures, and the risks entailed, and therefore take personal responsibility for any negative consequences of participation. In many research studies participants are required to read and sign a consent form, which would usually include the following:

- name, address and contact number of the person carrying out the study (if appropriate, the name of the research supervisor may be included);
- a description of the aims of the study;

- information about procedures, and what will be demanded of the participant;
- description of any potential risks to the participant;
- account of measures that will be taken to ensure confidentiality;
- information about what will be done with the data;
- statement about the right to withdraw from the study at any time;
- the name, address and contact number of the person or professional association to whom the research participant could make a complaint if necessary;
- information about the arrangements for de-briefing at the end of the study.

Participants would routinely be given their own copy of this contract to keep, after it had been signed by both parties.

However, although informed consent is a powerful tool that researchers can employ in coping with a wide array of ethical problems, the concept of informed consent is itself by no means straightforward (Lindsey, 1984). It is generally accepted that genuine informed consent depends on the fulfilment of three criteria: competence, provision of adequate information and voluntariness. The competence of the person giving consent refers to the capacity he or she has to make an informed and rational decision on the matter in question. In much psychological and medical research, for example, it is taken for granted that children are not able to consent to take part in research. The age at which a child becomes able to understand what is entailed by agreeing to be a research subject is open to debate. Also, many people would question the morality of a parent or other adult taking such a decision without consulting the child at all.

In counselling research, there are many situations in which the competence of the client may be temporarily impaired. People seeking counselling may be in a state of crisis, or highly distressed or anxious, and may find it hard to assimilate the information contained in a consent form. Large numbers of people have reading problems, which they may be reluctant to admit, and might therefore be considered not competent to enter into a research contract unless it was read out to them.

The second basic dimension of informed consent concerns the provision of adequate information, particularly information about possible risks or harm. For example, for anyone taking part in an outcome study, being fully informed about what might happen would require reading a book. The researcher could only really know that the participant was fully informed by giving him or her a test of knowledge on the type of therapy they were to receive. This is clearly ludicrous, and in practice the information that would be given to research participants would be limited to around two or three paragraphs, with an opportunity to ask questions.

Finally, proper informed consent requires that the consent is voluntary. There are clearly different degrees of voluntariness in different cases. For the participants in a 'cooperative inquiry' group (see Chapter 6), there is a high degree of commitment to the research, which is an activity they have perhaps been actively involved in initiating. By contrast, people in some distress arriving at a counselling agency for the first time may be so numb, anxious or needy that they would agree to almost anything. Dilemmas around autonomy and voluntariness can also be experiencd by counsellors and psychotherapists invited to participate in research studies. For example, if the other therapists in an agency have all agreed to take part in a piece of research, it could be hard for an individual to resist the pressure to conform, even if he or she was for some reason uncomfortable about the implications of the study.

It can be seen, therefore, that many situations can arise in counselling research where informed consent procedures may conceal some elements of coercion and persuasion. Research may often be carried out under time pressure, with very tangible rewards in the nature of employment prospects, a Doctorate or publications resting on the ability to find enough research subjects. The force of these pressures may lead to behaviour that conflicts with the needs of research participants, and so it is essential not only to set up informed consent procedures at the beginning of a study, but to monitor that they are being appropriately implemented throughout the duration of the research.

Ensuring confidentiality

There are a number of strategies available for making sure that the confidentiality of information given by research participants is not at risk. In principle, these strategies are similar to the steps a counsellor would take to protect the confidentiality of client information. In research, however, the intention to publish and disseminate findings adds a new dimension to the task of respecting the interests of the research informant. A basic necessity in all research is to disconnect information about client identity (e.g. name, address, occupation) from any other research data (e.g. interview tapes or notes, test results). In this way, even if an unauthorised person found access to the research data, it would be very difficult for him or her to know from whom the data had been collected. It is important that research data is identified only by a neutral code number, with the key to the code, along with biographical information about research informants, stored in a secure place. Other techniques for safeguarding confidentiality include:

- remembering to lock rooms that contain research data;
- checking that research assistants or technicians understand the importance of confidentiality;
- destroying notes and tapes after the completion of a study, or offering to return tapes to informants;
- omitting information from a report if it will compromise the identity of an informant.

There are legal restrictions over computerised records that contain personal information. These data protection regulations have been drafted in recognition of the dangers of unauthorised access to computer files. Any researcher working in a college or university, or for a human service agency of any size, will find that there will be someone in his or her organisation who is responsible for implementing a data protection policy, and who can give advice over the confidentiality issues associated with research data files. It is usual for researchers in these settings to be required to sign a declaration binding them to the agreed institutional policy. Researchers working independently are required to register with the appropriate government department.

In qualitative or case study research, which may rely on detailed descriptive material provided by research participants, it may be necessary to use quotes from informants in published articles or reports, or to write at length about the life of a particular person. In these circumstances it can be all too easy inadvertently to reveal the identity of the informant. It is valuable, whenever possible, to ask the informant to read a pre-publication draft of the report so that he or she can make up his or her own mind about whether sufficient anonymity has been achieved, and if necessary make suggestions for further amendments. It is worth noting that not all informants are concerned about whether or not they are identifiable in research reports – some are proud to share their 'story' with others. However, it is not appropriate to assume that the informant will adopt this attitude, and every effort should be made to allow clients appropriate control over this aspect of a study.

Like other ethical issues, there are situations where the need to preserve confidentiality conflicts with other moral and ethical rules. For example, research into well-known or famous cases presents specific problems. It would have made little sense for Lewis et al. (1992), in their study of the National Marriage Guidance Council (NMGC), to pretend that they were looking at any other agency, or to make up an invented name for the organisation to preserve anonymity. As in counselling, serious dilemmas arise in maintaining confidentiality if information about abusive or criminal behaviour is revealed. For instance, a researcher interviewing clients who uncovered instances of counsellor incompetence or exploitation would be bound by the ethical rule of nonmaleficence to take some kind of action.

The significance of these strategies for maintaining confidentiality lies not only in the basic moral imperative to respect and prevent harm to research participants, but in the role that perceived ethicality plays in counselling research. If the research participant can see that the researcher is doing everything possible to protect confidentiality, then he or she will be more willing to be open, honest and forthcoming in the information that he or she discloses. It is therefore good practice to explain to informants at the start of a study, for example through informed consent procedures, the methods that will be employed to ensure confidentiality.

Ethical issues in practitioner research

Research carried out by practitioners on their own clients raises a distinctive set of ethical dilemmas. These issues have received little attention in the literature, probably because most discussion of research ethics has focused on large-scale studies published in mainstream academic journals. However, there are many smaller-scale studies that are published 'locally' in the form of dissertations, projects or articles in professional magazines, that are based on data gathered by counsellors on their own clients. The main ethical problem in this type of research arises from potential conflict between the therapeutic and researcher roles taken by the practitioner. As a therapist, the practitioner has a duty to act in the service of the well-being of the client. As a researcher, the practitioner has a duty to collect data and make a contribution to knowledge and understanding. Much of the time, these roles may complement and enhance each other. On some occasions, however, they may be in conflict.

The kind of conflict that may occur can be exemplified through hypothetical cases drawn from different theoretical orientations. A psychodynamic counsellor may have a special interest in developing a theory of the unconscious motives and fantasies involved in suicidal intention. If a client begins to explore this kind of material in a session, the research interest of the counsellor may lead him or her subtly to encourage further exploration of the topic, or to seek to return to the theme in future sessions, even if to do so was not clinically necessary. Similarly, a cognitive-behavioural counsellor may have an interest in gathering case material on the use of a particular intervention technique, or a humanistic counsellor may be looking for opportunities to generate case data on the use of an experiential exercise. In all these examples, there is the possibility for a divergence to open up between therapeutic and research goals.

The ethical dilemma described here is equivalent to the problem of the existence of 'dual relationships' in therapy (Pope, 1991). When the therapist is also a friend, business partner, colleague or family member to the client, the relationship may all too easily tip in the direction of fulfilling the needs of the therapist rather than those of the client. In the researcher–therapist dual relationship, there is the added complication that it may be difficult to employ the standard research safeguard of informed consent. It would not be sensible, for example, for a counsellor interested in suicidal fantasies to tell *every* new client that he or she was a potential participant in a research study on this topic. Another complication arises from the awareness of the client that he or she is being studied by the counsellor, and the effect that this awareness might have on the therapeutic relationship. The client may believe at some level that he or she is special to the counsellor or has been chosen as the favourite client of the counsellor. The client may strive to produce the 'right' (or 'wrong') material for the counsellor, or may even find a way of ending in time for the counsellor to write up a dissertation. It could be argued that the emergence of such issues in a counselling relationship offers valuable material that the counsellor and client can work through. It could equally be argued that these issues merely interfere with a therapeutic task that is sufficiently challenging without the addition of a new layer of intricacy.

The message is not that practitioner research should be abandoned. In Chapter 11 it is argued that more practitioner studies are necessary if research is to become alive and relevant for counsellors. The implication is that great care should be taken by therapists who introduce a research component into their practice. It is important to talk through the impact of the research on the practice with not only the research supervisor but also with the counselling supervisor, and to endeavour to find ways of building in to practitioner studies as much informed consent as possible, even if this consent is obtained after the therapy is completed.

Membership of a research community

The moral and ethical dimension of research stretches beyond the actual immediate participants in a study, to include the research community as a whole. It is clearly unethical to distort or amend research data for personal gain, or to plagiarise from studies carried out by other people. It is immoral, and probably illegal, to misuse research funds. There is a moral duty to acknowledge in any publication the sources of all ideas and techniques and of any substantial assistance given by colleagues or friends. The nature of the power and authority relationships between Doctoral supervisors and their students, and between senior researchers and their technical staff or research assistants, can often lead to concerns that the work of junior researchers is exploited by their being denied first authorship of papers they have written, or even denied any authorship at all. Brannen observes that in research teams there is often:

> a sharply segregated division of labour . . . this tends to occur where research is organized in terms of the autonomous tenured academic (usually male) who is serviced by the contract research assistant (usually female) . . . the hired hand researcher is not usually around for the development or writing-up of the report. (1992b: 21)

The division of labour, status and power in research can therefore be seen to mirror the structure of inequality in the workplace in general, and as such is difficult to shift. Heppner et al. (1999) present a detailed discussion of the rules laid down by the American Psychological Association regarding publication credit.

The social responsibility of the researcher

There is social responsibility in research that transcends the academic discipline or profession to which the researcher belongs. The ultimate moral justification for research is that it makes a contribution to a greater public good, by easing suffering or promoting truth. This wider horizon introduces further challenges and demands on researchers. It is important to carry out research in a way that enhances public perceptions of and attitudes toward research. Within social psychology, for example, the spate of deception experiments carried out by Milgram, Zimbardo and others has certainly contributed to a public view of psychologists as duplicitous and not to be trusted. At a more local level, many people have had personal experiences of taking part in research studies that were either unpleasant, boring or irritating, and who would never want to have anything to do with research again. There is, therefore, an ethical responsibility on researchers not to spoil it for others, and to invest as much care and attention into negotiating the ending of a research project as they would into negotiating access at the start of a study.

In counselling and psychotherapy research, there are major questions about who the research is for. Many feminist and qualitative researchers argue that one of the aims of research should be to empower those who participate in it. However, most therapy research has taken the moral view that the primary responsibility to research participants is to prevent harm to them (nonmaleficence) rather than necessarily enhancing their well-being. Moreover, one might suppose that, if research was conducted for the greater social good, there would be a proliferation of studies into counselling issues associated with oppressed groups such as black, gay, lesbian, elderly and disabled people. Yet these are just the areas of research in which there is an absence of studies.

Conclusions

In the end, there are four key questions that the counselling researcher must address, in order to be able to anticipate and deal with ethical issues that might arise.

1   What harm might possibly occur to any of the participants in the study, or to those excluded from the research?
2   What procedures can be established to minimise harm and also to respond appropriately to distress or needs stimulated by participation in the study?
3   How can the confidentiality of information gathered during the research be safeguarded and respected?
4   What are the broader moral implications of the study, in terms of the ways that results will be used?

It is always helpful to submit any plans for a piece of research to external scrutiny, whether through the formal procedures of an established Ethics Committee, or by informal consultation with colleagues.

Further reading

The context for any discussion of research ethics in counselling and psychotherapy is the ethical and moral basis of therapy practice. An authoritative review of ethical issues in practice is provided by:

Bond, T. (2000) *Standards and Issues for Counselling in Action*, 2nd edn. London: Sage.
Corey, G., Corey, M.S. and Callanan, P. (2003) *Issues and Ethics in the Helping Professions*, 6th edn. Belmont, CA: Wadsworth.

Detailed discussion of ethical issues in counselling and psychotherapy research is available in:

Heppner, P.P., Kivlighan Jr, D.M. and Wampold, B.E. (1999) *Research Design in Counseling*, 2nd edn. Belmont, CA: Brooks/Cole.

Meara, N.M. and Schmidt, L.D. (1991) 'The ethics of researching the counseling/therapy process', in C.E. Watkins and L.J. Schneider (eds), *Research in Counseling*. Hillsdale, NJ: Lawrence Erlbaum.

The application of qualitative methods, which may involve the development of close relationships with research informants, and the handling of sensitive personal information, can raise difficult moral issues. Valuable exploration of these issues can be found in:

Grafanaki, S. (1996) 'How research can change the researcher: the need for sensitivity, flexibility and ethical boundaries in conducting qualitative research in counselling/psychotherapy', *British Journal of Guidance and Counselling*, 24: 329–38.

Josselson, R. (ed.) (1996) *Ethics and Process in the Narrative Study of Lives*. Thousand Oaks, CA: Sage.

Most professional associations, such as the British Association for Counselling and Psychotherapy (BACP), British Psychological Society (BPS) and American Psychological Association (APA) publish useful guidelines relating to ethical issues in research.

11 Critical Issues in Counselling Research

Many different topics have been studied within counselling and psychotherapy research, and many diverse methods and techniques have been employed to investigate these topics. However, although this sprawling mass of literature may sometimes appear chaotic, structureless and directionless, it returns again and again to the same core questions about how we gain knowledge. There are perhaps three broad issues that recur throughout the literature. The first concerns *epistemology*: the kind of knowledge that is considered valid, useful or acceptable. Do we need data based on precise measurements taken in order to test experimental hypotheses? Or do we need knowledge based on people's stories and experiences? If we need both types of knowledge, how can we integrate them? The second big issue is around relevance for *practice*: what is the role of the researcher, and what is the role of research, in an applied discipline such as counselling? The third major issue involves the place of *theory* in therapy research. There are many theories of therapy, but there are also strong pressures to integrate these ideas, to agree on a generic approach. It is not clear how therapists actually apply theory in practice. In a post-modern world, are 'grand' theories still relevant? These questions have their parallels in the world of research. Can meaningful research rely only on description and observation? Do theoretical models blind researchers to the complexity of what really happens in counselling and psychotherapy? The purpose of this chapter is to reflect on these issues, and, where possible, to suggest potential ways forward.

Methodological pluralism

The Handbook of Psychotherapy and Behavior Change, edited by Alan Bergin and Sol Garfield (1994), is essential reading for anyone doing counselling research. The list of contributors to Bergin and Garfield (1994) comprises 40 of the leading scholars in this field. As far as can be discovered from the information about their qualifications and institutional affiliations supplied in the book, all of these people are psychologists or psychiatrists. The view, presented in Chapter 1, that counselling and psychotherapy is an *interdisciplinary* activity, drawing on the arts, philosophy and theology as well as psychology and medicine, is not supported by this array of scholars. Yet, at the same time, in the final chapter of the *Handbook*, the editors write encouragingly about the concept of *methodological pluralism*:

the growing endorsement of narrative, descriptive, and qualitative approaches represents a rather significant shift in attitude that is likely to become more and more manifest in the conduct and reporting of inquiries. We find ourselves endorsing a kind of pluralism that does not throw out the virtues of the traditional approaches to research, but complements these with a variety of more flexible techniques for getting at the complexity of the phenomena we deal with. (1994: 828)

But what does this mean? Is pluralism possible if one approach is used merely to 'complement' another? To what extent is methodological pluralism viable within a single-discipline area of inquiry? What is at stake here?

Earlier chapters of this book have attempted to set out the methodological alternatives open to anyone undertaking counselling research. On the one hand is the quantitative, largely positivistic, traditional approach to research that is dominant within psychology and medicine. This approach is looking for causal relationships between variables. On the other hand is qualitative research, largely hermeneutic or interpretive in style, heavily influenced by classical phenomenology. This is a 'human science' approach that has its home in literary criticism, history, some branches of sociology and social anthropology, and women's studies. Its aim is to describe and interpret meanings. Methodological pluralism, therefore, must represent some combination or blending of these approaches.

In counselling research, the idea of methodological pluralism appears to have been introduced by Howard (1983), in a paper commenting on the case study by Hill et al. (1983a). At the heart of his argument, Howard proposes that:

a complete understanding of humans needs to consider a range of ontological perspectives, a variety of views of the nature of humans, and consequently it must employ a multiplicity of empirical research methods. I believe that a thorough understanding of humans will be facilitated by 'methodological pluralism'. (1983: 20)

Later in his paper, Howard arrives at a 'slippery question': '*How* are we to combine the findings from different perspectives into a coherent picture of human action?' (1983: 21, emphasis added). His answer is that there are no rules:

researchers are left to draw their own rough conclusions regarding whether or not the pictures emerging from different perspectives, on the same research question, yield complementary or contradictory findings. (p. 21)

Howard identifies here the tension inherent in a pluralist research. It holds the promise of a more 'complete' understanding, yet at the same time the very different philosophical assumptions implicit in each approach raise the risk of contradiction or confusion.

The issues associated with methodologically pluralist research can be exemplified by considering some effective examples of this strategy in action. Pluralist approaches have been applied largely in process research, and the studies by Hill (1989) and Elliott and Shapiro (1992) represent serious attempts to combine quantitative and qualitative data in the same study.

Hill (1989) carried out eight intensive case studies of brief therapy offered to women who were anxious and depressed. In each case, a battery of quantitative process and outcome measures was used, including the Experiencing Scale, Working Alliance Inventory, MMPI, SCL-90 and many others. However, a great deal of qualitative material was also collected from both clients and therapists, through interviews and open-ended questionnaires. Two points can be made about the methodological pluralism of this study. Firstly, the author gives no rationale for combining methods, except to argue that an appreciation of thera-peutic process requires a 'holistic' approach encompassing client, therapist and observer perspectives. There is no discussion of the basis on which decisions were made about how quantitative and qualitative data were to be compared or combined in individual case reports. It would appear that the research team met and talked about these matters in their formulation of a case report, but no explicit procedures are described. Secondly, a reading of the actual cases suggests that the analysis of each case is essentially based on the patterns emerging in the quantitative data, and the qualitative material is used to expand on, contextualise or give examples in support of the numbers.

The Hill (1989) book provides a fascinating account of the therapeutic pro-cesses that were instrumental in facilitating change in these cases. It may not achieve Howard's (1983) ambition of 'complete' understanding, but it certainly offers a more complete understanding of these phenomena than many other studies have done. Nevertheless, the use of qualitative methods in this study is very limited when set alongside the principles of qualitative methodology or criteria for evaluating qualitative research discussed in Chapter 6. It would be hard to describe the use of qualitative data in the Hill study as naturalistic, inductive or reflexive.

The Elliott and Shapiro (1992) study offers an example of Comprehensive Process Analysis of a key change event in one therapy session with a male client. The procedures employed in this study are described in some detail in Chapter 9, and involve using qualitative accounts as well as quantitative ratings from the therapist, client, and external observers. The experience of the therapist and client during the event is unfolded through an IPR interview. In the case discussed in the Elliott and Shapiro (1992) paper, quantitative data is virtually invisible. The analysis of the event is carried out through a grounded theory and phenom-enological analysis of the qualitative data, leading to a set of interpretive con-clusions. Again, as in the Hill (1989) study, the rules for combining quantitative and qualitative information are not made explicit, but in this instance the former is effectively subsumed into an essentially qualitative approach.

These two examples of pluralist research studies illustrate the difficulties in combining methods and philosophies. One view is that methods can be combined in a pragmatic manner, depending on the needs of the particular project (e.g. Miles and Huberman, 1994; Patton, 1990). Another view is that the logic, assumptions and values of positivist and constructionist methods of inquiry are so great that meaningful combination is impossible (e.g. Smith and Heshusius, 1986). The most constructive attempt to resolve this dilemma within the field of counselling and psychotherapy research has been the work of Rennie and

Toukmanian (1992). These writers have employed the terminology of *paradigmatic* to describe quantitative, positivist research and *narrative* to refer to qualitative, constructivist studies, following Bruner (1986) (see also Chapter 1). They suggest that, to be useful, methodological pluralism 'requires its practitioners not to violate the strengths of each approach to explanation' (Rennie and Toukmanian, 1992: 247). Each of the approaches possesses its own distinctive 'logic of justification', which includes values, rules of evidence and criteria for soundness. Rennie and Toukmanian (1992) suggest two ways of combining narrative and paradigmatic modes of knowing. First, research teams might include among their members individuals expert in each mode, so that integration or combination becomes a matter for discussion and negotiation in the research group, rather than being carried out individually. This strategy is similar to the 'diagnostic council' developed by Murray (1938) (see Chapter 7). Another strategy for achieving pluralism would be to give more attention to the development of theory, and to be open to the possibility that some aspects of the theory could only be satisfactorily tested using paradigmatic methods, while other facets would call for narrative exploration. Thus, data from both narrative and paradigmatic methods could be employed at different phases of a programme of research. Rennie and Toukmanian (1992) echo the sentiments of Bergin and Garfield (1994) in noting that the assimilation of qualitative methods into therapy research is only beginning. The field has been dominated by the positivist-paradigmatic monolith for so long that there is a long way to go before we will know what a truly pluralist methodology would look like, or even whether it is possible.

In their struggle to achieve methodological pluralism, counselling researchers may find some consolation and assistance in the experiences of sociological researchers, who have been grappling with this problem for some time (see reviews by Brannen, 1992a; and Bryman, 1984, 1988b). There have been many examples of combining qualitative and quantitative approaches in sociological studies, and Bryman (1992) has identified four distinct pluralist strategies that have been employed by researchers (Box 11.1). From this list it can be seen that the majority of pluralist research is mainly based in one approach, and uses data from the other approach to 'fill in the gaps'. So, most pluralist research in sociology resembles the Hill (1989) and Elliott and Shapiro (1992) studies in so far as one kind of data is used to complement the other. Studies that go further than this, and explicitly attempt to integrate data from both approaches, are viewed by Bryman (1992) as relying on triangulation. However, as he points out, it is naive to expect that different methods will produce convergent data:

quantitative and qualitative research have different preoccupations and highly contrasting strengths and weaknesses. The very fact that the quantitative approach emphasises causality, variables, and a heavily pre-structured approach to research, while qualitative research is concerned with the elucidation of subjects' perspectives, process, and contextual detail, means that the ensuing data may not be as comparable as is sometimes proposed by the advocates of triangulation. In other words,

> *it is highly questionable whether quantitative and qualitative research are tapping the same things even when they are examining apparently similar issues.* (1992: 64, emphasis added)

Moreover, the concept of triangulation is itself defined and understood in different ways by researchers from different traditions. Within quantitative psychology it is taken to mean the correlation between different measures of the same construct (Campbell and Fiske, 1959). In qualitative sociology it refers to a more holistic comparison of multiple perspectives (Denzin, 1978), based on the informed judgement of the researcher rather than on the application of statistical techniques.

The sociological literature exhibits an acceptance of combined or pluralist approaches. For example, it is acknowledged that access to some research sites may be facilitated by the use of pluralist research design, since the combination of both numbers and stories may engage the interests and agendas of different stakeholders or decision-makers. Also, the impression is that in sociology the professional gatekeepers, such as editors of important journals, are open to methodological pluralism in a way that the guardians of psychological rigour are

---

Box 11.1 Strategies for combining qualitative and quantitative research

The logic of triangulation. The findings from one type of study are checked against findings derived from the other type.

Qualitative research facilitates quantitative research. Qualitative research may provide background information, act as a source of hypotheses, or contribute to the construction of tests of survey questionnaires. Qualitative data may be used in the interpretation of relationships between variables found in a quantitative study.

Quantitative research facilitates qualitative research. For example, subjects for a qualitative study are selected on the basis of results from a quantitative survey or experiment.

Different approaches focus on different perspectives. Quantitative methods are used to examine 'structural' or 'macro' features of the topic, while qualitative research is used to explore the 'micro' or process level of experience. Quantitative research is usually driven by the concerns and interests of the researcher, while qualitative research emphasises the perspective of the subject or research participant. These contrasting emphases may be brought together in a single study.

Source: Bryman (1992)

---

not. There is also a sense that there is no single best way of doing research. Some research questions call for quantitative methods, some for qualitative. Hammersley (1992) has called for a 'deconstruction' of the qualitative–quantitative divide, arguing that the use of this dichotomy, resonant of an opposition between 'good' and 'bad', operates to obscure a complex set of issues and arguments involved in making methodological choices.

One of the fundamental issues that has permeated this discussion of methodo-logical pluralism has been the distinction between data-gathering techniques and epistemological assumptions. At a pragmatic level, quantitative data involves numbers and qualitative data involves words. However, at this level there is a fair amount of permeability between the two types of data. Words or text can be quantified through content analysis or rating. Numbers can be converted to a narrative. By contrast, at the level of philosophy and epistemology, the concepts and 'logics of justification' of both the natural and human sciences can be experienced as irreducible to the other. It is in this context that the observations of Brannen, a sociological researcher who has worked extensively from a plural-ist perspective, have special significance:

> a multi-method strategy . . . can serve as an exercise in clarification: in particular it can help to clarify the formulation of the research problem and the most appropriate ways in which problems or aspects of problems may be theorised and studied. With a single method the researcher is not forced to consider the issues in quite the same way. With multiple methods the researcher has to confront the tensions between different theoretical perspectives while at the same time considering the relationship between the data sets produced by the different methods . . . the process of con-sidering these issues has given me a new set of spectacles through which I have seen, with a sudden clarity and freshness, those 'deep down things' – the main issues of the research endeavour, namely the relationship between theory, method and data. (1992b: 32–3)

A good example of a psychotherapy research study in which researchers using multiple methods were forced to 'confront the tensions between different per-spectives' was the well-known but seldom read study of the effectiveness of client-centred therapy with hospitalised 'schizophrenic' patients carried out by Carl Rogers and his colleagues (Rogers et al., 1967). The challenge of integrating findings generated by different methods led this group of researchers to a set of conclusions that significantly shifted their assumptions about the 'core conditions' (see McLeod, 2002b).

The underlying issue here concerns the attitude of the researcher toward knowledge. Useful research knowledge is not manufactured through the mech-anical application of method. Rather, method is used to assist the basic human impulse to know and learn. Perhaps the real significance of the 'shift in attitude' detected by Bergin and Garfield (1994) lies in the rejection of what has been called 'methodolatry' in psychotherapy research and the beginnings of a move-ment in the direction of a greater readiness to 'confront the tensions' inherent in the research process.

The relevance of research for practice

The field of counselling and psychotherapy research has been highly productive, generating many hundreds of published studies on a wide array of topics. Yet, given that therapy is an applied discipline, what impact has all this research had on the activities and attitudes of practitioners? To answer this question, Morrow-Bradley and Elliott (1986) conducted a large-scale survey of therapists in the USA. These researchers sent a questionnaire on research utilisation to a 10 per cent sample of Division 29 (Psychotherapy) of the American Psychological Association (APA), receiving 279 (73 per cent) replies. A large majority of the sample (88 per cent) had PhD degrees, so had carried out substantial research projects during their training. One section of the survey questionnaire asked these therapists about their consumption and production of research. More than 75 per cent had read at least one research article in the preceding month. Around 40 per cent had published at least one research article. So, this group of therapists had a reasonable amount of research experience and awareness. However, when asked to indicate the source of information about psychotherapy that they found most useful, they reported that on-going experience with clients, supervision, the experience of being a client and practical books were significantly more valuable than reading research articles or doing research. This group of therapists had many criticisms of therapy research, with more than half of them agreeing with all the statements listed in Box 11.2. It is of special interest that the first item in this list, which was endorsed by 75 per cent of the sample, flies in the face of contemporary developments in the use of treatment manuals in research (see Chapter 8).

These findings were largely confirmed in an interview study of 30 child therapists carried out by Cohen, Sargent and Sechrest (1986). In this research, informants were asked not only about their consumption of research but also about their *conceptual* use of research. The actual question they were asked was: 'In what way, if at all, has the general research literature on clinical child practice affected your own clinical child work? The issue here is not a particular study, but a more diffuse influence of research in this area.' The aim of this question was to explore the possibility that research might have a 'gradual, indirect and diffuse effect . . . on awareness of problems, conceptualization of issues, consideration of options, and the like' (1986: 199). However, 37 per cent denied that research had even influenced their work in this incidental manner.

It is generally accepted that a serious research–practice 'gap' exists, despite the attempts by a number of leading researchers to communicate with practitioners (Elliott, 1983b; Strupp, 1989). The fact that this is happening in the USA is particularly significant, since clinical psychology training there has been dominated by a 'scientist-practitioner' model (Barlow et al., 1984), which emphasises the ability of therapists to be able to apply scientific methods in the evaluation of their work. Also, the proportion of counsellors and psychotherapists with Doctoral degrees is much higher in the USA than in European countries. If such a gap exists in the USA, therefore, it is likely to be even more pronounced in Britain and Europe.

Box 11.2   Criticisms of therapy research made by practitioners

1   Research that treats all therapists or all responses by therapists as interchangeable obscures essential differences.

2   Practical, relevant and scientifically sound measures of psychological change due to therapy often are unavailable.

3   Studies designed to try to incorporate the complexities of psychotherapy rarely are done.

4   In an effort to make studying psychotherapy more manageable, researchers often ignore important variables.

5   Often researchers focus on specific techniques while ignoring the importance of the relationship between therapist and client.

6   Traditional research methodologies, those derived from the physical sciences, are not for the most part appropriate for the investigation of psychotherapy.

7   Psychotherapy researchers often use criteria that are either too global or too specific.

8   Clinically meaningful questions about psychotherapy often are not studied or selected.

9   The frequent use of only aggregate statistics (means, F values, etc.) does not include important results, for example how many are changed.

10   Often, the therapists, clients and settings studied in research are vastly different from those found in clinical practice.

Source: Morrow-Bradley and Elliott (1986)

There are a number of solutions to the problem of the gulf between therapy research and practice. The proponents of intensive process studies (e.g. Elliott, 1983b) argue that they produce research outputs that practitioners will find useful. Increasingly, researchers carrying out large-scale extensive studies are publishing case studies to exemplify themes of interest to clinicians. The series of case studies written by Strupp (1980a, 1980b, 1980c, 1980d) is a good example of this approach. It may be that improvements in research training and in the availability of research articles (as on-line databases become affordable) will eventually make a difference.

There are, however, other ways of looking at the relationship between research and practice in counselling and psychotherapy. These involve reframing the relationship between researchers and practitioners. The debate over the research–practice gap is presented as though researchers create knowledge which clinicians can then feed into their work with clients. However, as pointed out in Chapter 1, counselling and psychotherapy are not like medicine. In medicine, researchers in universities and institutes develop new drugs or physical treatments that are then evaluated through clinical trials. In medicine, the new ideas come from the scientists. In therapy, the new ideas come from practitioners. All of the key figures in the development of psychotherapy (Freud, Jung,

Rogers, Perls, Moreno, Wolpe, Ellis, Beck) made their important discoveries in the clinic, even if some of them then went on to test the validity of these discoveries through systematic research.

Another facet of this issue is that, for therapy researchers, there is no *personal* research–practice gap. Virtually all contemporary therapy researchers are also active practitioners, even if their clinical work represents a relatively small portion of their work time. Reading between the lines of many research papers, it is apparent that the experience of actually doing research (formulating hypotheses, defining concepts, listening to tapes, making sense of patterns in the data) is enormously enriching in terms of giving opportunities for reflecting on practice and talking to other people about practice. Many students on counselling courses also have this experience: the research they actually do themselves informs their practice, even if their review of the literature means little to them.

What is being suggested here is that everyone might benefit from a fresh look at the researcher–practitioner relationship. Rather than merely disseminating results to practitioners, it would be useful for researchers to find out what practitioners want to know. What are the research questions that front-line counsellors and psychotherapists want answered? It is very difficult for hard-working therapists in agencies or in private practice to combine the roles of scientist and practitioner as recommended by Barlow et al. (1984). Perhaps they need researchers who will act as consultants, supplying them with the technical expertise and awareness of the literature that will enable them to carry out research that is relevant to them. In other applied fields, such as management and education, consultants feed back evaluation data with the aim of helping organisations to be more effective. Could this happen in the world of counselling and psychotherapy? Why are outcome studies one-off scientific exercises? What would happen if further research such as that by Lambert et al. (2001) was carried out, in which outcome data was fed back to counsellors so that they could learn from their successes and failures? Finally, might it not be time for researchers to find creative ways of utilising their practitioner side? Presumably most researchers set up studies at least partially because the research makes some connection with dilemmas and questions arising from their own practice. Their research findings would make more sense to readers if they were truly *reflexive*, if they communicated not only the 'hard' data but the personal meaning.

There is also an important area awaiting further development in relation to the actual therapeutic value, for clients, of participating in research. On the whole, counsellors and psychotherapists tend to fear that the introduction of research interviews and questionnaires will interfere with the therapeutic process, and be resented by clients. The evidence from clients is quite the contrary. Marshall et al. (2001) explored the subjective experience of clients who had participated in an outcome study of the effectiveness of psychodynamic psychotherapy. They found that clients did not find the research intrusive or disruptive, and adjusted quickly to the taping of sessions. The majority of clients reported that 'question-naires and interviews were slightly to moderately helpful in . . . facilitating therapy' (2001: 319). The therapists in this study, by contrast, consistently believed that the research had been harmful to their clients. Berger and Mallison

(2000) discuss several aspects of the therapeutic potential of research participation for clients. Some therapists have explicitly incorporated research exercises into their work with clients. For example, Madigan (1999) describes a case
in which a client was invited to collect information about how other people
perceived him (through letters) and then to use methods of qualitative analysis to
identify themes and categories within this data set.

The politics of research

The relevance of research for practice is not merely a matter of practitioners
reading research papers and adjusting their approach in line with up-to-date
research findings. Research also plays a role in the politics of service delivery.
The kind of therapy that is made available through state-funded agencies is
determined, to an increasing extent, by the conclusions that can be drawn from
systematic reviews of the research literature. In some countries, not only access
to therapy, but also access to training, is controlled by consideration of which
approaches are 'empirically validated'. The committees which commission and
publish lists of 'validated' treatments have, up to now, been dominated by a
medical model approach which gives most credibility to evidence derived from
randomised controlled trials, and less value to naturalistic, qualitative and cases
study evidence relating to outcome. The positive aspect of evidence-based treatment policy is that it forces the profession to address questions of accountability,
quality and value for money. The negative dimension of the policy arises from the
significant limitations of the existing research base. There are many widely
practised approaches to therapies which have not been evaluated. There are
issues, rehearsed in Chapter 8, about whether the randomised trials represent
the most appropriate strategy for evaluating the effectiveness of therapy. It can
be questioned whether symptom change (the most commonly utilised outcome
measure) truly captures the kind of learning that at least some people can acquire
from the experience of therapy. And there is evidence that the therapist, and the
therapeutic relationship, not the approach to therapy, are the factors that contribute most to outcome. It would seem important for counselling and psychotherapy practitioners to engage constructively with the political process around
evidence-based care, and to define the kind of evidence that they consider most
relevant to the task of making decisions about the social resourcing of therapy
services.

The contribution of counselling to research

The discourse on research methods in counselling and psychotherapy places
great emphasis on what research can offer to counselling. It is also worth thinking
about what counselling can offer to research. Any research that involves meaningful contact with people, for example carrying out interviews, running a focus

or human inquiry group, explaining what will happen in an experiment, calls on many of the skills and competencies that are central to counsellor training. Good researchers should be able to establish rapport, listen, respond non-defensively to questions, and engage in appropriate challenging. Counselling training offers a good grounding in these areas, upon which specific research skills can be built. However, going further than this, counselling theories also provide valuable tools for making sense of the relationship between researcher and informant. Person-centred theory suggests that people will collaborate more effectively when a relationship characterised by the 'core conditions' of empathy, acceptance and congruence is established (Mearns and McLeod, 1984). Psychodynamic theory is a source of insight into the distortions that can occur in the research relationship, through the operation of transference, counter-transference and resistance. Finally, the practice in counselling of using supervision not only for task-management purposes but to explore the underlying dynamics of the therapist–client relationship is clearly applicable to many research situations where the topic has a personal meaning for the researcher.

The role of theory

One of the issues that has been a matter of some debate in counselling and psychotherapy research has occurred around the role of theory. There have been three approaches to the use of theory in counselling research. First, some researchers have been explicitly guided by a theoretical model, and their work has been designed to test or extend that model. An example of this approach would be the programme of research carried out by Rogers and his colleagues (Rogers and Dymond, 1954; Rogers et al., 1967) into the processes and outcomes of client-centred counselling and psychotherapy. Another example would be the psychoanalytically oriented research of Luborsky and his colleagues (1986) into transference and interpretation. In these theory-informed studies, researchers not only explored hypotheses derived from theory, but developed techniques and instruments that would allow them to measure theoretical constructs such as the self-concept (Rogers) or core conflictual relationship themes (Luborsky). In contrast, other researchers have intentionally designed their studies in order to generate knowledge that is not tied to any specific theory. A good example of this approach can be found in the work of Clara Hill, who describes her research programme as 'trans-theoretical', by which she means that it draws upon a generally integrative approach that respects the relevance of all the major theoretical orientations. The research carried out by Hill and her group has been characterised by the use of common-sense, everyday language terms such as 'therapist intentions' or 'things not said'.

A third perspective on the role of theory is to conduct research according to the 'grounded theory' methodology advocated by Glaser and Strauss (1967) and Strauss and Corbin (1998). This approach involves gathering descriptive accounts of personal experience, and then coding the material in a way that allows the meanings within it to emerge into a model or theory that is firmly and precisely 'grounded' in the original data. Rennie (1992) has used this approach to generate a model of the experience of clients and therapists in the therapy hour. However, this type of systematic qualitative theory-building has not been widely employed so far in counselling and psychotherapy research.

It would appear that therapy research has become less informed or driven by theory in recent years. Omer and Dar (1992) surveyed the proportion of research articles published in the *Journal of Consulting and Clinical Psychology* that included a theoretical rationale. They found that in 1968, 69 per cent of research articles were contextualised within some theoretical frame of reference, while in 1988 this proportion had fallen to 31 per cent. There are a number of factors that may have contributed to this decline in the use of theory. Over this period, integrationist approaches to counselling and psychotherapy were gaining in importance. The pressure of cut-backs in health and welfare funding occurring throughout industrial societies during the 1980s could have focused the attention of researchers on practical rather than theoretical issues. It could be argued that dwindling interest in 'grand' theories was a symptom of the emergence of 'postmodern' ways of thinking (Kvale, 1992).

The role and significance of theory in counselling research can be viewed in a number of different ways. A philosopher of science such as Popper (1959, 1962, 1972) would argue that it is impossible to make observations without engaging in some assumptions about what is being observed, or what it might mean. The notion that one can merely 'observe' things would, for Popper, be meaningless. The attention of the observer must be focused on *what* to observe, and this very act of focusing attention introduces a selectivity that is guided by a cognitive understanding or model of the world. So, for Popper and other philosophers of science, all scientific observation is driven by theory, but sometimes this theory is made explicit and sometimes it remains implicit. The argument here would be that research that does not place itself within a theoretical context, or calls itself trans-theoretical, is indeed employing theoretical assumptions but is doing so in an implicit or hidden manner. Another position is represented by the idea that any well-established theory offers a detailed and structured interpretive map of the territory it sets out to explain. A theory allows productive links to be made between different observations, and enables connections be made of the type 'if I observe A, then it is likely that B will happen too'. This facet of theory-use can be seen by reflecting on the nature of psychoanalytic theory, which is probably the most comprehensive theoretical model in use in the domain of counselling and psychotherapy. Psychoanalytic theory comprises a network or paradigm of linked concepts that enable meaningful connections to be made between observations such as what the client says about his mother, the non-verbal behaviour of the client in the therapy session, and the content of a dream he recounts. Without the theory, the therapist would be able to make a list of these observations, but would not be able to fit them together into a coherent whole. Similarly, the researcher who eschews theory may be in danger of ending up with patchwork fragments of observations that are impossible to combine together into a meaningful overall picture.

It is not easy to disentangle these contrasting attitudes toward and uses of theory. One of the leading figures in social psychology, Kurt Lewin, asserted that 'there is nothing as practical as a good theory'. Some of the leading figures in therapy research might reply: 'there is nothing as practical as a valid rating scale'. This discussion has attempted to set out the theoretical choices facing researchers. As in the world of therapy practice, the choice of theory is influenced by many factors, including the availability of a network of like-minded people who share the same theoretical language. It is probably true to say that it is *safer* to carry out a-theoretical or trans-theoretical research. There is always a risk that a theory will be wrong.

Counselling in non-counselling settings

One of the gaps in this book, because it remains a gap in the research literature as a whole, concerns the exploration and evaluation of the use of counselling in non-counselling settings. The vast majority of published studies of counselling refer to what goes on when a person who explicitly enters the role of client meets with another person who is solely in the role of 'counsellor'. There is very little research into counselling carried out by nurses, social workers, teachers or clergy. From a user-oriented understanding of counselling (McLeod, 2003), counselling is something that takes place when a person asks another person to listen, and help them to explore a problem in living, under conditions of confidentiality. From this perspective, moments of counselling can be understood to take place in many non-counselling settings. While it is clear that large numbers of members of health and other human service occupations receive training in counselling skills, little is known about the processes that take place when these skills are applied in practice, or the outcomes of applying them. The neglect of research into counselling in non-counselling settings can perhaps be attributed to the pressure on counselling to establish itself as an autonomous profession, separate from nursing, social work and other professions. However, from the point of view of people who seek help, the quality of what they receive from non-specialist counsellors is crucial.

The search for perfect knowledge

The issues and debates over the proper role of theory in counselling and psychotherapy research are influenced by the myth of the search for perfect knowledge. One of the most widely quoted phrases in the therapy literature is the statement by Paul (1967) that the aim of research should be to identify '*what* treatment, by *whom*, is most effective for *this* individual with *that* specific condition, and under *which* set of circumstances' (Paul, 1967: 111, emphasis in original). On the face of it, these aims appear to be reasonable and laudable, and the vast factory of therapy research has tooled itself up to achieve them.

However, what would happen if these goals were ever attained? If a form of psychological intervention ever existed that could meet these criteria, it would represent a technology for shaping human behaviour that would inevitably be used to further political objectives. No authoritarian state could resist this temptation. But is such an outcome even imaginable? What would the world be like if there was a highly effective treatment that could be specified for every 'problem in living'? Would everyone be happy all the time?

Within medicine, it makes some sense to imagine that science might eradicate malaria, or find a cure for cancer or AIDS. But can anxiety and depression ever be eradicated? What would it be like to live in a world where there was a cure for guilt?

The psychologist David Bakan (1969) suggests that one of the main impediments to the development of true psychological understanding is what he calls the 'mystery–mastery complex':

> the complex of which I speak consists in the simultaneous pursuit of two objectives: to keep the nature of human personality from being understood, to preserve it under a cloak of mystery; and to master, or predict and control, the behavior of human beings. (1969: 37)

Bakan argues that the origins of this complex lie in the growth of urbanisation and industrialisation in the nineteenth and twentieth centuries, and the spread of the Protestant ethic. These developments brought individuals into interaction with strangers. Secrecy, privacy and individualism became valued and protected. People found new ways of controlling others, as relationships became more formal and contractual. The Protestant ethic and capitalism provided the driving force to master the world through industry and by means of scientific discovery and invention.

The mystery–mastery complex is alive in therapy research, in debates over the role of theory and in much else. Theorising about people makes human personality more mysterious, since as soon as this process of theoretical reflection even begins it becomes apparent that there are many alternative ways of understanding or seeing that can be applied to any event. Yet theorising makes that mystery bearable, in showing that there are at least some maps that can be employed to guide the exploration of what can never be fully known. Empirical research that conforms to the aims outlined by Paul (1967), or at least to the literal meaning of his statement, is attempting to gain mastery without understanding.

Bakan (1969) relates a story of a successful young research psychologist who came to see him and complained about becoming a 'hollow man'. He was doing well professionally, but felt empty inside. Any therapist reading that story would have lots of ideas about what this story might mean, and how this young man could be helped. An effective outcome for that young man would be to find a set of meanings that transcended both mystery and mastery, that integrated both sides of the schism, that allowed him to become more whole.

My own view is that the most important role that research can play is to contribute to the reconstruction of therapy. The activities that we know as 'counselling' and 'psychotherapy' are relatively recent inventions. 'Psychotherapy' has been in existence for less than 120 years, but has only been widely available (in Western industrial societies) for the last 50 years or so. In any culture, there are always socially recognised ways in which people can be helped by others to resolve their personal and emotional difficulties. In our society, at this time, the most popular way of doing this is through psychology and therapy. But even in the last 50 years, the type of therapy that is acceptable to people has changed in response to cultural shifts. For example, feminist and multicultural orientations in therapy, brief therapy, and email counselling were all unheard of in the 1950s but are centrally important today. Counselling and psychotherapy must be continually reconstructed or reinvented (McLeod, 2001c) in the face of social change, and as old therapeutic ideas lose their power to make a difference.

This, I believe, is why a balance between mystery and mastery is essential. As a practitioner, it is always necessary to develop expertise and mastery, to carry out the tasks of therapy as well as one can. But there is always a sense of mystery too – no matter how well researched and 'evidence-based' an approach to therapy may be, it is only a temporary 'clearing', not a final answer.

Conclusions

In a book such as this it is not possible to do much more than briefly convey a felt sense of where the coming together of mystery and mastery might lead. There are perhaps six emerging strands that can be identified in counselling and psychotherapy research.

1 **Greater awareness of the relationship between research and practice** Research and practice are interlinked in counselling and psychotherapy. Much previous research has broken this link, and acted as though research was conducted in an abstract, 'pure' environment. There is, perhaps, a growing awareness that research needs to be grounded in the messy world of everyday practice, and that 'practice-based evidence' is as important as evidence-based practice.

2 **Permission to be reflexive** Most therapy is based on the presupposition that both client and counsellor are able to reflect on their personal experience. In the past, research has been conducted in a way that denied reflexivity. Willingness to explore the meaning of the research for both researcher and participant adds an important dimension to therapy research.

3 **Openness to new methods of inquiry** The traditional mode of therapy research relied on the masterful use of quasi-experimental designs. The recent acceptance of different styles of research drawn from other disciplines, encompassed by the broad category of 'qualitative' methods, has forced therapy researchers to examine the goals and assumptions underpinning their work.

4 **Research oriented to discovery rather than verification** In the past few years, researchers have turned to heuristic or discovery-oriented forms of research, in recognition of the fact that research that generates ideas about what

is possible is equally as valuable as research that tests or verifies what is known or believed to be 'factually' true.

5 **Appreciation of the power relationship between researcher and researched** One of the invaluable contributions made by feminist writers on research methodology has been to draw attention to the ways that the conventional relationship between researcher and informant operates to make invisible the true concerns and experiences of the latter. The question 'who is research for?' introduces a greater appreciation of issues around empowerment and social responsibility in research.

6 **Displacement of an over-psychological concept of the person** Almost all counselling and psychotherapy research has been carried out from within the discipline of psychology. In a robust challenge to this view, Heaton suggests that:

> psychotherapy should not be based on psychology . . . theoretical work in psychotherapy must foster the recognition of the limits of language and the contexts in which words come to represent. It should combat the craving for generalizations about human nature which besets therapists when they theorize and should help them to see the part that different therapeutic practices play in the life of people and societies. (1979: 194)

The case being made here is that only an interdisciplinary perspective can enable counselling and psychotherapy to generate adequate understandings of persons. Heaton (1979) demonstrates the value of philosophical insights in this endeavour. Other disciplines, such as sociology, anthropology, theology and the arts all have an equal part to play. The work of Cushman (1995) represents a powerful example of the value of an interdisciplinary orientation in developing a new way of seeing the evolution of psychotherapy.

These trends represent steps in the re-alignment of counselling and psycho-therapy research toward human science. In human science there is no objective truth. All of us, therapists, clients, researchers, are engaged in negotiating and co-constructing shared understandings of events. These understandings are best seen as local knowledges rather than universal truths, as a way of contributing to a never-ending dialogue and conversation abouth the meaning of things and the basis for right action. The starting point and well-spring of this type of inquiry is in the fundamental human experience of *not knowing*: the best researchers are those with the best questions, not the best answers.

Further reading

Anyone who has reached this final chapter, having read through the seemingly endless lists of practical and methodological issues associated with research in psychotherapy and counselling, will no doubt have a firm sense of the com-plexity of this kind of work. Doing counselling research is not a straightforward matter. It involves making *choices* in relation to goals, ideas and procedures. One of the best ways to become more familiar with the texture of this decision-making process is to 'listen in' to the debates that take place between professional therapy researchers. Some good examples of researchers 'thinking aloud' about their craft, can be found in:

Hoshmand, L.T. and Martin, J. (eds) (1995) *Research as Praxis: Lessons from Programmatic Research in Therapeutic Psychology.* New York: Teachers' College Press.
Polkinghorne, D.E. (1999) 'Traditional research and psychotherapy practice', *Journal of Clinical Psychology*, 55: 1429–40.
Russell, R.L. (ed.) (1994) *Reassessing Psychotherapy Research.* New York: Guilford Press.
Talley, P.F., Strupp, H.H. and Butler, S.F. (eds) (1994) *Research Findings and Clinical Practice: Bridging the Chasm.* New York: Basic Books.

Almost all of the writers who appear in these edited books are based in North America, reflecting the cultural domination of the counselling and psycho-therapy research literature by the American imagination.

References

Addis, M.E. and Krasnow, A.D. (2000) 'A national survey of practicing psychologists' attitudes toward psychotherapy treatment manuals', *Journal of Consulting and Clinical Psychology*, 68: 331–9.

Adler, P.A. and Adler, P. (1994) 'Observational techniques', in N.K. Denzin and Y.S. Lincoln (eds), *Handbook of Qualitative Research*. London: Sage.

Agnew-Davies, R. (1999) 'Learning from research into the counselling relationship', in C. Feltham (ed.), *Understanding the Counselling Relationship*. London: Sage.

Allman, L.S., De La Rocha, O., Elkins, D.N. and Weathers, R.S. (1992) 'Psychotherapists' attitudes toward clients reporting mystical experiences', *Psychotherapy*, 29: 564–9.

Allport, G. (1942) *The Use of Personal Documents in Psychological Science*. New York: Social Science Research Council.

Altheide, D.L. and Johnson, J.M. (1994) 'Criteria for assessing interpretive validity in qualitative research', in N.K. Denzin and Y.S. Lincoln (eds), *Handbook of Qualitative Research*. London: Sage.

Altshuler, K.Z. (1989) 'Will the psychotherapies yield different results? A look at assumptions in therapy trials', *American Journal of Psychotherapy*, 63 (3): 310–20.

Anderson, R. (1998) 'Intuitive inquiry: a transpersonal approach', in W. Braud and R. Anderson (eds), *Transpersonal Research Methods for the Social Sciences: Honoring Human Experience*. Thousand Oaks, CA: Sage.

Anderson, T. and Strupp, H.H. (1996) 'The ecology of psychotherapy research', *Journal of Consulting and Clinical Psychology*, 64: 776–82.

Angus, L. (1996) 'An intensive analysis of metaphor themes in psychotherapy', in J.S. Mio and A. Katz (eds), *Metaphor: Pragmatics and Applications*. New York: Erlbaum.

Angus, L. and Hardtke, K. (1994) 'Narrative processes in psychotherapy', *Canadian Psychology*, 35 (2): 190–203.

Angus, L., Levitt, H. and Hardtke, K. (1999) 'The Narrative Processes Coding System: research applications and implications for psychotherapy practice', *Journal of Clinical Psychology*, 55 (10): 1255–70.

Angus, L.E. and Rennie, D.L. (1988) 'Therapist participation in metaphor generation: collaborative and noncollaborative styles', *Psychotherapy*, 25: 552–60.

Angus, L.E. and Rennie, D.L. (1989) 'Envisioning the representational world: the client's experience of metaphoric expressiveness in psychotherapy', *Psychotherapy*, 26: 373–9.

Argyrous, G. (2000) *Statistics for Social and Health Research*. London: Sage.

Arthern, J. and Madill, A. (1999) 'How do transition objects work? The therapist's view', *British Journal of Medical Psychology*, 72: 1–21.

Atkinson, P. and Hammersley, M. (1994) 'Ethnography and participant observation', in N.K. Denzin and Y.S. Lincoln (eds), *Handbook of Qualitative Research*. London: Sage.

Attkisson, C.C. and Greenfield, T.K. (1994) 'Client Satisfaction Questionnaire-8 and Service Satisfaction Scale-30', in M.E. Maruish (ed.), *The Use of Psychological Testing for Treatment Planning and Outcome Assessment*. Hillsdale, NJ: Lawrence Erlbaum.

Attkinson, C.C. and Zwick, R. (1982) 'The client satisfaction questionnaire: psychometric properties and correlations with service utilization and psychotherapy outcome', *Evaluation and Program Planning*, 5: 233–7.

Auerbach, A.H. (1983) 'Assessment of psychotherapy outcome from the viewpoint of expert observer', in M.J. Lambert, E.R. Christensen and S.S. DeJulio (eds), *The Assessment of Psychotherapy Outcome*. New York: Wiley.

Axline, V. (1950) 'Play therapy experiences as described by child participants', *Journal of Consulting Psychology*, 14: 53–63.

Bachelor, A. (1988) 'How clients perceive therapist empathy: a content analysis of "received" empathy', *Psychotherapy*, 25: 277–40.

Bachrach, H.M. (1976) 'Empathy', *Archives of General Psychiatry*, 33: 35–8.

Bachrach, H., Curtis, H., Escoll, P., Graff, H., Huxster, H., Ottenberg, P. and Pulver, S. (1981) 'Units of observation and perspectives on the psychoanalytic process', *British Journal of Medical Psychology*, 54: 25–33.

Bakan, D. (1969) *On Method: Toward a Reconstruction of Psychological Investigation*. San Francisco, CA: Jossey-Bass.

Barker, C. (1985) 'Interpersonal Process Recall in clinical training and research', in F.N. Watts (ed.), *New Developments in Clinical Psychology*. Chichester: Wiley/BPS.

Barkham, M., Margison, F., Leach, C., Lucock, M., Mellor-Clark, J., Evans, C., Benson, L., Connell, J. and McGrath, G. (2001) 'Service profiling and outcomes benchmarking using the CORE OM: toward practice-based evidence in the psychological therapies', *Journal of Consulting and Clinical Psychology*, 69: 184–96.

Barkham, M. and Mellor-Clark, J. (2000) 'Rigour and relevance: the role of practice-based evidence in the psychological therapies', in N. Rowland and S. Goss (eds), *Evidence-based Counselling and Psychological Therapies: Research and Applications*. London: Routledge.

Barkham, M.J. and Shapiro, D.A. (1986) 'Counselor verbal response modes and experienced empathy', *Journal of Counseling Psychology*, 33 (1): 3–10.

Barkham, M.J. and Shapiro, D.A. (1990) 'Exploratory therapy in two-plus-one sessions: a research model for studying the process of change', in G. Lietaer, J. Rombouts and R. Van Balen (eds), *Client-centered and Experiential Psychotherapy in the Nineties*. Leuven: Leuven University Press.

Barkham, M., Shapiro, D.A. and Firth-Cozens, J. (1989) 'Personal questionnaire changes in prescriptive vs. exploratory psychotherapy', *British Journal of Clinical Psychology*, 28: 97–107.

Barkham, M., Stiles, W.B., Hardy, G.E. and Field, S.F. (1996) 'The assimilation model: theory, research and practical guidelines', in W. Dryden (ed.), *Research in Counselling and Psychotherapy: Practical Applications*. London: Sage.

Barlow, D.H., Hayes, S.C. and Nelson, R.O. (1984) *The Scientist Practitioner: Research and Accountability in Clinical and Educational Settings*. New York: Pergamon.

Barlow, D.H. and Hersen, M. (1986) *Single Case Experimental Designs: Strategies for Studying Behavior Change*, 2nd edn. New York: Pergamon.

Barrett-Lennard, G.T. (1979) 'The client-centered system unfolding', in F.J. Turner (ed.), *Social Work Treatment: Interlocking Theoretical Approaches*, 2nd edn. New York: Free Press.

Barrett-Lennard, G.T. (1981) 'The empathy cycle – refinement of a nuclear concept', *Journal of Counseling Psychology*, 28: 91–100.

Barrett-Lennard, G.T. (1986) 'The Relationship Inventory now: issues and advances in theory, method and use', in L.S. Greenberg and W.M. Pinsof (eds), *The Psychotherapeutic Process: A Research Handbook*. New York: Guilford Press.

Barrett-Lennard, G.T. (1998) *Carl Rogers' Helping System: Journey and Substance*. London: Sage.

Bartram, D. (1990) 'Measuring differences between people', in J.R. Beech and L. Harding (eds), *Testing People: A Practical Guide to Psychometrics*. Windsor: NFER-Nelson.

Basham, R.B. (1986) 'Scientific and practical advantages of comparative design in psychotherapy outcome research', *Journal of Consulting and Clinical Psychology*, 54 (1): 88–94.

Battle, C.C., Imber, S.D., Hoehn-Saric, R., Stone, A.R., Nash, E.R. and Frank, J.D. (1966) 'Target complaints as a criteria of improvement', *American Journal of Psychotherapy*, 20: 184–92.

Beauchamp, T.L. and Childress, J.F. (1979) *Principles of Biomedical Ethics*. Oxford: Oxford University Press.

Beck, A.T., Rush, A.J., Shaw, B.J. and Emery, G.D. (1979) *Cognitive Therapy of Depression: A Treatment Manual*. New York: Guilford Press.

Beck, A.T., Steer, R.A. and Garbin, M.G. (1988) 'Psychometric properties of the Beck Depression Inventory: twenty-five years of evaluation', *Clinical Psychology Review*, 8: 77–100.

Beck, A.T., Ward, C.H., Mendelson, M. et al. (1961) 'Inventory for measuring depression', *Archives of General Psychiatry*, 4: 561–71.

Becker, C.S. (1992) *Living and Relating: An Introduction to Phenomenology*. London: Sage.

Becker, H.S. (1986) *Writing for Social Scientists: How to Start and Finish Your Thesis, Book or Article*. Chicago: University of Chicago Press.

Beech, J.R. and Harding, L. (eds) (1990) *Testing People: A Practical Guide to Psychometrics*. Windsor: NFER-Nelson.

Bell, C. and Newby, H. (eds) (1977) *Doing Sociological Research*. London: George Allen and Unwin.

Bell, J. (1993) *Doing Your Research Project*. Buckingham: Open University Press.

Berger, M. (1983) 'Toward maximising the utility of consumer satisfaction as an outcome', in M.J. Lambert, E.R. Christensen and S.S. DeJulio (eds), *The Assessment of Psychotherapy Outcome*. New York: Wiley.

Berger, R. and Mallison, R. (2000) '"Therapeutizing" research: the positive impact of family-focused research on participants', *Smith College Studies in Social Work*, 27: 307–14.

Bergin, A.E. (1963) 'The effects of psychotherapy: negative results revisited', *Journal of Counseling Psychology*, 10: 244–50.

Bergin, A.E. and Garfield, S.L. (eds) (1994) *Handbook of Psychotherapy and Behavior Change*, 4th edn. Chichester: Wiley.

Bergin, A.E. and Strupp, H.H. (1972) *Changing Frontiers in the Science of Psychotherapy*. Chicago: Aldine Atherton.

Bertaux, D. (ed.) (1981) *Biography and Society*. London: Sage.

Berzon, B., Pious, C. and Farson, R.E. (1963) 'The therapeutic event in group psychotherapy: a study of subjective reports by group members', *Journal of Individual Psychology*, 19: 204–12.

Bettelheim, B. (1960) *The Informed Heart*. London: Thames and Hudson.

Beutler, L.E. and Crago, M. (1983) 'Self-report measures of psychotherapy outcome', in M.J. Lambert, E.R. Christensen and S.S. DeJulio (eds), *The Assessment of Psychotherapy Outcome*. New York: Wiley.

Bickman, L. and Rog, D.J. (eds) (1998) *Handbook of Applied Social Research Methods*. London: Sage.

Binder, J.L. (1993) 'Observations on the training of therapists in time-limited dynamic psychotherapy', *Psychotherapy*, 30 (4): 592–8.

Blatt, S.J., Sanislow, C.A., Zuroff, D.C. and Pilkonis, P.A. (1996) 'Characteristics of effective therapists: further analysis of data from the National Institute of Mental Health Treatment of Depression Collaborative Research Program', *Journal of Consulting and Clinical Psychology*, 64 (6): 1276–84.

Bloch, S., Reibtein, J., Crouch, E., Holroyd, P. and Themen, J. (1979) 'A method for the study of therapeutic factors in group psychotherapy', *British Journal of Psychiatry*, 134: 257–63.

Bloor, M., Frankland, J., Thomas, M. and Robson, K. (2000) *Focus Groups in Social Research*. London: Sage.

Bohart, A. (2000) 'A qualitative "adjudicational" model for assessing psychotherapy outcome'. Paper presented at meeting of Society for Psychotherapy Research, Chicago, IL.

Bohart, A.C. and Greenberg, L.S. (eds) (1997) *Empathy Reconsidered: New Directions in Psychotherapy*. Washington, DC: American Psychological Association.

Bolgar, H. (1965) 'The case study method', in B. Wolman (ed.), *Handbook of Clinical Psychology*. New York: McGraw-Hill.

Bond, T. (2000) *Standards and Issues for Counselling in Action*, 2nd edn. London: Sage.

Bordin, E. (1979) 'The generalizability of the psychoanalytic concept of the working alliance', *Psychotherapy: Theory, Research and Practice*, 16: 252–60.

Bower, P., Rowland, N., Mellor-Clark, J., Heywood, P., Godfrey, C. and Hardy, R. (2002) 'Effectiveness and cost-effectiveness of counselling in primary care (Cochrane Review)', *Cochrane Library*, 1, Oxford: Update Software

Bowling, A. (1997) *Measuring Health: A Review of Quality of Life Measurement Scales*, 2nd edn. Buckingham: Open University Press.

Bowling, A. (2001) *Measuring Disease: A Review of Disease-specific Quality of Life Measurement Scales*, 2nd edn. Buckingham: Open University Press.

Brannen, J. (ed.) (1992a) *Mixing Methods: Qualitative and Quantitative Research*. Aldershot: Avebury, pp. 38–55.

Brannen, J. (1992b) 'Combining qualitative and quantitative approaches: an overview', in J. Brannen (ed.), *Mixing Methods: Qualitative and Quantitative Research*. Aldershot: Avebury.

Brannen, J. and Collard, J. (1982) *Marriages in Trouble: The Process of Seeking Help*. London: Tavistock.

Branthwaite, A. and Lunn, T. (1985) 'Projective techniques in social and market research', in R. Walker (ed.), *Applied Qualitative Research*. Aldershot: Gower.

Braud, W. (1998) 'Integral inquiry: complementary ways of knowing, being and expression', in W. Braud and R. Anderson (eds), *Transpersonal Research Methods for the Social Sciences: Honoring Human Experience*. Thousand Oaks, CA: Sage.

Braud, W. and Anderson, R. (eds) (1998) *Transpersonal Research Methods for the Social Sciences: Honoring Human Experience*. Thousand Oaks, CA: Sage.

Breakwell, G.M., Hammond, S.and Fife-Schaw, C. (eds) (2000) *Research Methods in Psychology*, 2nd edn. London: Sage.

Brewin, C. and Bradley, C. (1989) 'Patient preferences and randomised clinical trials', *British Medical Journal*, 299: 313–15.

Bridges, K. and Goldberg, D. (1989) 'Self-administered scales of neurotic symptoms', in C. Thompson (ed.), *The Instruments of Psychiatric Research*. Chichester: Wiley.

Bromley, D. (1981) *Personality Description in Ordinary Language*. Chichester: Wiley.

Bromley, D. (1986) *The Case-Study Method in Psychology and Related Disciplines*. Chichester: Wiley.

Bruner, J. (1986) *Actual Minds, Possible Worlds*. Cambridge, MA: Harvard University Press.

Bryman, A. (1984) 'The debate about quantitative and qualitative research: a question of method or epistemology?', *British Journal of Sociology*, 35 (1): 75–93.

Bryman, A. (ed.) (1988a) *Doing Research in Organizations*. London: Routledge.

Bryman, A. (1988b) *Quantity and Quality in Social Research*. London: Unwin Hyman.

Bryman, A. (1992) 'Quantitative and qualitative research: further reflections on their integration', in J. Brannen (ed.), *Mixing Methods: Qualitative and Quantitative Research*. Aldershot: Avebury, pp. 57–8.

Buzan, T. (1974) *Use Your Head*. London: BBC Publications.

Cain, D.J. and Seeman, J. (eds) (2002) *Humanistic Psychotherapies: Handbook of Research and Practice*. Washington, DC: American Psychological Association.

Campbell, D.T. and Fiske, D.W. (1959) 'Convergent and discriminant validation by the multitrait-multimethod approach', *Psychological Bulletin*, 56: 81–105.

Campbell, D.T. and Stanley, J.C. (1963) *Experimental and Quasi-Experimental Designs for Research*. Chicago: Rand McNally.

Charmaz, K. (2000) 'Grounded theory: objectivist and constructivist methods', in N.K. Denzin and Y.S. Lincoln (eds), *Handbook of Qualitative Research*, 2nd edn. Thousand Oaks, CA: Sage.

Chassan, J.B. (1979) *Research Design in Clinical Psychology and Psychiatry*, 2nd edn. New York: Wiley.

Cheyne, A. and Kinn, S. (2001a) 'A pilot study for a randomised controlled trial of the use of the schedule for the evaluation of individual quality of life (SEIQoL) in an alcohol counselling setting', *Addiction Research and Theory*, 9 (2): 165–78.

Cheyne, A. and Kinn, S. (2001b) 'Counsellors' perspectives on the use of the Schedule for the Evaluation of Individual Quality of Life (SEIQoL) in an alcohol counselling setting', *British Journal of Guidance and Counselling*, 29 (1): 35–46.

Cohen, J. (1960) 'A coefficient of agreement for nominal scales', *Educational and Psychological Measurement*, 20: 37–46.

Cohen, L.H., Sargent, M.M. and Sechrest, L.B. (1986) 'Use of psychotherapy research by professional psychologists', *American Psychologist*, 41: 198–206.

Cohen, S. and Taylor, L. (1972) *Psychological Survival*. Harmondsworth: Penguin.

Colbourn, C.J. (1996) 'Using computers', in G. Parry and F.N. Watts (eds), *Behavioural and Mental Health Research: A Handbook of Skills and Methods*, 2nd edn. London: Lawrence Erlbaum.

Combs, A.W. (1986) 'What makes a good helper? A person-centered approach', *Person-Centered Review*, 1: 51–61.

Cone, J.D. (2001) *Evaluating Outcomes: Empirical Tools for Effective Practice*. Washington, DC: American Psychological Association.

Coolidge, F.L. (2000) *Statistics: A Gentle Introduction*. Thousand Oaks, CA: Sage.

Corey, G., Corey, M.S. and Callanan, P. (2003) *Issues and Ethics in the Helping Professions*, 6th edn. Belmont, CA: Wadsworth.

Cornelius III, E.T. (1983) 'The use of projective techniques in personnel selection', in K. Rowland and G. Ferris (eds), *Research in Personnel and Human Resources Management*, vol. 1. London: JAI Press.

Cozby, P.C. (1985) *Methods in Behavioral Research*, 3rd edn. Palo Alto, CA: Mayfield.

Cramer, D. (1990) 'The necessary conditions for evaluating client-centered therapy', in G. Lietaer, J. Rombauts and R. Van Balen (eds), *Client-Centered and Experiential Therapy in the Nineties*. Leuven: University of Leuven Press.

Cramer, D. (1992) *Personality and Psychotherapy: Theory, Practice and Research*. Buckingham: Open University Press.

Crits-Christoph, P., Baranackie, K. and Kurcias, J. (1991) 'Meta-analysis of therapist effects in psychotherapy outcome studies', *Psychotherapy Research*, 1 (2): 81–91.

Cronbach, L. (1970) *Essentials of Psychological Testing*, 3rd edn. New York: Harper and Row.

Crosby, F. (1979) 'Evaluating psychohistorical explanations', *Psychohistory Review*, 7 (4): 6–16.

Cunningham, I. (1988) 'Interactive holistic research: researching self managed learning', in P. Reason (ed.), *Human Inquiry in Action*. London: Sage.

Curtis, J.T., Weiss, J., Silberschatz, G., Sampson, H. and Rosenberg, S.E. (1988) 'Developing reliable psychodynamic case formulations: an illustration of the plan diagnosis method', *Psychotherapy*, 25: 256–65.

Cushman, P. (1995) *Constructing the Self, Constructing America: A Cultural History of Psychotherapy*. Reading, MA: Addison-Wesley.

Cytrynbaum, S., Ginath, Y., Birdwell, J. and Brandt, L. (1979) 'Goal attainment scaling: a critical review', *Evaluation Quarterly*, 3 (1): 5–40.

Dale, P., Allen, J. and Measor, L. (1998) 'Counselling adults who were abused as children: clients' perceptions of efficacy, client–counsellor communication, and dissatisfaction', *British Journal of Guidance and Counselling*, 26: 141–58.

Danziger, K. (1990) *Constructing the Subject: Historical Origins of Psychological Research*. Cambridge: Cambridge University Press.

Dar, R. (1987) 'Another look at Meehl, Lakatos and the scientific practices of psychologists', *American Psychologist*, 42 (2): 145–51.

Dar, R., Serlin, R.C. and Omer, H. (1994) 'Misuse of statistical tests in three decades of psychotherapy research', *Journal of Consulting and Clinical Psychology*, 62 (1): 75–82.

Davidson, C.V. and Davidson, R.H. (1983) 'The significant other as data source and data problem in psychotherapy outcome research', in M.J. Lambert, E.R. Christensen and S.S. DeJulio (eds), *The Assessment of Psychotherapy Outcome*. New York: Wiley.

de Vaus, D.A. (1990) *Surveys in Social Research*, 3rd edn. London: Allen and Unwin.

Deane, F.P., Spicer, J. and Todd, D.M. (1997) 'Validity of a simplified target complaints measure', *Psychological Assessment*, 4: 119–30.

Denker, P.G. (1937) 'Prognosis and life expectancy in the psychoneuroses', *Proceedings of the Association of Life Insurance Medical Directors of America*, 24: 179.

Denzin, N.K. (1978) *The Research Act: A Theoretical Introduction to Sociological Methods*, 2nd edn. New York: McGraw-Hill.

Denzin, N. (1989) *Interpretive Interactionism*. London: Sage.

Denzin, N.K. (1994) 'The art and politics of interpretation', in N.K. Denzin and Y.S. Lincoln (eds), *Handbook of Qualitative Research*. London: Sage.

Denzin, N.K. and Lincoln, Y.S. (1994) 'Introduction: entering the field of qualitative research', in N.K. Denzin and Y.S. Lincoln (eds), *Handbook of Qualitative Research*. London: Sage.

Denzin, N.K. and Lincoln, Y.S. (eds) (2000) *Handbook of Qualitative Research*, 2nd edn. Thousand Oaks, CA: Sage.

Derogatis, L.R. and Melisaratos, N. (1983) 'The Brief Symptom Inventory: an introductory report', *Psychological Medicine*, 13: 595–605.

Devereaux, G. (1967) *From Anxiety to Method in the Behavioural Sciences*. The Hague: Mouton.

DeWaele, J. and Harré, R. (1976) 'The personality of individuals', in R. Harré (ed.), *Personality*. Oxford: Blackwell.

DiMascio, A., Klerman, G.L., Weissman, M.N., Prusoff, B.A., Nev, C. and Moore, P. (1979) 'A control group for psychotherapy research in acute depression: one solution to ethical and methodologic issues', *Journal of Psychiatric Research*, 15: 189–97.

Dineen, T. (1999) *Manufacturing Victims: What the Psychology Industry is Doing to People*. London: Constable.

Dobson, K.S. and Shaw, B.F. (1993) 'The training of cognitive therapists: what have we learned from treatment manuals?', *Psychotherapy*, 30 (4): 573–7.

Douglas, J.D. and Johnson, J.M. (eds) (1977) *Existential Sociology*. Cambridge: Cambridge University Press.

Douglass, B.G. and Moustakas, C. (1985) 'Heuristic inquiry: the internal search to know', *Journal of Humanistic Psychology*, 25 (3): 39–55.

Dryden, W. (ed.) (1987) *Key Cases in Psychotherapy*. London: Croom Helm.

Dryden, W. (ed.) (1996) *Research in Counselling and Psychotherapy: Practical Applications*. London: Sage.

Dryden, W. and Yankura, J. (1992) *Daring to be Myself*. Buckingham: Open University Press.

DuBois, F.H. (1970) *A History of Psychological Testing*. Boston, MA: Allyn and Bacon.

Duckworth, J.C. (1990) 'The Minnesota Multiphasic Personality Inventory', in C.E. Watkins Jr, and V.L. Campbell (eds), *Testing in Counseling Practice*. Hillsdale, NJ: Lawrence Erlbaum.

Eames, V. and Roth, A. (2000) 'Patient attachment orientation and the early working alliance: a study of patient and therapist reports of alliance quality and ruptures', *Psychotherapy Research*, 10: 421–34.

Edwards, A.L. (1957) *The Social Desirability Variable in Personality Research*. New York: Dryden Press.

Edwards, D.J.A. (1998) 'Types of case study work: a conceptual framework for case-based research', *Journal of Humanistic Psychology*, 38 (3): 36–70.

Elkin, I. (1999) 'A major dilemma in psychotherapy outcome research: disentangling therapists from therapies', *Clinical Psychology: Science and Practice*, 6: 10–32.

Elliott, R. (1983a) '"That in your hands . . .": a comprehensive process analysis of a significant event in psychotherapy', *Psychiatry*, 46: 113–29.

Elliott, R. (1983b) 'Fitting process research to the practicing psychotherapist', *Psychotherapy*, 20 (1): 47–55.

Elliott, R. (1984) 'A discovery-oriented approach to significant change events in psychotherapy: Interpersonal Process Recall and Comprehensive Process Analysis', in L.N. Rice and L.S. Greenberg (eds), *Patterns of Change: Intensive Analysis of Psychotherapy Process*. New York: Guilford Press.

Elliott, R. (1986) 'Interpersonal Process Recall (IPR) as a psychotherapy process research method', in L.S. Greenberg and W.M. Pinsof (eds), *The Psychotherapeutic Process: A Research Handbook*. New York: Guilford Press.

Elliott, R. (1991) 'Five dimensions of therapy process', *Psychotherapy Research*, 1: 92–103.

Elliott, R. (1998) 'A guide to the empirically supported treatments controversy', *Psychotherapy Research*, 8: 115–25.

Elliott, R. (2001) 'Hermeneutic single-case efficacy design: an overview', in K.J. Schneider, J. Bugental and J.F. Pierson (eds), *The Handbook of Humanistic Psychology: Leading Edges in Theory, Research and Practice*. Thousand Oaks, CA: Sage.

Elliott, R. (2002a) 'The effectiveness of humanistic therapies: a meta-analysis', in D.J. Cain and J.

Seeman (eds), *Humanistic Psychotherapies: Handbook of Research and Practice*. Washington, DC: American Psychological Association.

Elliott, R. (2002b) 'Hermeneutic single-case efficacy design', *Psychotherapy Research*, 12: 1–23.

Elliott, R., Barker, C.B., Caskey, N. and Pistrang, N. (1982) 'Differential helpfulness of counselor verbal response modes', *Journal of Counseling Psychology*, 29: 354–61.

Elliott, R., Fischer, C.T. and Rennie, D.L. (1999) 'Evolving guidelines for the publication of qualitative research studies in psychology and related fields', *British Journal of Clinical Psychology*, 38: 215–29.

Elliott, R., Hill, C.E., Stiles, W.B., Friedlander, M.L., Mahrer, A.R. and Margison, F.R. (1987) 'Primary therapist response modes: comparison of six rating systems', *Journal of Consulting and Clinical Psychology*, 55: 223–8.

Elliott, R. and James, E. (1989) 'Varieties of client experience in psychotherapy: an analysis of the literature', *Clinical Psychology Review*, 9: 443–67.

Elliott, R. and Shapiro, D.A. (1988) 'Brief Structured Recall: a more efficient method for studying significant therapy events', *British Journal of Medical Psychology*, 61: 141–53.

Elliott, R. and Shapiro, D.A. (1992) 'Client and therapist as analysts of significant events', in S.G. Toukmanian and D.L. Rennie (eds), *Psychotherapy Process Research: Paradigmatic and Narrative Approaches*. London: Sage.

Elliott, R., Davis, K.L. and Slatick, E. (1998) 'Process-experiential therapy for posttraumatic stress difficulties', in L.S. Greenberg, J.C. Watson and G. Lietaer (eds), *Handbook of Experiential Psychotherapy*. New York: Guilford Press.

Ellis, C. and Bochner, A.P. (2000) 'Auto-ethnography, personal narrative, reflexivity: researcher as subject', in N.K. Denzin and Y.S. Lincoln (eds), *Handbook of Qualitative Research*, 2nd edn. Thousand Oaks, CA: Sage.

Ellis, C. and Flaherty, M. (eds) (1992) *Investigating Subjectivity: Research on Lived Experience*. Thousand Oaks, CA: Sage.

Ellis, C., Kiesinger, C.E. and Tillmann-Healy, L.M. (1997) 'Interactive interviewing: talking about emotional experience', in R. Hertz (ed.), *Reflexivity and Voice*. Thousand Oaks, CA: Sage.

Etherington, K. (2000) *Narrative Approaches to Working with Adult Male Survivors of Child Sexual Abuse: The Client's, the Counsellor's and the Researcher's Story*. London: Jessica Kingsley.

Evans, C., Mellor-Clark, J. et al. (2000) 'CORE: Clinical Outcomes in Routine Evaluation', *Journal of Mental Health*, 9, 247–55.

Evans, I.M. and Robinson, C.H. (1978) 'Behavior therapy observed: the diary of a client', *Cognitive Therapy and Research*, 2 (4): 335–55.

Eysenck, H.J. (1952) 'The effects of psychotherapy: an evaluation', *Journal of Consulting Psychology*, 16: 319–24.

Eysenck, H.J. (1960) 'The effects of psychotherapy', in H.J. Eysenck (ed.), *Handbook of Abnormal Psychology*. New York: Basic Books.

Eysenck, H.J. (1965) 'The effects of psychotherapy', *International Journal of Psychiatry*, 1: 97–178.

Eysenck, H.J. (1992) 'The outcome problem in psychotherapy', in W. Dryden and C. Feltham (eds), *Psychotherapy and its Discontents*. Buckingham: Open University Press.

Ferguson, B. and Tyrer, P. (1989) 'Rating instruments in psychiatric research', in C. Freeman and P. Tyrer (eds), *Research Methods in Psychiatry: A Beginners' Guide*. London: Gaskell.

Fetterman, D.M. (1998) 'Ethnography', in J.L. Bickman and D.J. Rog (eds), *Handbook of Social Research Methods*. Thousand Oaks, CA: Sage.

Fiedler, F.E. (1950) 'A comparison of psychoanalytic, nondirective and Adlerian therapeutic relationships', *Journal of Consulting Psychology*, 14: 436–45.

Fielding, N. (1993) 'Ethnography', in N. Gilbert (ed.), *Researching Social Life*. London: Sage.

Fielding, N.G. and Lee, R.M. (eds) (1991) *Using Computers in Qualitative Research*. London: Sage.

Finch, J. (1984) '"It's great to have someone to talk to": ethics and politics of interviewing women', in C. Bell and H. Roberts (eds), *Social Researching: Politics, Problems, Practice*. London: Routledge.

Finch, J. (1987) 'Research note: the vignette technique in survey research', *Sociology*, 21: 105–14.

Fink, A. (1998) *Conducting Research Literature Reviews: From Paper to the Internet*. Thousand Oaks, CA: Sage.

Firth, J., Shapiro, D. and Parry, G. (1986) 'The impact of research on the practice of psychotherapy', *British Journal of Psychotherapy*, 2 (3): 169–79.

Fishman, D.B. (1999) *The Case for a Pragmatic Psychology*. New York: NYU Press.

Fishman, D.B. (2000, May 3) 'Transcending the efficacy versus effectiveness research debate: proposal for a new, electronic "Journal of Pragmatic Case Studies"', *Prevention & Treatment*, 3, Article 8. http://journals.apa.org/prevention/volume3/pre0030008a.html.

Fitts, W. (1965) *The Experience of Psychotherapy: What It's Like for Client and Therapist*. Princeton, NJ: Van Nostrand.

Flick, U. (1998) *An Introduction to Qualitative Research*. London: Sage.

Frank, J.D. (1973) *Persuasion and Healing: A Comparative Study of Psychotherapy*. Baltimore, MD: Johns Hopkins University Press.

Freud, S. (1901/1979) 'The case of Dora', *Pelican Freud Library*, vol. 8: *Case Histories I*. Harmondsworth: Penguin.

Freud, S. (1909/1979) 'Notes upon a case of obsessional neurosis (the "Rat Man")', *Pelican Freud Library*, vol. 9: *Case Histories II*. Harmondsworth: Penguin.

Freud, S. (1910/1979) 'Psychoanalytic notes on an autobiographical account of a case of paranoia (Dementia Paranoides) (Schreber)', *Pelican Freud Library*, vol. 9: *Case Histories II*. Harmondsworth: Penguin.

Friedlander, M.L., Ellis, M.V., Siegel, S.M., Raymond, L., Haase, R.F. and Highlen, P.S. (1988) 'Generalizing from segments to sessions: should it be done?', *Journal of Counseling Psychology*, 35 (3): 243–50.

Friedli, K., King, M.B., Lloyd, M. (2000) 'The economics of employing a counsellor in general practice: analysis of data from a randomised control trial', *British Journal of General Practice*, 50: 276–83.

Frommer, J. and Rennie, D.L. (eds) (2001) *Qualitative Psychotherapy Research: Methods and Methodology*. Lengerich, Germany: Pabst.

Galassi, J.P. and Gersh, T.L. (1991) 'Single-case research in counseling', in C.E. Watkins and L.J. Schneider (eds), *Research in Counseling*. Hillsdale, NJ: Lawrence Erlbaum.

Garfield, S.L. (1984) 'The evaluation of research: an editorial perspective', in A. Bellack and M. Hersen (eds), *Research Methods in Clinical Psychology*. New York: Pergamon.

Garfield, S.L. and Bergin, A.E. (1994) 'Introduction and historical overview', in A.E. Bergin and S.L. Garfield (eds), *Handbook of Psychotherapy and Behavior Change*, 4th edn. Chichester: Wiley.

Garfield, S.L. and Kurtz, R. (1974) 'A survey of clinical psychologists: characteristics, activities and orientations', *The Clinical Psychologist*, 28: 7–10.

Geertz, C. (1973) *The Interpretation of Culture: Selected Essays*. New York: Basic Books.

Gendlin, E. (1986) 'What comes after traditional psychotherapy research?', *American Psychologist*, 41: 131–6.

Gendlin, E.T. (1966) 'Experiential explication and truth', *Journal of Existentialism*, 6: 131–46.

Gendlin, E.T., Beebe, J., Cassens, J., Klein, M. and Oberlander, M. (1968) 'Focusing ability in psychotherapy, personality and creativity', in J.M. Shlien (ed.), *Research in Psychotherapy*, vol. 3. Washington, DC: American Psychological Association.

Gendlin, E.T. and Tomlinson, T.M. (1967) 'The process conception and its measurement', in C.R. Rogers, E.T. Gendlin, D.J. Kiesler and C.B. Truax (eds), *The Therapeutic Relationship and its Impact: A Study of Psychotherapy with Schizophrenics*. Madison, WI: University of Wisconsin Press.

Gerber, L. (1992) 'Intimate politics: connectedness and the social-political self', *Psychotherapy*, 29 (4): 626–30.

Gergen, K.J. (1985) 'The social constructionist movement in modern psychology', *American Psychologist*, 40 (3): 266–75.

Gergen, K.J. (1999) *An Invitation to Social Construction*. Thousand Oaks, CA: Sage.

Glaser, B.G. (1978) *Theoretical Sensitivity: Advances in the Methodology of Grounded Theory*. Mill Valley, CA: Sociology Press.

Glaser, B.G. and Strauss, A. (1967) *The Discovery of Grounded Theory*. Chicago: Aldine.

Golden, C., Sawicki, R. and Franzen, M. (1984) 'Test construction', in A. Bellack and M. Hersen (eds), *Research Methods in Clinical Psychology*. New York: Pergamon.

Grafanaki, S. (1996) 'How research can change the researcher: the need for sensitivity, flexibility and ethical boundaries in conducting qualitative research in counselling/psychotherapy', *British Journal of Guidance and Counselling*, 24: 329–38.

Grafanaki, S. (2001) 'What counselling research has taught us about the concept of congruence: main discoveries and unresolved issues', in G. Wyatt (ed.), *Rogers' Therapeutic Conditions: Evolution, Theory and Practice*. Vol. 1: *Congruence*. Ross-on-Wye: PCCS Books.

Greenbaum, T.L. (1998) *The Handbook for Focus Group Research*, 2nd edn. Thousand Oaks, CA: Sage.

Greenberg, L.S. (1984a) 'A task analysis of intrapersonal conflict resolution', in L.N. Rice and L.S. Greenberg (eds), *Patterns of Change: Intensive Analysis of Psychotherapy Process*. New York: Guilford Press.

Greenberg, L.S. (1984b) 'Task analysis: the general approach', in L.N. Rice and L.S. Greenberg (eds), *Patterns of Change: Intensive Analysis of Psychotherapy Process*. New York: Guilford Press.

Greenberg, L.S. (1992) 'Task analysis: identifying components of interpersonal conflict resolution', in S.G. Toukmanian and D.L. Rennie (eds), *Psychotherapy Process Research: Paradigmatic and Narrative Approaches*. London: Sage.

Greenberg, L.S. and Geller, S. (2001) 'Congruence and therapeutic presence', in G. Wyatt (ed.), *Rogers' Therapeutic Conditions: Evolution, Theory and Practice*. Vol. 1: *Congruence*. Ross-on-Wye: PCCS Books.

Greenberg, L.S. and Pinsof, W.M. (eds) (1986) *The Psychotherapeutic Process: A Research Handbook*. New York: Guilford Press.

Greenberg, L.S., Rice, L.N. and Elliott, R. (1993) *Facilitating Emotional Change: The Moment-by-Moment Process*. New York: Guilford Press.

Greenberg, L.S., Watson, J.C. and Goldman, R. (1998) 'Process-experiential therapy of depression', in L.S. Greenberg, J.C. Watson and G. Lietaer (eds), *Handbook of Experiential Psychotherapy*. New York: Guilford Press.

Greenberg, L.S., Watson, J.C. and Lietaer, G. (eds) (1998) *Handbook of Experiential Psychotherapy*. New York: Guilford Press.

Greene, J. and d'Oliveira, M. (1999) *Learning to Use Statistical Tests in Psychology*, 2nd edn. Buckingham: Open University Press

Grencavage, L.N. and Norcross, J.C. (1990) 'Where are the commonalities among the therapeutic common factors?', *Professional Psychology: Research and Practice*, 21: 372–8.

Gurland, B.J., Yorkston, N.J., Stone, A.R. et al. (1972) 'The Structured and Scaled Interview to Assess Maladjustment (SSIAM) Parts I & II', *Archives of General Psychiatry*, 27: 259–67.

Guthrie, E., Moorey, J., Barker, H., Margison, F. and McGrath, G. (1999) 'Cost-effectiveness of brief psychodynamic–interpersonal therapy in high utilizers of psychiatric services', *Archives of General Psychiatry*, 56: 519–26.

Hammersley, M. (1992) 'Deconstructing the qualitative–quantitative divide', in J. Brannen (ed.), *Mixing Methods: Qualitative and Quantitative Research*. Aldershot: Avebury.

Hardy, G.E., Aldridge, J., Davidson, C., Rowe, C., Reilly, S. and Shapiro, D.A. (1999) 'Therapist responsiveness to client attachment styles and issues observed in client-identified significant events in psychodynamic–interpersonal psychotherapy', *Psychotherapy Research*, 9: 36–53.

Hart, C. (1998) *Doing a Literature Review: Releasing the Social Science Research Imagination*. London: Sage.

Hasenfeld, Y. (ed.) (1992) *Human Services as Complex Organizations*. London: Sage.

Hattie, J.A., Sharpley, C.F. and Rogers, H.J. (1984) 'Comparative effectiveness of professional and paraprofessional helpers', *Psychological Bulletin*, 95: 534–41.

Heaton, J.M. (1979) 'Theory in psychotherapy', in N. Bolton (ed.), *Philosophical Problems in Psychology*. London: Methuen.

Henry, W.P. (1998) 'Science, politics, and the politics of science: the use and misuse of empirically validated treatment research', *Psychotherapy Research*, 8: 126–40.

Henry, W.P., Strupp, H.H., Schact, T.E. and Gaston, L. (1994) 'Psychodynamic approaches', in

A.E. Bergin and S.L. Garfield (eds), *Handbook of Psychotherapy and Behavior Change*, 4th edn. New York: Wiley.

Heppner, P.P., Kivlighan Jr, D.M. and Wampold, B.E. (1999) *Research Design in Counseling*, 2nd edn. Belmont, CA: Brooks/Cole.

Herbert, J.D. and Mueser, K.T. (1992) 'Eye movement desensitization: a critique of the evidence', *Journal of Behavior Therapy and Experimental Psychiatry*, 23 (3): 169–74.

Hesse, E. (1999) 'The Adult Attachment Interview: historical and current perspectives', in J. Cassidy and P.R. Shaver (eds), *Handbook of Attachment: Theory, Research and Clinical Applications*. New York: Guilford Press.

Hill, C.E. (1986) 'An overview of the Hill counselor and client verbal response modes category systems', in L.S. Greenberg and W.M. Pinsof (eds), *The Psychotherapeutic Process: A Research Handbook*. New York: Guilford Press.

Hill, C.E. (1989) *Therapist Techniques and Client Outcomes: Eight Cases of Brief Psychotherapy*. London: Sage.

Hill, C.E. (1991) 'Almost everything you ever wanted to know about how to do process research on counseling and psychotherapy but didn't know who to ask', in C.E. Watkins and L.J. Schneider (eds), *Research in Counseling*. Hillsdale, NJ: Lawrence Erlbaum.

Hill, C.E., Carter, J.A. and O'Farrell, M.K. (1983a) 'A case study of the process and outcome of time-limited counseling', *Journal of Counseling Psychology*, 30 (1): 3–18.

Hill, C.E., Carter, J.A. and O'Farrell, M.K. (1983b) 'Reply to Howard and Lambert: case study methodology', *Journal of Counseling Psychology*, 30 (1): 26–30.

Hill, C.E. and Corbett, M.M. (1993) 'A perspective on the history of process and outcome research in counseling psychology', *Journal of Counseling Psychology*, 40 (1): 3–24.

Hill, C.E., Helms, J.E., Tichenor, V., Spiegel, S.B., O'Grady, K.E. and Perry, E.S. (1988) 'Effects of therapist response modes in brief psychotherapy', *Journal of Counseling Psychology*, 35: 222–33.

Hill, C.E. and O'Grady, K.E. (1985) 'List of therapist intentions illustrated by a case study and with therapists of varying theoretical orientations', *Journal of Counseling Psychology*, 32: 3–22.

Hill, C.E., Nutt-Williams, E., Heaton, K.J., Thompson, B.J. and Rhodes, R.H. (1996) 'Therapist retrospective recall of impasses in long-term psychotherapy: a qualitative analysis', *Journal of Counseling Psychology*, 43: 207–17.

Hill, C.E., Thompson, B.J., Nutt-Williams, E. (1997) 'A guide to conducting consensual qualitative research', *Counseling Psychologist*, 25: 517–72.

Hilliard, R.B. (1993) 'Single-case methodology in psychotherapy process and outcome research', *Journal of Consulting and Clinical Psychology*, 61 (3): 373–80.

Hinton, P. (1995) *Statistics Explained: A Guide for Social Science Students*. London: Routledge.

Hodgson, R. and Rollnick, S. (1996) 'More fun, less stress: how to survive in research', in G. Parry and F.N. Watts (eds), *Behavioural and Mental Health Research: A Handbook of Skills and Methods*, 2nd edn. London: Psychology Press.

Holloman, R. (1974) 'Ritual opening and individual transformation: rites of passage at Esalen', *American Anthropologist*, 76: 265–80.

Holstein, J.A. and Gubrium, J.F. (1994) 'Phenomenology, ethnomethodology and interpretive practice', in N.K. Denzin and Y.S. Lincoln (eds), *Handbook of Qualitative Research*. London: Sage.

Honos-Webb, L., Stiles, W.B., Greenberg, L.S., and Goldman, R. (1998) 'Assimilation analysis of process-experiential psychotherapy: a comparison of two cases', *Psychotherapy Research*, 8: 264–86.

Honos-Webb, L., Surko, M., Stiles, W.B. and Greenberg, L.S. (1999) 'Assimilation of voices in psychotherapy: the case of Jan', *Journal of Counseling Psychology*, 46: 448–60.

Hope, D. (1989) 'The evaluation of counselling services and counsellors in the United States', *Counselling*, 69 (August): 19–30.

Horowitz, M.J. (1982) 'Strategic dilemmas and the socialization of psychotherapy researchers', *British Journal of Clinical Psychology*, 21: 119–27.

Horowitz, M.J., Stinson, C., Curtis, D. et al. (1993) 'Topics and signs: defensive control of emotional expression', *Journal of Consulting and Clinical Psychology*, 61 (3): 421–30.

Horvath, A.O. and Greenberg, L.S. (1986) 'Development of the Working Appliance Inventory', in L.S. Greenberg and W.M. Pinsof (eds), *The Psychotherapeutic Process: A Research Handbook*. New York: Guilford Press.

Horvath, A.O. and Greenberg, L.S. (1989) 'Development and validation of the Working Alliance Inventory', *Journal of Counseling Psychology*, 36: 223–33.

Hoshmand, L.T. and Martin, J. (eds) (1994) *Method Choice and Inquiry Process: Lessons from Programmatic Research in Therapeutic Practice*. New York: Teachers' College Press.

Houghton, S. (1991) 'A multi-component intervention with an Olympic archer displaying performance-related anxiety: a case study', *Behavioural Psychotherapy*, 19 (3): 289–92.

Howard, G.S. (1983) 'Toward methodological pluralism', *Journal of Counseling Psychology*, 30 (1): 19–21.

Howard, K.I., Kopta, S.M., Krause, M.S. and Orlinsky, D.E. (1986) 'The dose–effect relationship in psychotherapy', *American Psychologist*, 41: 159–64.

Howard, K.I., Krause, M.S. and Orlinsky, D.E. (1986) 'The attrition dilemma: toward a new strategy for psychotherapy research', *Journal of Consulting and Clinical Psychology*, 54 (1): 106–10.

Howe, D. (1989) *The Consumer's View of Family Therapy*. Aldershot: Gower.

Huberman, A.M. and Miles, M.B. (1994) 'Data management and analysis methods', in N.K. Denzin and Y.S. Lincoln (eds), *Handbook of Qualitative Research*. London: Sage.

Hunt, P. (1985) *Clients' Responses to Marriage Counselling*. Rugby: NMGC.

Jacobson, N.S., Follette, W.C. and Revenstorf, D. (1984) 'Psychotherapy outcome research: methods for reporting variability and evaluating clinical significance', *Behavior Therapy*, 15: 336–52.

Jacobson, N.S. and Revenstorf, D. (1988) 'Statistics for assessing the clinical significance of psychotherapy techniques: issues, problems and new developments', *Behavioral Assessment*, 10: 133–45.

Jones, E.E. (1993) 'Introduction to Special Section: single-case research in psychotherapy', *Journal of Consulting and Clinical Psychology*, 61 (3): 371–2.

Jones, E.E., Ghannam, J., Nigg, J.T. and Dyer, J.E. (1993) 'A paradigm for single-case research: the time series study of a long-term psychotherapy for depression', *Journal of Consulting and Clinical Psychology*, 61 (3): 381–94.

Jones, P. (1975) *Philosophy and the Novel*. Oxford: Clarendon Press.

Josselson, R. (ed.) (1996) *Ethics and Process in the Narrative Study of Lives*. Thousand Oaks, CA: Sage.

Kagan, N. (1980) 'Influencing human interaction: 18 years with IPR', in A.K. Hess (ed.), *Psychotherapy Supervision: Theory, Research and Practice*. Chichester: Wiley.

Kagan, N. (1984) 'Interpersonal Process Recall: basic methods and recent research', in D. Larsen (ed.), *Teaching Psychological Skills*. Monterey, CA: Brooks/Cole.

Kagan, N., Krathwohl, D.R. and Miller, R. (1963) 'Stimulated recall in therapy using videotape – a case study', *Journal of Counseling Psychology*, 10: 237–43.

Kaschak, E. (1978) 'Therapist and client: two views of the process and outcome of psychotherapy', *Professional Psychology*, 9: 271–7.

Kazdin, A.E. (1981) 'Drawing valid inferences from case studies', *Journal of Consulting and Clinical Psychology*, 49 (2): 183–92.

Kazdin, A.E. (1986) 'Comparative outcome studies of psychotherapy: methodological issues and strategies', *Journal of Consulting and Clinical Psychology*, 54 (1): 95–105.

Kazdin, A.E. (1994) 'Methodology, design and evaluation in psychotherapy research', in A.E. Bergin and S.L. Garfield (eds), *Handbook of Psychotherapy and Behavior Change*, 4th edn. Chichester: Wiley.

Kemmis, S. and McTaggart, R. (2000) 'Participatory action research', in N.K. Denzin and Y.S. Lincoln (eds), *Handbook of Qualitative Research*, 2nd edn. Thousand Oaks, CA: Sage.

Kendall, P.C. and Hollon, S.D. (eds) (1981) *Assessment Strategies for Cognitive-Behavioral Interventions*. New York: Academic Press.

Kerr, A.W., Hall, H.K. and Kozub, S.A. (2002) *Doing Statistics with SPSS*. London: Sage.

Kirk, J. and Miller, M.L. (1986) *Reliability and Validity in Qualitative Research*. London: Sage.

Kitchener, K.S. (1984) 'Intuition, critical evaluation and ethical principles: the foundation for ethical decisions in counseling psychology', *Counseling Psychologist*, 12: 43–55.

Kivlighan, D.M., Patton, M.J. and Foote, D. (1998) 'Moderating effects of client attachment on the counselor experience–working alliance relationship', *Journal of Counseling Psychology*, 45: 274–8.

Klein, M.H., Mathieu, P.L., Gendlin, E.T. and Kiesler, D.J. (1969) *The Experiencing Scale: A Research and Training Manual*, vol. 1. Madison, WI: University of Wisconsin Bureau of Audiovisual Instruction.

Klein, M.H., Mathieu-Coughlan, P. and Kiesler, D.J. (1986) 'The Experiencing Scales', in L.S. Greenberg and W.M. Pinsof (eds), *The Psychotherapeutic Process: A Research Handbook*. New York: Guilford Press.

Kline, P. (1981) *Fact and Fantasy in Freudian Theory*, 2nd edn. London: Methuen.

Kline, P. (1992) 'Problems of methodology in studies of psychotherapy', in W. Dryden and C. Feltham (eds), *Psychotherapy and its Discontents*. Buckingham: Open University Press.

Kordy, H., Hannover, W. and Richard, M. (2001) 'Computer-assisted feedback-driven quality management for psychotherapy: the Stuttgart–Heidelberg model', *Journal of Consulting and Clinical Psychology*, 69: 173–83.

Kratochwill, T., Mott, S. and Dodson, C. (1984) 'Case study and single-case research in clinical and applied psychology', in A. Bellack and M. Hersen (eds), *Research Methods in Clinical Psychology*. New York: Pergamon, pp. 55–99.

Krueger, R.A. (1988) *Focus Groups: A Practical Guide for Applied Research*. London: Sage.

Krueger, R.A. and Casey, M.A. (2000) *Focus Groups: A Practical Guide for Applied Research*, 3rd edn. Thousand Oaks, CA: Sage.

Kuhn, T. (1962) *The Structure of Scientific Revolutions*. Chicago: University of Chicago Press.

Kutash, I.L. and Wolf, A. (eds) (1986) *The Psychotherapists' Casebook*. San Francisco, CA: Jossey-Bass.

Kvale, S. (1983) 'The qualitative research interview: a phenomenological and hermeneutical mode of understanding', *Journal of Phenomenological Psychology*, 14 (2): 171–96.

Kvale, S. (1996) *InterViews: An Introduction to Qualitative Research Interviewing*. London: Sage.

Kvale, S. (ed.) (1992) *Postmodernism and Psychology*. London: Sage.

Laitila, A., Aaltonen, J., Wahlstroem, J. and Angus, L. (2001) 'Narrative Process Coding System in marital and family therapy: an intensive case analysis of the formation of a therapeutic system', *Contemporary Family Therapy: An International Journal*, 23 (3): 309–22.

Lambert, M.J. (1983) 'Comments on "A case study of the process and outcome of time-limited counseling"', *Journal of Counseling Psychology*, 30 (1): 22–5.

Lambert, M.J. (1989) 'The individual therapist's contribution to psychotherapy process and outcome', *Clinical Psychology Review*, 9: 469–85.

Lambert, M.J. (1999) 'Use of psychological tests for outcome assessment', in M.E. Maruish (ed.), *The Use of Psychological Testing for Treatment Planning and Outcome Assessment*, 2nd edn. Mahwah, NJ: Lawrence Erlbaum.

Lambert, M.J., Burlingame, G.M., Umphress, V., Hansen, N., Yanchar, S.C., Vermeersch, D. and Clouse, G.C. (1996) 'The reliability and validity of a new psychotherapy outcome questionnaire', *Clinical Psychology and Psychotherapy*, 3 (4): 249–58.

Lambert, M.J. and Finch, A.E. (1999) 'Outcome Questionnaire', in M.E. Maruish (ed.), *The Use of Psychological Testing for Treatment Planning and Outcome Assessment*, 2nd edn. Mahwah, NJ: Lawrence Erlbaum.

Lambert, M.J., Hansen, N.B. and Finch, A.E. (2001) 'Patient-focused research: using patient outcome data to enhance treatment effects', *Journal of Consulting and Clinical Psychology*, 69: 159–72.

Lambert, M.J. and Hill, C.E. (1994) 'Assessing psychotherapy processes and outcomes', in A.E. Bergin and S.L. Garfield (eds), *Handbook of Psychotherapy and Behavior Change*, 4th edn. New York: Wiley.

Lambert, M.J., Masters, K.S. and Ogles, B.M. (1991) 'Outcome research in counseling', in C.E. Watkins and L.J. Schneider (eds), *Research in Counseling*. Hillsdale, NJ: Lawrence Erlbaum, pp. 51–84.

Lambert, M.J. and Ogles, B.M. (1988) 'Treatment manuals: problems and promise', *Journal of Integrative and Eclectic Psychotherapy*, 7 (2): 187–204.

Lambert, M.J., Whipple, J.L., Smart, D.W., Vermeesch, D.A., Nielsen, S.L. and Hawkins, E.J. (2001) 'The effects of providing therapists with feedback on patient progress: are outcomes enhanced?', *Psychotherapy Research*, 11: 49–68.

Landis, C. (1938) 'Statistical evaluation of psychotherapeutic methods', in S.E. Hinsie (ed.), *Concepts and Problems of Psychotherapy*. London: Heinemann, pp. 155–65.

Larsen, D.L., Attkinson, C.C., Hargreaves, W.A. and Nguyen, T.D. (1979) 'Assessment of client/patient satisfaction: development of a general scale', *Evaluation and Program Planning*, 2: 197–207.

Larson, V.A. (1987) 'An exploration of psychotherapeutic resonance', *Psychotherapy*, 24: 321–4.

Lebow, J. (1982) 'Consumer satisfaction with mental health treatment', *Psychological Bulletin*, 91: 244–59.

Levitt, H. and Angus, L. (1999) 'Psychotherapy process measure research and the evaluation of psychotherapy orientation: a narrative analysis', *Journal of Psychotherapy Integration*, 9 (3): 279–300.

Lewis, J., Clark, D. and Morgan, D. (1992) *Whom God Hath Joined Together: The Work of Marriage Guidance*. London: Routledge.

Liddle, B.J. (1996) 'Therapist sexual orientation, gender, and counseling practices as they relate to ratings of helpfulness by gay and lesbian clients', *Journal of Counseling Psychology*, 43 (4): 394–401.

Liddle, B.J. (1997) 'Gay and lesbian clients' selection of therapists and utilization of therapy', *Psychotherapy*, 34: 11–18.

Lieberman, M., Yalom, I. and Miles, M. (1973) *Encounter Groups: First Facts*. New York: Basic Books.

Lieblich, A. and Josselson, R. (eds) (1997) *Narrative Studies of Lives*, vol. 5. Thousand Oaks, CA: Sage.

Lietaer, G. (1990) 'The client-centered approach after the Wisconsin project: a personal view on its evolution', in G. Lietaer, J. Rombauts and R. Van Balen (eds), *Client-Centered and Experiential Therapy in the Nineties*. Leuven: University of Leuven Press, pp. 19–46.

Lietaer, G. (1992) 'Helping and hindering processes in client-centered/experiential psychotherapy: a content analysis of client and therapist postsession perceptions', in S.G. Toukmanian and D.L. Rennie (eds), *Psychotherapy Process Research: Paradigmatic and Narrative Approaches*. London: Sage, pp. 134–62.

Lincoln, Y.S. and Guba, E.G. (1985) *Naturalistic Inquiry*. London: Sage.

Lincoln, Y.S. and Guba, E.G. (1989) 'Judging the quality of case study reports', *Qualitative Studies in Education*, 3: 53–9.

Lindsey, R.T. (1984) 'Informed consent and deception in psychotherapy research: an ethical analysis', *Counseling Psychologist*, 12 (3): 79–86.

Lipkin, S. (1948) 'The client evaluates nondirective psychotherapy', *Journal of Consulting Psychology*, 12: 137–46.

Llewelyn, S.P., Elliott, R., Shapiro, D.A., Hardy, G. and Firth-Cozens, J. (1988) 'Client perceptions of significant events in prescriptive and exploratory periods of individual therapy', *British Journal of Clinical Psychology*, 27: 105–14.

Lofland, J. (1971) *Analysing Social Settings*. Belmont, CA: Wadsworth.

Lofland, J. and Lofland, L. (1984) *Analyzing Social Settings: A Guide to Qualitative Observation and Analysis*, 2nd edn. Belmont, CA: Wadsworth.

Lott, D.A. (1999) *In Session: The Bond between Women and their Therapists*. New York: W.H. Freeman.

Luborsky, L. (1984) *Principles of Psychotherapy: A Manual for Supportive-Expressive Treatment*. New York: Basic Books.

Luborsky, L. (1993) 'Recommendations for training therapists based on manuals for psychotherapy research', *Psychotherapy*, 30 (4): 578–80.

Luborsky, L., Crits-Christoph, P. and Mellon, J. (1986) 'Advent of objective measures of the transference concept', *Journal of Consulting and Clinical Psychology*, 54: 39–47.

Luborsky, L. and DeRubeis, R.J. (1984) 'The use of psychotherapy treatment manuals: a small revolution in psychotherapy research style', *Clinical Psychology Review*, 4: 5–14.

Luborsky, L., Diguer, L., Seligman, D.A. et al. (1999) 'The researcher's own therapy allegiances: a "wild card" in comparisons of treatment efficacy', *Clinical Psychology: Science and Practice*, 6: 95–106.

Luborsky, L., McLellan, A.T., Diguer, L., Woody, G. and Seligman, D.A. (1997) 'The psychotherapist matters: comparison of outcomes across twenty-two therapists and seven patient samples', *Clinical Psychology: Science and Practice*, 4: 53–65.

Luborsky, L., Popp, C., Luborsky, E. and Mark, D. (1994) 'The Core Conflictual Relationship Theme', *Psychotherapy Research*, 4: 172–83.

Luborsky, L., Singer, B. and Luborsky, L. (1975) 'Comparative outcome studies of psychotherapy', *Archives of General Psychiatry*, 32: 995–1008.

Lucas, R.W., Mullins, P.J., Luna, C.B.X. and McInroy, D.C. (1977) 'Psychiatrists and a computer as interrogators of patients with alcohol-related diseases: a comparison', *British Journal of Psychiatry*, 131: 160–7.

Lueger, R.J. (1998) 'Using feedback on patient progress to predict the outcome of psychotherapy', *Journal of Clinical Psychology*, 54: 383–93.

Lueger, R.J., Howard, K.I., Martinovich, Z., Lutz, W., Anderson, E.E. and Grissom, G. (2001) 'Assessing treatment progress of individual patients using expected treatment response models', *Journal of Consulting and Clinical Psychology*, 69: 150–8.

Lueger, R.J., Saunders, S.M., Howard, K.I., Vessey, J.T. and Nunez, P.R. (1999) 'Entering psychotherapy: probabilities, routes and finances', in N.E. Miller and K.M. Magruder (eds), *Cost-effectiveness of Psychotherapy: A Guide for Practitioners, Researchers and Policymakers*. New York: Oxford University Press.

Macaskill, N. and Macaskill, A. (1992) 'Psychotherapists-in-training evaluate their personal therapy: results of a UK survey', *British Journal of Psychotherapy*, 9 (2): 133–8.

Mace, C., Moorey, S. and Roberts, B. (eds) (2001) *Evidence in the Psychological Therapies: A Critical Guide for Practitioners*. London: Brunner-Routledge.

Mackay, H.C., West, W., Moorey, J., Guthrie, E. and Margison, F. (2001) 'Counsellors' experiences of changing their practice: learning the psychodynamic–interpersonal model of therapy', *Counselling and Psychotherapy Research*, 1: 29–40.

Madigan, S. (1999) 'Inscription, description and deciphering chronic identities', in I. Parker (ed.), *Deconstructing Psychotherapy*. London: Sage.

Madill, A. and Barkham, M. (1997) 'Discourse analysis of a theme in one successful case of brief psychodynamic–interpersonal psychotherapy', *Journal of Counseling Psychology*, 44: 232–44.

Madill, A. and Doherty, K. (1994) '"So you did what you wanted then": discourse analysis, personal agency, and psychotherapy', *Journal of Community and Applied Social Psychology*, 4: 261–73.

Mahrer, A., Dessaulles, A., Nadler, W.P., Gervaize, P.A. and Sterner, I. (1987) 'Good and very good moments in psychotherapy: content, distribution and facilitation', *Psychotherapy*, 24: 7–14.

Mahrer, A. and Nadler, W. (1986) 'Good moments in psychotherapy: a preliminary review, a list and some promising research avenues', *Journal of Consulting and Clinical Psychology*, 54 (1): 10–5.

Mahrer, A., Nadler, W., Gervaize, P. and Markow, R. (1986) 'Discovering how one therapist obtains some very good moments in psychotherapy', *Voices*, 22: 72–83.

Mahrer, A., Nifakis, D., Abhukara, L. and Sterner, I. (1984) 'Microstrategies in psychotherapy: the patterning of sequential therapist statements', *Psychotherapy*, 21 (4): 465–72.

Mahrer, A., Sterner, I., Lawson, K. and Dessaulles, A. (1986) 'Microstrategies: distinctively patterned sequences of therapist statements', *Psychotherapy*, 23 (1): 50–6.

Main, M. (1991) 'Metacognitive knowledge, metacognitive monitoring, and singular (coherent) versus multiple (incoherent) model of attachment: findings and directions for future research', in C.M Parkes, J. Stevenson-Hinde and P. Marris (eds), *Attachment across the Life-cycle*. London: Routledge.

Malan, D. (1973) 'The outcome problem in psychotherapy research – a historical review', *Archives of General Psychiatry*, 29: 719–29.

Mallett, P. (1991) 'Cost–benefit analyses of psychotherapeutic treatments', *Psychiatric Bulletin*, 15: 575–6.

Maluccio, A. (1979) *Learning from Clients: Interpersonal Helping as Viewed by Clients and Social Workers*. New York: Free Press.

Mangen, S. (1988) 'Assessing cost-effectiveness', in F.N. Watts (ed.), *New Developments in Clinical Psychology*, vol. II. Chichester: Wiley.

Marshall, C. and Rossman, G.B. (1999) *Designing Qualitative Research*, 3rd edn. London: Sage.

Marshall, R.D., Spitzer, R.L. et al (2001) 'Assessing the subjective experience of being a participant in psychiatric research', *American Journal of Psychiatry*, 158: 3019–21.

Martin, J. and Stelmazonek, K. (1988) 'Participants' identification and recall of important events in counseling', *Journal of Counseling Psychology*, 35 (4): 385–90.

Martin, J., Martin, W. and Slemon, A.G. (1989) 'Cognitive-mediational models of action–act sequences in counseling', *Journal of Counseling Psychology*, 36: 8–16.

Maruish, M.E. (ed.) (1999) *The Use of Psychological Testing for Treatment Planning and Outcome Assessment*, 2nd edn. Mahwah, NJ: Lawrence Erlbaum.

Masson, J. (1988) *Against Therapy: Emotional Tyranny and the Myth of Psychological Healing*. Glasgow: Collins.

Mayer, J. and Timms, N. (1970) *The Client Speaks: Working-Class Impressions of Casework*. London: Routledge and Kegan Paul.

McAdams, D.P., Josselson, R. and Lieblich, A. (eds) (2001) *Turns in the Road: Narrative Studies of Lives in Transition*. Washington, DC: American Psychological Association.

McCallum, M. and Piper, W.E. (1997) 'The Psychological Mindedness Assessment Procedure', in M. McCallum and W.E. Piper (eds), *Psychological Mindedness: A Contemporary Understanding*. Mahwah, NJ: Lawrence Erlbaum.

McCann, D.L. (1992) 'Post-traumatic stress disorder due to devastating burns overcome by a single session of eye movement desensitization', *Journal of Behaviour Therapy and Experimental Psychiatry*, 23 (4): 319–23.

McClelland, D.C. (1980) 'Motive dispositions: the merits of operant and respondent measures', in L. Wheeler (ed.), *Review of Personality and Social Psychology*. Beverley Hills, CA: Sage.

McClelland, D.C. (1981) 'Is personality consistent?', in A.I. Rabin, J. Aronoff, A.M. Barclay and R.A. Zucher (eds), *Further Explorations in Personality*. New York: Wiley.

McClelland, D.C. and Boyatzis, R.E. (1980) 'Opportunities for counselors from the competency assessment movement', *Personnel and Guidance Journal*, 58: 368–72.

McGrath, G. and Lowson, K. (1986) 'Assessing the benefits of psychotherapy: the economic approach', *British Journal of Psychiatry*, 150: 65–71.

McLellan, A.T., Woody, G.E., Luborsky, L. and Gohl, L. (1988) 'Is the counselor an "active ingredient" in substance abuse rehabilitation? An examination of treatment success among four counselors', *Journal of Nervous and Mental Disease*, 176: 423–30.

McLeod, J. (1990) 'The client's experience of counselling: a review of the research literature', in D. Mearns and W. Dryden (eds), *Experiences of Counselling in Action*. London: Sage, pp. 1–19.

McLeod, J. (1992) 'The story of Henry Murray's diagnostic council: a case study in the demise of a scientific method', *Clinical Psychology Forum*, 44 (June): 6–12.

McLeod, J. (1994) 'The research agenda for counselling', *Counselling*, 5 (1): 41–3.

McLeod, J. (1997) 'Reading, writing and research', in I. Horton and V. Varma (eds), *The Needs of Counsellors and Psychotherapists*. London: Sage.

McLeod, J. (1998) *An Introduction to Counselling*, 2nd edn. Buckingham: Open University Press.

McLeod, J. (1999a) *Practitioner Research in Counselling*. London: Sage.

McLeod, J. (1999b) 'A narrative social constructionist approach to therapeutic empathy', *Counselling Psychology Quarterly*, 12: 377–84.

McLeod, J. (2000) 'The contribution of qualitative research to evidence-based counselling and psychotherapy', in N. Rowland and S. Goss (eds), *Evidence-based Counselling and Psychological Therapies: Research and Applications*. London: Routledge.

McLeod, J. (2001a) 'An administratively created reality: some problems with the use of self-report questionnaire measures of adjustment in counselling/psychotherapy outcome research', *Counselling and Psychotherapy Research*, 1: 215–26.

McLeod, J. (2001b) *Counselling in the Workplace: the Facts. A Systematic Study of the Research Evidence*. Rugby: British Association for Counselling and Psychotherapy.

McLeod, J. (2001c) *Qualitative Research in Counselling and Psychotherapy*. London: Sage.

McLeod, J. (2002a) 'Qualitative research methods in counselling psychology', in R. Woolfe, W. Dryden and S. Strawbridge (eds), *Handbook of Counselling Psychology*, 2nd edn. London: Sage.

McLeod, J. (2002b) 'Research policy and practice in person-centred and experiential therapy: restoring coherence', 1/2: 87–101.

McLeod, J. (2003) *An Introduction to Counselling*, 3rd edn. Buckingham: Open University Press.

McLeod, J. and Balamoutsou, S. (2000) 'Narrative process in the assimilation of a problematic experience: qualitative analysis of a single case', *Zeitschrift für Qualitative Bildungs – Beratungs – und Sozialforschung*, 2: 283–302.

McLeod, J. and Balamoutsou, S. (2001) 'A method for qualitative narrative analysis of psychotherapy transcripts', in J. Frommer and D.L. Rennie (eds), *Qualitative Psychotherapy Research: Methods and Methodology*. Lengerich, Germany: Pabst.

McLeod, J. and Lynch, G. (2000) '"This is our life": strong evaluation in psychotherapy narrative', *European Journal of Psychotherapy, Counselling and Health*, 3: 389–406.

McLeod, J. and Machin, L. (1998) 'Contexts of counselling: a neglected dimension of theory, research and practice', *British Journal of Guidance and Counselling*, 26: 325–36.

Meara, N.M. and Schmidt, L.D. (1991) 'The ethics of researching the counseling/therapy process', in C.E. Watkins and L.J. Schneider (eds), *Research in Counseling*. Hillsdale, NJ: Lawrence Erlbaum, pp. 237–59.

Mearns, D. and McLeod, J. (1984) 'A person-centred approach to research', in R. Levant and J. Shlien (eds), *Client-Centered Therapy and the Person-Centered Approach: New Directions in Theory, Research and Practice*. New York: Praeger, pp. 370–89.

Mearns, D. and Thorne, B. (1988) *Person-Centred Counselling in Action*. London: Sage.

Meehl, P.E. (1967) 'Theory testing in psychology and in physics: a methodological paradox', *Philosophy of Science*, 34: 103–15.

Meehl, P.E. (1978) 'Theoretical risks and tabular asterisks: Sir Karl, Sir Ronald and the slow progress in soft psychology', *Journal of Consulting and Clinical Psychology*, 46: 806–34.

Mellor-Clark, J., Barkham, M., Connell, J. and Evans, C. (1999) 'Practice-based evidence and standardized evaluation: informing the design of the CORE system', *European Journal of Psychotherapy, Counselling and Health*, 2: 357–74.

Mellor-Clark, J., Connell, J., Barkham, M. and Cummins, P. (2001) 'Counselling outcomes in primary health care: a CORE system data profile', *European Journal of Psychotherapy, Counselling and Health*, 4: 65–86.

Messer, S.B., Sass, L.A. and Woolfolk, R.L. (eds) (1988) *Hermeneutics and Psychological Theory: Interpretive Perspectives on Personality, Psychotherapy and Psychopathology*. New Brunswick, NJ: Rutgers University Press.

Mies, M. (1983) 'Towards a methodology for feminist research', in G. Bowles and R.D. Klein (eds), *Theories for Women's Studies*. London: Routledge and Kegan Paul.

Miles, M. and Huberman, A. (1984) *Qualitative Data Analysis: A Sourcebook of New Methods*. London: Sage.

Miles, M. and Huberman, A. (1994) *Qualitative Data Analysis: A Sourcebook of New Methods*, 2nd edn. London: Sage.

Miles, M.B. and Huberman, A.M. (eds) (2002) *The Qualitative Researcher's Companion*. Thousand Oaks, CA: Sage.

Miller, N.E., Luborsky, L., Barber, J.P. and Docherty, J.P. (eds) (1993) *Psychodynamic Treatment Research: A Handbook for Clinical Practice*. New York: Basic Books.

Miller, N.E. and Magruder, K.M. (eds) (1999) *Cost-effectiveness of Psychotherapy: A Guide for Practitioners, Researchers and Policymakers*. New York: Oxford University Press.

Mintz, J., Auerbach, A.H., Luborsky, L. and Johnson, M. (1973) 'Patients', therapists' and observers' views of psychotherapy: a "Rashomon" experience or reasonable consensus?', *British Journal of Medical Psychology*, 46: 83–9.

Mintz, J. and Luborsky, L. (1971) 'Segments vs. whole sessions: which is the better unit for psychotherapy research?', *Journal of Abnormal Psychology*, 78: 180–91.

Mischel, W. (1968) *Personality and Assessment*. New York: Wiley.

Moras, K. (1993) 'The use of treatment manuals to train psychotherapists: observations and recommendations', *Psychotherapy*, 30 (4): 581–6.

Morley, S. (1996) 'Single case research', in G. Parry and F.N. Watts (eds), *Behavioural and Mental Health Research: A Handbook of Skills and Methods*, 2nd edn. London: Lawrence Erlbaum, pp. 233–64.

Morley, S. and Snaith, P. (1989) 'Principles of psychological assessment', in C. Freeman and P. Tyrer (eds), *Research Methods in Psychiatry: A Beginners' Guide*. London: Gaskell, pp. 133–47.

Morrow-Bradley, C. and Elliott, R. (1986) 'Utilization of psychotherapy research by practicing psychotherapists', *American Psychologist*, 41 (2): 188–97.

Moustakas, C. (1967) 'Heuristic research', in J. Bugental (ed.), *Challenges of Humanistic Psychology*. New York: McGraw-Hill.

Moustakas, C. (1990a) *Heuristic Research: Design, Methodology and Applications*. Thousand Oaks, CA: Sage.

Moustakas, C. (1990b) 'Heuristic research, design and methodology', *Person-Centered Review*, 5: 170–90.

Moustakas, C. (1994) *Phenomenological Research Methods*. London: Sage.

Mulhall, D. (1976) 'Systematic self-assessment by PQRST', *Psychological Medicine*, 6: 591–7.

Murphy, S. and Tyrer, P. (1989) 'Rating scales for special purposes. I: Psychotherapy', in C. Freeman and P. Tyrer (eds), *Research Methods in Psychiatry: A Beginners' Guide*. London: Gaskell, pp. 176–97.

Murray, H.A. (1938) *Explorations in Personality: A Clinical and Experimental Study of Fifty Men of College Age*. New York: Oxford University Press.

Murray, H.A. and Morgan, C.D. (1945) 'A clinical study of sentiments', *Genetic Psychology Monographs*, 32: 3–311.

Neimeyer, G. and Resnikoff, A. (1982) 'Qualitative strategies in counseling research', *Counseling Psychologist*, 10 (4): 75–85.

Nelson, R.O. (1981) 'Realistic dependent measures for clinical use', *Journal of Consulting and Clinical Psychology*, 49 (2): 168–82.

Newman, L.E. (1983) 'Therapists' evaluation of psychotherapy', in M.J. Lambert, E.R. Christensen and S.S. DeJulio (eds), *The Assessment of Psychotherapy Outcome*. New York: Wiley, pp. 498–536.

Nicholson, P. (1989) 'Counselling women with post natal depression: implications from recent qualitative research', *Counselling Psychology Quarterly*, 2 (2): 123–32.

Niederland, W.G. (1959) 'Schreber: father and son', *Psychoanalytic Quarterly*, 28: 151–69.

Nunnally, J.C. (1978) *Psychometric Theory*, 2nd edn. New York: McGraw-Hill.

Oakley, A. (1981) 'Interviewing women: a contradiction in terms', in H. Roberts (ed.), *Doing Feminist Research*. London: Routledge and Kegan Paul.

Ogles, B.M., Lambert, M.J., Weight, D.G. and Payne, I.R. (1990) 'Agoraphobia outcome measurement: a review and meta-analysis', *Journal of Consulting and Clinical Psychology*, 59: 317–25.

Ogles, B., Lunnen, K. and Bonesteel, K. (2001) 'Clinical significance: history, application, and current practice', *Clinical Psychology Review*, 21: 421–46.

Omer, H. and Dar, R. (1992) 'Changing trends in three decades of psychotherapy research: the flight from theory into pragmatics', *Journal of Consulting and Clinical Psychology*, 60: 88–93.

Orlinsky, D.E. (1989) 'Researchers' images of psychotherapy: their origins and influence on research', *Clinical Psychology Review*, 9: 413–41.

Orlinsky, D.E., Grawe, K. and Parks, B.K. (1994) 'Process and outcome in psychotherapy: noch einmal', in A.E. Bergin and S.L. Garfield (eds), *Handbook of Psychotherapy and Behavior Change*, 4th edn. Chichester: Wiley.

Orlinsky, D.E. and Howard, K.I. (1975) *Varieties of Psychotherapeutic Experience: Multivariate Analyses of Patients' and Therapists' Reports*. New York: Teachers' College Press.

Orlinsky, D.E. and Howard, K.I. (1986) 'The psychological interior of psychotherapy: explorations with the Therapy Session reports', in L.S. Greenberg and W.M. Pinsof (eds), *The Psychotherapeutic Process: A Research Handbook*. New York: Guilford Press.

Osborne, J.W. (1990) 'Some basic existential-phenomenological research methodology for counsellors', *Canadian Journal of Counselling*, 24 (2): 79–91.

Parry, G. (1992) 'Improving psychotherapy services: applications of research, audit and evaluation', *British Journal of Clinical Psychology*, 31: 3–19.

Parry, G. (1996) 'Writing a research report', in G. Parry and F.N. Watts (eds), *Behavioural and Mental Health Research: A Handbook of Skills and Methods*, 2nd edn. London: Psychology Press.

Parry, G., Shapiro, D.A. and Firth, J. (1986) 'The case of the anxious executive: a study from the research clinic', *British Journal of Medical Psychology*, 59: 221–33.

Parry, G. and F.N. Watts (eds) (1996) *Behavioural and Mental Health Research: A Handbook of Skills and Methods*, 2nd edn. London: Psychology Press.

Partyka, R., Amer, M., Elliott, R. et al. (2002) 'An adjudicated hermeneutic single case efficacy study of experiential therapy for borderline personality processes'. Paper presented at meeting of Society for Psychotherapy Research, Santa Barbara, CA, USA.

Paterson, C. (1996) 'Measuring outcomes in primary care: a patient-generated measure, MYMOP, compared with the SF-36 health survey', *British Medical Journal*, 312: 1016–20.

Patterson, C.H. (1984) 'Empathy, warmth and genuineness in psychotherapy: a review of reviews', *Psychotherapy*, 21: 431–8.

Patton, M.Q. (1990) *Qualitative Evaluation and Research Methods*, 2nd edn. New York: Sage.

Paul, G.L. (1967) 'Strategy of outcome research in psychotherapy', *Journal of Consulting Psychology*, 31: 109–18.

Paulson, B., Everall, R.D. and Stuart, J. (2001) 'Client perceptions of hindering experiences in counselling', *Counselling and Psychotherapy Research*, 1: 53–61.

Peck, D.F. (1989) 'Research with single (or few) patients', in C. Freeman and P. Tyrer (eds), *Research Methods in Psychiatry: A Beginners' Guide*. London: Gaskell.

Phillips, J.P.N. (1986) 'Shapiro Personal Questionnaire and generalized personal questionnaire techniques: a repeated measures individualized outcome measurement', in L.S. Greenberg and W.M. Pinsof (eds), *The Psychotherapeutic Process: A Research Handbook*. New York: Guilford Press, pp. 557–89.

Polkinghorne, D.E. (1989) 'Phenomenological research methods', in R.S. Valle and S. Halling (eds), *Existential-Phenomenological Perspectives in Psychology*. New York: Plenum Press, pp. 41–60.

Polkinghorne, D.E. (1991a) 'Qualitative procedures for counseling research', in C.E. Watkins and L.J. Schneider (eds), *Research in Counseling*. Hillsdale, NJ: Lawrence Erlbaum, pp. 163–204.

Polkinghorne, D.E. (1991b) 'Two conflicting calls for methodological reform', *Counseling Psychologist*, 19 (1): 103–14.

Polkinghorne, D.E. (1999) 'Traditional research and psychotherapy practice', *Journal of Clinical Psychology*, 55: 1429–40.

Pope, K.S. (1991) 'Dual relationships in psychotherapy', *Ethics and Behavior*, 1: 21–34.

Popper, K.R. (1959) *The Logic of Scientific Discovery*. New York: Basic Books.

Popper, K.R. (1962) *Conjectures and Refutations*. New York: Basic Books.

Popper, K.R. (1972) *Objective Knowledge*. Oxford: Oxford University Press.

Powell, G.E. (1989) 'Selecting and developing measures', in G. Parry and F.N. Watts (eds), *Behavioural and Mental Health Research: A Handbook of Skills and Methods*. London: Lawrence Erlbaum, pp. 27–54.

Prioleau, L., Murdock, M. and Brody, N. (1983) 'An analysis of psychotherapy versus placebo studies', *Behavioral and Brain Sciences*, 6: 275–310.

Rasmussen, B. and Angus, L. (1996) 'Metaphor in psychodynamic psychotherapy with borderline and non-borderline clients: a qualitative analysis', *Psychotherapy*, 33: 521–30.

Rawlinson, J.G. (1981) *Creative Thinking and Brainstorming*. Aldershot: Gower.

Reason, P. (ed.) (1988a) *Human Inquiry in Action: Developments in New Paradigm Research*. London: Sage.

Reason, P. (1988b) 'Whole person medical practice', in P. Reason (ed.), *Human Inquiry in Action: Developments in New Paradigm Research*. London: Sage, pp. 102–26.

Reason, P. (1994) 'Three approaches to participative inquiry', in N.K. Denzin and Y.S. Lincoln (eds), *Handbook of Qualitative Research*. London: Sage, pp. 324–39.

Reason, P., Chase, H.D., Desser, A. et al. (1992) 'Towards a clinical framework for collaboration between general and complementary practitioners: discussion paper', *Journal of the Royal Society of Medicine*, 85: 161–4.

Reason, P. and Heron, J. (1986) 'Research with people: the paradigm of cooperative experiential inquiry', *Person-Centered Review*, 1 (4): 456–76.

Reason, P. and Rowan, J. (eds) (1981) *Human Inquiry: A Sourcebook of New Paradigm Research*. Chichester: Wiley.

Rennie, D.L. (1990) 'Toward a representation of the client's experience of the psychotherapy hour', in G. Lietaer, J. Rombauts and R. Van Balen (eds), *Client-Centered and Experiential Therapy in the Nineties*. Leuven: University of Leuven Press, pp. 155–72.

Rennie, D.L. (1992) 'Qualitative analysis of the client's experience of psychotherapy: the unfolding of reflexivity', in S.G. Toukmanian and D.L. Rennie (eds), *Psychotherapy Process Research: Paradigmatic and Narrative Approaches*. London: Sage, pp. 211–33.

Rennie, D.L. (1994a) 'Clients' deference in psychotherapy', *Journal of Counseling Psychology*, 41: 427–37.

Rennie, D.L. (1994b) 'Storytelling in psychotherapy: the client's subjective experience', *Psychotherapy*, 31: 234–43.

Rennie, D.L. (1994c) 'Clients' accounts of resistance in counselling: a qualitative analysis', *Canadian Journal of Counselling*, 28: 43–57.

Rennie, D.L. (1994d) 'Strategic choices in a qualitative approach to psychotherapy process research: a personal account', in L.T. Hoshmand and J. Martin (eds), *Method Choice and Inquiry Process: Lessons from Programmatic Research in Therapeutic Practice*. New York: Teachers' College Press.

Rennie, D.L. (1994e) 'Human science and counselling psychology: closing the gap between research and practice', *Counselling Psychology Quarterly*, 7: 235–50.

Rennie, D.L. (2001) 'The client as self-aware agent in counselling and psychotherapy', *Counselling and Psychotherapy Research*, 1: 82–9.

Rennie, D.L. (2002) 'Experiencing psychotherapy: grounded theory studies', in D.J. Cain and J. Seeman (eds), *Humanistic Psychotherapies: Handbook of Research and Practice*. Washington, DC: American Psychological Association.

Rennie, D.L., Phillips, J.R. and Quartaro, J.K. (1988) 'Grounded theory: a promising approach for conceptualization in psychology?', *Canadian Psychology* 29: 139–50.

Rennie, D.L. and Toukmanian, S.G. (1992) 'Explanation in psychotherapy process research', in S.G. Toukmanian and D.L. Rennie (eds), *Psychotherapy Process Research*. London: Sage, pp. 234–51.

Rice, L.N. (1992) 'From naturalistic observation of psychotherapy process to micro theories of change', in D.L. Rennie and S.G. Toukmanian (eds), *Psychotherapy Process Research: Narrative and Paradigmatic Approaches*. London: Sage.

Rice, L.N. and Greenberg, L.S. (eds) (1984a) *Patterns of Change: Intensive Analysis of Psychotherapy Process*. New York: Guilford Press.

Rice, L.N. and Greenberg, L.S. (1984b) 'The new research paradigm', in L.N. Rice and L.S. Greenberg (eds), *Patterns of Change: Intensive Analysis of Psychotherapy Process*. New York: Guilford Press.

Rice, L.N and Saperia, E.P. (1984) 'Task analysis of the resolution of problematic reactions', in L.N. Rice and L.S. Greenberg (eds), *Patterns of Change: Intensive Analysis of Psychotherapy Process*. New York: Guilford Press.

Rice, L.N. and Kerr, G.P. (1986) 'Measures of client and therapist voice quality', in L.S. Greenberg and W.M. Pinsof (eds), *The Psychotherapeutic Process: A Research Handbook*. New York: Guilford Press.

Richards, T.J. and Richards, L. (1994) 'Using computers in qualitative research', in N.K. Denzin and Y.S. Lincoln (eds), *Handbook of Qualitative Research*. London: Sage, pp. 445–62.

Richardson, L. (1991) *Writing Strategies: Reaching Diverse Audiences*. London: Sage.

Robson, C. (2002) *Real World Research: A Resource for Social Scientists and Practitioner-Researchers*, 2nd edn. Oxford: Blackwell.

Rogers, A., Pilgrim, D. and Lacey, R. (1993) *Experiencing Psychiatry: Users' Views of Services*. London: Macmillan.

Rogers, C.R. (1942a) *Counseling and Psychotherapy*. Boston, MA: Houghton Miflin.

Rogers, C.R. (1942b) 'The use of electrically recorded interviews in improving psychotherapy techniques', *American Journal of Orthopsychiatry*, 12: 429–34. Reprinted in H. Kirschenbaum and V. Henderson (eds) (1990) *The Carl Rogers Reader*. London: Constable.

Rogers, C.R. (1951) *Client-Centered Therapy: Its Current Practice, Implications and Theory*. London: Constable.

Rogers, C.R. (1957) 'The necessary and sufficient conditions of therapeutic personality change', *Journal of Consulting Psychology*, 21: 95–103.

Rogers, C.R. (1958) 'A process conception of psychotherapy', *American Psychologist*, 13: 142–9.

Rogers, C.R. and Dymond, R.F. (eds) (1954) *Psychotherapy and Personality Change*. Chicago: University of Chicago Press.

Rogers, C.R., Gendlin, E.T., Kiesler, D.J. and Truax, C.B. (eds) (1967) *The Therapeutic Relationship and its Impact: A Study of Psychotherapy with Schizophrenics*. Madison, WI: University of Wisconsin Press.

Rosenthal, R. and Rubin, D.B. (1978) 'Interpersonal expectancy effects: the first 345 studies', *Behavioral and Brain Sciences*, 3: 377–415.

Ross, P. (1989) 'Counselling and accountability', *Counselling*, 69 (August): 11–18.

Ross, P. (1994) 'The impact of research upon practice', *Counselling*, 5 (1): 35–7.

Roth, A. and Fonagy, P. (1996) *What Works for Whom? A Critical Review of Psychotherapy Research*. New York: Guilford Press.

Rowland, N. and Goss, S. (eds) (2000) *Evidence-based Counselling and Psychological Therapies: Research and Applications*. London: Routledge.

Rubino, G., Barker, C., Roth, T. and Fearon, P. (2000) 'Therapist empathy and depth of interpretation in response to potential alliance ruptures: the role of patient and therapist attachment styles', *Psychotherapy Research*, 10: 408–20.

Runyan, W.M. (1980) 'Alternative accounts of lives: an argument for epistemological relativism', *Biography*, 3: 209–24.

Runyan, W.M. (1981a) 'Why did Van Gogh cut off his ear? The problem of alternative explanations in psychobiography', *Journal of Personality and Social Psychology*, 40 (6): 1070–7.

Runyan, W.M. (1981b) *Life Histories and Psychobiography: Explorations in Theory and Method*. New York: Oxford University Press.

Runyan, W.M. (1997) 'Studying lives: psychobiography and the conceptual structure of personality psychology', in R. Hogan, J. Johnson and S. Briggs (eds), *Handbook of Personality Psychology*. San Antonio, TX: Psychology Corporation.

Russell, R.L. (1989) 'Language and psychotherapy', *Clinical Psychology Review*, 9: 505–20.

Russell, R.L. (ed.) (1994) *Reassessing Psychotherapy Research*. New York: Guilford Press.

Rust, J. and Golombok, S. (1989) *Modern Psychometrics: The Science of Psychological Assessment*. London: Routledge.

Rycroft, C. (1966) 'Causes and meaning', in C. Rycroft (ed.), *Psychoanalysis Observed*. London: Constable.

Ryder, J. and Lowenthal, D. (2001) 'Psychotherapy for lesbians: the influence of therapist sexuality', *Counselling and Psychotherapy Research*, 1: 42–52.

Sachs, J.S. (1983) 'Negative factors in brief psychotherapy: an empirical assessment', *Journal of Consulting and Clinical Psychology*, 51: 557–64.

Sachse, R. and Elliott, R. (2002) 'Process–outcome research on humanistic therapy variables', in D.J. Cain and J. Seeman (eds), *Humanistic Psychotherapies: Handbook of Research and Practice*. Washington, DC: American Psychological Association.

Salkind, N.J. (2000) *Statistics for People Who (Think They) Hate Statistics*. Thousand Oaks, CA: Sage.

Sampson, H. and Weiss, J. (1986) 'Testing hypotheses: the approach of the Mount Zion Psychotherapy Research Group', in L.S. Greenberg and W.M. Pinsof (eds), *The Psychotherapeutic Process: A Research Handbook*. New York: Guilford Press.

Sampson Jr, J.P. (1990) 'Computer applications and issues in using tests in counseling', in C.E. Watkins Jr, and V.L. Campbell (eds), *Testing in Counseling Practice*. Hillsdale, NJ: Lawrence Erlbaum.

Sandell, R., Blomberg, J., Lazar, A., Carlsson, J., Broberg, J. and Schubert, J. (2000) 'Varieties of long-term outcome among patients in psychoanalysis and long-term psychotherapy. A review of findings of the Stockholm Outcome of Psychoanalysis and Psychotherapy Project (STOPPP)', *International Journal of Psychoanalysis*, 81: 921–42.

Schatzman, M. (1973) *Soul Murder: Persecution in the Family*. London: Allen Lane.

Schneider, K.J. (1999) 'Multiple-case depth research', *Journal of Clinical Psychology*, 55: 1531–40.

Schneider, K.J., Bugental, J.F.T. and Pierson, J.F. (eds) (2001) *The Handbook of Humanistic Psychology: Leading Edges in Theory, Research and Practice*. Thousand Oaks, CA: Sage.

Sechrest, L. (1984) 'Reliability and validity', in A. Bellack and M. Hersen (eds), *Research Methods in Clinical Psychology*. New York: Pergamon.

Seligman, M.E.P. (1995) 'The effectiveness of psychotherapy: the *Consumer Reports* study', *American Psychologist*, 50: 965–74.

Semeonoff, B. (1976) *Projective Techniques*. Chichester: Wiley.

Serlin, R.C. and Lapsley, D.K. (1985) 'Rationality in psychological research: the good-enough principle', *American Psychologist*, 40: 73–83.

Shadish, W.R., Matt, G.E., Navarro, A.M. et al. (1997) 'Evidence that therapy works in clinically representative conditions', *Journal of Consulting and Clinical Psychology*, 65: 355–65.

Shapiro, D.A. (1977) 'The "double standard" in evaluation of psychotherapies', *Bulletin of the British Psychological Society*, 30: 209–10.

Shapiro, D.A. (1996) 'Outcome research', in G. Parry and F.N. Watts (eds), *Behavioural and Mental Health Research: A Handbook of Skills and Methods*, 2nd edn. London: Lawrence Erlbaum.

Shapiro, D.A., Barkham, M., Hardy, G. and Morrison, L. (1990) 'The Second Sheffield Psychotherapy Project: rationale, design and preliminary outcome data', *British Journal of Medical Psychology*, 63: 97–108.

Shapiro, D.A., Barkham, M., Rees, A., Hardy, G.E., Reynolds, S. and Startup, M. (1994) 'Effects of treatment duration and severity of depression on the effectiveness of cognitive-behavioral and psychodynamic-interpersonal psychotherapy', *Journal of Consulting and Clinical Psychology*, 62: 522–34.

Shapiro, M.B. (1961) 'A method of measuring psychological changes specific to the individual psychiatric patient', *British Journal of Medical Psychology*, 34: 151–5.

Shaw, M. and Miles, I. (1979) 'The social roots of statistical knowledge', in J. Irvine, I. Miles and J. Evans (eds), *Demystifying Social Statistics*. London: Pluto Press.

Shotter, J. (1975) *Images of Man in Psychological Research*. London: Methuen.

Shrout, P.E. and Fleiss, J.L. (1979) 'Intraclass correlations: uses in assessing rater reliability', *Psychological Bulletin*, 86: 420–8.

Silberschatz, G., Curtis, J.T. and Nathans, S. (1989) 'Using the patients' plan to assess progress in psychotherapy', *Psychotherapy*, 26: 40–6.

Silberschatz, G., Fretter, P.B. and Curtis, J.T. (1986) 'How do interpretations influence the progress of psychotherapy?', *Journal of Consulting and Clinical Psychology*, 54: 646–52.

Skovholt, T.M. and Ronnestad, M.H. (1992) *The Evolving Professional Self: Stages and Themes in Therapist and Counselor Development*. New York: Wiley.

Slade, A. (1999) 'Attachment theory and research: implications for the theory and practice of individual psychotherapy with adults', in J. Cassidy and P.R. Shaver (eds), *Handbook of Attachment: Theory, Research and Clinical Applications*. New York: Guilford Press.

Sloane, R.B., Staples, F.R., Cristol, A.H., Yorkston, N.J. and Whipple, K. (1975) *Psychotherapy vs Behavior Therapy*. Cambridge, MA: Harvard University Press.

Sloboda, J.A., Hopkins, J.S., Turner, A., Rogers, D. and McLeod, J. (1993) 'An evaluated staff counselling programme in a public sector organization', *Employee Counselling Today*, 5 (5): 4–12.

Smith, J.K. and Heshusius, L. (1986) 'Closing down the conversation: the end of the qualitative–quantitative debate among educational researchers', *Educational Researcher*, 15: 4–12.

Smith, M., Glass, G. and Miller, T. (1980) *The Benefits of Psychotherapy*. Baltimore, MD: Johns Hopkins University Press.

Sorensen, R.L., Gorusch, R.K. and Mintz, J. (1985) 'Moving targets: patients changing complaints during psychotherapy', *Journal of Consulting and Clinical Psychology*, 53: 49–54.

Spence, D.P. (1982) *Narrative Truth and Historical Truth: Meaning and Interpretation in Psychoanalysis*. New York: Norton.

Spence, D.P. (1986) 'Narrative smoothing and clinical wisdom', in T.R. Sarbin (ed.), *Narrative Psychology: The Storied Nature of Human Conduct*. New York: Praeger.

Spence, D.P. (1989) 'Rhetoric vs. evidence as a source of persuasion: a critique of the case study genre', in M.J. Packer and R.B. Addison (eds), *Entering the Circle: Hermeneutic Investigation in Psychology*. Albany, NY: State University of New York Press.

Spence, D.P. (2001) 'Dangers of anecdotal reports', *Journal of Clinical Psychology*, 57: 37–41.

Spiegelberg, H. (1960) *The Phenomenological Movement: A Historical Introduction*. The Hague: Martinus Nijhoff.

Spielberger, C.D., Gorsuch, R.L. and Lushene, R. (1970) *Manual for the State–Trait Anxiety Inventory*. Palo Alto, CA: Consulting Psychologists Press.

Spitzer, R.L., Endicott, J., Fleiss, J.L. and Cohen, J. (1970) 'The Psychiatric Status Schedule: a technique for evaluating psychopathology and impairment in functioning', *Archives of General Psychiatry*, 23: 41–55.

Stanton, A.L. and New, M.J. (1988) 'Ethical responsibilities to depressed research participants', *Professional Psychology: Research and Practice*, 19: 279–85.

Steenbarger, B.N. (1992) 'Toward science–practice integration in brief counseling and psychotherapy', *Counseling Psychologist*, 20: 403–50.

Steier, F. (ed.) (1991) *Research and Reflexivity*. London: Sage.

Sternberg, R.J. (ed.) (1988) *The Nature of Creativity: Contemporary Psychological Perspectives*. Cambridge: Cambridge University Press.

Stevenson, I. (1961) 'Processes of "spontaneous recovery" from the psychoneuroses', *American Journal of Psychiatry*, 117: 1057–64.

Stewart, D.W. and Shamdasani, P.N. (1990) *Focus Groups: Theory and Practice*. London: Sage.

Stiles, W.B. (1980) 'Measurement of the impact of psychotherapy sessions', *Journal of Consulting and Clinical Psychology*, 48: 176–85.

Stiles, W.B. (1986) 'Development of a taxonomy of verbal response modes', in L.S. Greenberg and W.M. Pinsof (eds), *The Psychotherapeutic Process: A Research Handbook*. New York: Guilford Press, pp. 161–200.

Stiles, W.B. (1993) 'Quality control in qualitative research', *Clinical Psychology Review*, 13: 593–618.

Stiles, W.B. (2001) 'Assimilation of problematic experiences', *Psychotherapy: Theory, Research, Practice and Training*, 38: 462–5.

Stiles, W.B. (2002) 'Assimilation of problematic experiences', in J.C. Norcross (ed.), *Psychotherapy Relationships that Work*. New York: Oxford University Press.

Stiles, W.B., Elliott, R., Llewelyn, S., Firth-Cozens, J., Margison, F., Shapiro, D.A. and Hardy, G. (1990) 'Assimilation of problematic experiences by clients in psychotherapy', *Psychotherapy*, 27: 411–20.

Stiles, W.B., Meshot, C.N., Anderson, T.M. and Sloan, W.W. (1992) 'Assimilation of problematic experiences: the case of John Jones', *Psychotherapy Research*, 2 (2): 81–101.

Stiles, W.B., Morrison, L.A., Haw, S.F., Harper, H., Shapiro, D.A. and Firth-Cozens, J. (1991) 'Longitudinal study of assimilation in exploratory psychotherapy', *Psychotherapy*, 28: 195–206.

Stiles, W.B. and Shapiro, D.A. (1989) 'Abuse of the drug metaphor in psychotherapy process–outcome research', *Clinical Psychology Review*, 9: 521–43.

Stiles, W.B. and Snow, J. (1984) 'Dimensions of psychotherapy session impact across sessions and across clients', *British Journal of Clinical Psychology*, 23: 59–63.

Strain, P. and Kerr, M. (1984) 'Writing grant applications: some general guidelines', in A. Bellack and M. Hersen (eds), *Research Methods in Clinical Psychology*. New York: Pergamon, pp. 370–94.

Strauss, A. and Corbin, J. (1990) *Basics of Qualitative Research: Grounded Theory Procedures and Techniques*. New York: Sage.

Strauss, A. and Corbin, J. (eds) (1997) *Grounded Theory in Practice*. Thousand Oaks, CA: Sage.

Strauss, A. and Corbin, J. (1998) *Basics of Qualitative Research: Techniques and Procedures for Developing Grounded Theory*, 2nd edn. Thousand Oaks, CA: Sage.

Strupp, H.H. (1980a) 'Success and failure in time-limited psychotherapy. A systematic comparison of two cases: comparison 1', *Archives of General Psychiatry*, 37: 595–603.

Strupp, H.H. (1980b) 'Success and failure in time-limited psychotherapy. A systematic comparison of two cases: comparison 2', *Archives of General Psychiatry*, 37: 708–16.

Strupp, H.H. (1980c) 'Success and failure in time-limited psychotherapy: with special reference to the performance of the lay counselor', *Archives of General Psychiatry*, 37: 831–41.

Strupp, H.H. (1980d) 'Success and failure in time-limited psychotherapy. Further evidence: comparison 4', *Archives of General Psychiatry*, 37: 947–54.

Strupp, H.H. (1989) 'Psychotherapy: can the practitioner learn from the researcher?', *American Psychologist*, 44: 717–24.

Strupp, H.H. (1993) 'The Vanderbilt psychotherapy studies: synopsis', *Journal of Consulting and Clinical Psychology*, 61 (3): 431–3.

Strupp, H.H. and Binder, J.L. (1984) *Psychotherapy in a New Key: A Guide to Time-Limited Dynamic Psychotherapy*. New York: Basic Books.

Strupp, H.H. and Hadley, S.W. (1977) 'A tripartite model of mental health and therapeutic outcome: with special reference to negative effects in psychotherapy', *American Psychologist*, 32: 187–96.

Strupp, H.H. and Hadley, S.W. (1979) 'Specific vs. non-specific factors in psychotherapy – a controlled study of outcome', *Archives of General Psychiatry*, 36: 1125–36.

Strupp, H.H., Wallach, M. and Wogan, M. (1964) 'Psychotherapy experience in retrospect: questionnaire survey of former patients and their therapists', *Psychological Monographs: General and Applied*, 78 (11), Whole Number 588.

Sudman, S. and Bradburn, N.M. (1982) *Asking Questions: A Practical Guide to Questionnaire Design*. San Francisco, CA: Jossey-Bass.

Suh, C.S., Strupp, H.H. and O'Malley, S.S. (1986) 'The Vanderbilt process measures: the Psychotherapy Process Scale (VPPS) and the Negative Indicators Scale (VNIS)', in L.S. Greenberg and W.M. Pinsof (eds), *The Psychotherapeutic Process: A Research Handbook*. New York: Guilford Press, pp. 285–324.

Sussman, S. (2001) 'The significance of psycho-peristalsis and tears within the therapeutic relationship', *Counselling and Psychotherapy Research*, 1: 90–100.

Sutton, C. (1987) 'The evaluation of counselling: a goal–attainment approach', *Counselling*, 5 (1): 35–7.

Swoyer, C. and Monson, T.C. (1975) 'Theory confirmation in psychology', *Philosophy of Science*, 42: 487–502.

Talley, P.F., Strupp, H.H. and Butler, S.F. (eds) (1994) *Research Findings and Clinical Practice: Bridging the Chasm*. New York: Basic Books.

Taylor, C. (1979) 'Interpretation and the science of man', in P. Rabinow and W. Sullivan (eds), *Interpretive Social Science: A Reader*. Berkeley, CA: University of California Press.

Taylor, I.A. and Getzels, J.W. (eds) (1975) *Perspectives in Creativity*. Chicago: Aldine.

Taylor, J.A. (1953) 'A personality scale of manifest anxiety', *Journal of Abnormal and Social Psychology*, 48: 285–90.

Taylor, J.B., Carithers, M. and Coyne, L. (1976) 'MMPI performance, response set and the "self-concept hypothesis"', *Journal of Consulting and Clinical Psychology*, 44: 351–62.

Thompson, C. (1989a) 'Affective disorders', in C. Thompson (ed.), *The Instruments of Psychiatric Research*. Chichester: Wiley.

Thompson, C. (1989b) 'Anxiety', in C. Thompson (ed.), *The Instruments of Psychiatric Research*. Chichester: Wiley.

Thompson, C. and Jenal, S. (1994) 'Interracial and intraracial quasi-counselling interactions: when counselors avoid discussing race', *Journal of Counseling Psychology*, 41: 484–91.

Thorne, B. and Dryden, W. (eds) (1993) *Counselling: Interdisciplinary Perspectives*. Buckingham: Open University Press.

Timms, N. and Blampied, A. (1985) *Intervention in Marriage: The Experience of Counsellors and their Clients*. University of Sheffield: Joint Unit for Social Services Research.

Tingey, R.C., Lambert, M.J., Burlingame, G.M. and Hansen, N.B. (1996) 'Assessing clinical significance: proposed extensions to method', *Psychotherapy Research*, 6: 109–23.

Tinsley, H.E. and Weiss, D.J. (1975) 'Interrater reliability and agreement of subjective judgements', *Journal of Counseling Psychology*, 22: 358–76.

Tolley, K. and Rowland, N. (1995) *Evaluating the Cost-effectiveness of Counselling in Health Care*. London: Routledge.

Toukmanian, S.G. (1986) 'A measure of client perceptual processing', in L.S. Greenberg and W.M. Pinsof (eds), *The Psychotherapeutic Process: A Research Handbook*. New York: Guilford Press, pp. 107–30.

Toukmanian, S.G. (1992) 'Studying the clients' perceptual processes and their outcomes in psychotherapy', in S.G. Toukmanian and D.L. Rennie (eds), *Psychotherapy Process Research: Paradigmatic and Narrative Approaches*. London: Sage.

Toukmanian, S.G. and Rennie, D.L. (eds) (1992) *Psychotherapy Process Research: Paradigmatic and Narrative Approaches*. London: Sage.

Treacher, A. (1983) 'On the utility or otherwise of psychotherapy research', in D. Pilgrim (ed.), *Psychology and Psychotherapy: Current Trends and Issues*. London: Routledge & Kegan Paul.

Truax, C.B. and Carkhuff, R.R. (1967) *Toward Effective Counseling and Psychotherapy: Training and Practice*. Chicago: Aldine.

Tuckwell, G. (2001) '"The threat of the Other": using mixed quantitative and qualitative methods to elucidate racial and cultural dynamics in the counselling process', *Counselling and Psychotherapy Research*, 1: 154–62.

Turpin, G. (2001) 'Single-case methodology and psychotherapy evaluation: from research to practice', in C. Mace, S. Moorey and B. Roberts (eds), *Evidence in the Psychological Therapies: A Critical Guide for Practitioners*. London: Brunner-Routledge.

Tyrrell, C.L., Dozier, M., Teague, G.B. and Fallot, R.D. (1999) 'Effective treatment relationships for persons with serious psychiatric disorders: the importance of attachment states of mind', *Journal of Consulting and Clinical Psychology*, 67: 725–33.

Valle, R.S. and Halling, S. (eds) (1989) *Existential-Phenomenological Perspectives in Psychology: Exploring the Breadth of Human Experience*. New York: Plenum.

Van Hasselt, V.B. and Hersen, M. (eds) (1996) *Sourcebook of Psychological Treatment Manuals for Adult Disorders*. New York: Plenum Press.

van Kaam, A. (1969) *Existential Foundations of Psychology*. New York: Image Books.

Vernon, P.E. (1963) *Personality Assessment: A Critical Survey*. London: Methuen.

Viens, M.J. and Hranchuk, K. (1992) 'The treatment of Bulimia Nervosa following surgery using a stimulus control procedure: a case study', *Journal of Behaviour Therapy and Experimental Psychiatry*, 23 (4): 313–17.

Von Wright, G.H. (1971) *Explanation and Understanding*. London: Routledge.

Waskow, I.E. and Parloff, M.B. (1975) *Psychotherapy Change Measures*. Washington, DC: US Government Printing Office.

Watkins Jr, C.E. and Campbell, V.L. (eds) (2000) *Testing and Assessment in Counseling Practice*, 2nd edn. Hillsdale, NJ: Lawrence Erlbaum.

Watson, D. and Friend, R. (1969) 'Measurement of social evaluative anxiety', *Journal of Consulting and Clinical Psychology*, 33: 448–57.

Watson, G. (1940) 'Areas of agreement in psychotherapy', *American Journal of Orthopsychiatry*, 10: 698–709.

Watson, N. (1984) 'The empirical status of Rogers's hypotheses of the necessary and sufficient conditions for effective psychotherapy', in R. Levant and J. Shlien (eds), *Client-Centered Therapy and the Person-Centered Approach: New Directions in Theory, Research and Practice*. New York: Praeger.

Webb, Y. (1993) 'Consumer surveys: an overview', in R. Leiper and V. Field (eds), *Counting for Something in Mental Health Services: Effective User Feedback*. Aldershot: Avebury.

Wedding, D. and Corsini, R. (eds) (1979) *Great Cases in Psychotherapy*. Itasca, IL: F.E. Peacock.

Weiss, D.S. and Marmar, C.R. (1993) 'Teaching time-limited psychotherapy for post-traumatic stress disorder and pathological grief', *Psychotherapy*, 30 (4): 587–91.

Wells, M.G., Burlingame, G.M. and Lambert, M.J. (1999) 'Youth Outcome Questionnaire', in M.E. Maruish (ed.), *The Use of Psychological Testing for Treatment Planning and Outcome Assessment*, 2nd edn. Mahwah, NJ: Lawrence Erlbaum.

West, M. and Reynolds, S. (1995) 'Employee attitudes to work-based counselling services', *Work and Stress*, 9: 31–44.

West, W.S. (1992) 'Client evaluations of Reichian therapy'. Unpublished MA Dissertation, Department of Applied Social Studies, University of Keele.

West, W.S. (1996) 'Using human inquiry groups in counselling research', *British Journal of Guidance and Counselling*, 24: 347–56.

West, W.S. (1997) 'Integrating psychotherapy and healing', *British Journal of Guidance and Counselling*, 25: 291–312.

West, W.S. (1998a) 'Passionate research: heuristics and the use of self in counselling research', *Changes*, 16: 60–6.

West, W.S. (1998b) 'Critical subjectivity: use of self in counselling research', *Counselling*, 9: 228–30.

West, W.S. (1998c) 'Developing practice in a context of religious faith: a study of psychotherapists who are Quakers', *British Journal of Guidance and Counselling*, 26: 365–75.

West, W.S. (2001) 'Beyond grounded theory: the use of a heuristic approach to qualitative research', *Counselling and Psychotherapy Research*, 1: 126–31.

Whiston, S.C. (2000) *Principles and Applications of Assessment in Counseling*. Belmont, CA: Brooks/Cole.

Wiener, M., Budney, S., Wood, L. and Russell, R.L. (1989) 'Nonverbal events and psychotherapy', *Clinical Psychology Review*, 9: 487–504.

Wilson, S.R. (1985) 'Therapeutic processes in a yoga ashram', *American Journal of Psychotherapy*, 39 (2): 253–62.

Wing, J. (1991) 'Ethics and psychiatric research', in S. Bloch and P. Chodoff (eds), *Psychiatric Ethics*, 2nd edn. Oxford: Oxford University Press.

Wolcott, H.F. (1990) *Writing up Qualitative Research*. London: Sage.

Wright, D.B. (2002) *First Steps in Statistics*. Thousand Oaks, CA: Sage.

Wright, T.L., Ingraham, L.J., Chemtob, H.J. and Perez-Arce, P. (1985) 'Satisfaction and things not said: clinical tools for group therapists', *Small Group Behavior*, 16 (4): 565–72.

Yalom, I.D. (1989) *Love's Executioner and Other Tales of Psychotherapy*. Harmondsworth: Penguin.

Yalom, I.D. and Elkin, G. (1974) *Every Day Gets a Little Closer: A Twice-Told Therapy*. New York: Basic Books.

Yin, R.K. (1994) *Case Study Research: Design and Methods*, 2nd edn. Thousand Oaks, CA: Sage.

Index

ABAB design, 106
abstract concepts, 18
abstracts of research, 17
abuse of clients by therapists, 2
academic freedom, 5–6
accountability of counsellors, 2
ad hoc rationalisations, 53
adult attachment interview (AAA) methodology, 163
Allman, L.S., 65
alpha levels, 47, 51–2; *see also* Cronbach's alpha
Altheide, D.L., 95
American Psychological Association, 175
analogue studies, 12
analysis of variance (ANOVA), 49
Anderson, R., 83–4
Anderson, T., 170
Angus, L.E., 150, 159
anxiety
    concepts of, 56
    measurement of, 58–9
aspectival readings of data, 91
'assimilation model' of client change, 101
Assimilation of Problematic Experience Scale (APES), 64
attachment theory, 161
attrition rates, 135
audiences for research, 24
Auerbach, A.H., 127
authenticity of research material, 95
autoethnography, 83, 97
autonomy, principle of, 167
axial coding, 89
Axline, V., 146

Bachelor, A., 79, 146
Bachrach, H., 165
Bakan, D., 191
Barkham, M., 133, 141, 150
Barlow, D.H., 186
Barrett-Lennard Relationship Inventory, 147
Basham, R.B., 132–3
Battle, C.C., 126
Beck Depression Inventory (BDI), 61, 133, 135

behavioural measures, 64, 127
benchmarking, 60
beneficence, principle of, 167
Berger, R., 186–7
Bergin, A.E., 13, 178, 183
Berzon, B., 146
Bettelheim, B., 87
Beutler, L.E., 67
Bloch, S., 79, 146
Bohart, A., 110
Boyatzis, R.E., 67
brainstorming, 25, 27
Brannen, J., 77, 159, 169, 175, 183
Braud, W., 83
brief structural recall, 150, 155
Brody, N., 131–2
Bromley, D., 103, 113
Bruner, J., 7–8
Bryman, A., 181

Carter, J.A., 100
case studies
    criteria for quality of, 114
    pluralist, 108–9
    research-informed, 108
    structure of reports, 113
case study research, 11, 31, 99–115
    advantages of, 99–100, 143
    central features of, 115
    doubts about, 100
    issues in, 111–15
    qualitative, 101–4
    types of, 101
catalytic validity, 96
categorical measurement, 42
categorisation of research data, 85–6
causality, direction of, 50
central tendency, measures of, 44
Chassan, J.B., 100
Cheyne, A., 127
chi-square (χ^2) test, 29, 48
client-centred counselling and psychotherapy, 63, 66, 79, 138, 150–4, 188
client-centred research, 11–12
client experience studies, 158–60

client groups for counselling, 2
client perceptual processing, 149
client satisfaction studies, 122–6, 130
clinically significant change, 134–5
Cochrane database, 13, 140
coding, 85, 89
Cohen, L.H., 184
Cohen, S., 80
Collard, J., 77, 159, 169
collective aspect of research, 9–10
Combs, A.W., 50
communication between therapists and clients,
    studies of, 153–4
comparison group designs, 132–3
comprehensive process analysis, 155, 180
computers, use of, 69, 92
Comte, A., 7
confidentiality, 172–3
contextual awareness, 72
contrast group studies, 28–9
control groups, 45, 118, 130–3
    typology of, 130–1
cooperative inquiry groups, 81–3, 92–3, 97,
    171
copyright, 69
Corbett, M.M., 12
Corbin, J., 88–9, 91, 188
core categories (in grounded theory), 91
CORE (clinical outcomes routine evaluation)
    scale, 60, 68–9, 129–30, 135
core conflictual relationship theme (CCRT)
    model, 160
Cornelius, E.T. III, 66
correlation coefficient, 49–50
cost-benefit analysis, 128–9
cost-effectiveness studies, 128–9
The Counseling Psychologist, 13
counselling in non-counselling settings, 190
counsellor response modes, 153–4
Crago, M., 67
creativity, 27
credibility of researchers, 94–5
critical inquiry, concept of, 4
criticisms of therapy research made by
    practitioners, 184–5
critique of research, 17–18
Crits-Christoph, P., 160
Cronbach's alpha, 57
Cunningham, I., 23
Curtis, J.T., 161
Cushman, P., 193
cyclical research processes, 23, 72, 82

Dar, R., 51–2, 189
data analysis, 35–6

data-gathering techniques, 32–5
data protection, 172
databases of academic literature, 13
Deane, F.P., 126–7
deconstruction of questions, 25–6
Denker, P.G., 118
dependent and independent variables, 46
Derogatis, L.R., 61
descriptive statistics, 43–6
design of research, 28–30, 36
Devereaux, G., 25
'Devil's advocate' role, 82
DeWaele, J., 103
Dilthey, W., 7
DiMascio, A., 130
dissemination of research results, 38–9
documentary research, 81
'double blind' studies, 123
drop-out rates, 127
drug metaphor in research, 142
'dual relationships' theory, 174
Dymond, R.F., 151, 165

effect size, 140
    concept of, 44–5
effectiveness of counselling and psychotherapy,
    research on, 11–12
efficacy studies, 110–11
Elkin, G., 102
Elliott, R., 65, 93, 110, 113, 148–50, 153–8,
    165, 180, 184
Ellis, C., 83, 154
epistemology, 178
equivalence paradox, 137
Etherington, K., 22, 84, 102
ethical issues, 33, 167–76
    in practitioner research, 173–5
ethics committees, 168
events paradigm, 154
evidence-based practice, 139–40, 187
experiencing scale, 63–4, 149
experiential knowing, 4
extensive research designs, 100
extreme scores, 45–6
Eysenck, H.J., 118, 130, 133

F tests, 49
facilitative conditions model, 152, 164
feedback from outcome questionnaires, 138–9
feminist analysis, 97
Finch, J., 76, 96
first-person writing, 17
Fishman, D., 101
Fitts, W., 146
focus groups, 78

Follette, W.C., 134–5
Frank, J.D., 132
frequency distributions, 44
Freud, S., 2, 99–100, 102, 113, 160
Friedli, K., 129
Friend, R., 56

Garfield, S.L., 13, 39, 178, 183
Geertz, C., 87
Gendlin, E.T., 27, 63, 108
generalisability of results, 18, 111
Gergen, K.J., 7
Gervaize, P., 157
Glaser, B.G., 88, 92, 188
Glass, G., 19
Goal Attainment Scaling, 126
'good moments' in therapy, 157–8
Grafanaki, S., 22
Grawe, K., 163–4
Greenberg, L.S., 156–8
grounded theory, 88–92, 95, 97, 159, 188–9
groups of research participants, 81–3
Guba, E.G., 93
Guthrie, E., 129

Hadley, S.W., 129, 170
Hammersley, M., 183
*Handbook of Psychotherapy and Behavior
    Change*, 178
Harré, R., 103
Hasenfeld, Y., 3
Hattie, J.A., 132
Heaton, J.M., 193
Heppner, P.P., 28, 106, 175
Herbert, J.D., 106
hermeneutic cycle, 87
hermeneutic studies, 7, 95, 110–11
hermeneutically-inspired theory, 29
Heron, J., 82
heuristic inquiry, 83–4, 97, 192–3
Hill, C.E., 12, 93, 100, 107, 110, 135, 147,
    150, 153–4, 180, 188
Hilliard, R.B., 101, 104, 108
Hodgson, R., 22
Holloman, R., 80–1
Hollon, S.D., 64
Hopkins Symptom Checklist, 61
Horowitz, M.J., 28, 143
Houghton, S., 105
Howard, G.S., 142, 179
Howard, R.I., 135
Hranchuk, K., 104–6
Huberman, A., 71, 92
human inquiry groups, 81
human science, 193

humanistic psychology, 83
Hunt, P., 130
hypothesis-testing, 16, 46–9

'images' of counselling and psychotherapy, 2,
    142
imaginative variation technique, 86
immersion in the research process, 27, 85, 92
inductive analysis, 72
'indwelling', 83–4
inferential statistics, 44, 46–51
informed consent, 170–4
inkblot test, 65, 79
innovations in theory and technique, 2
integral inquiry approach, 83
intensive research designs, 100
interaction effects, 49
interdisciplinarity, 4, 8, 193
internal consistency of scales, 57–8
internet, the, 13
interpersonal process recall (IPR), 76, 148–50,
    155–6, 159–60, 165, 169, 180
interpretation of research, 18, 85–8
inter-rater reliability, 58, 62
interval scaling, 42–3, 48
interviewers, 74–6
interviews, 35, 74–8
  on client experience, 159
  structured, 127
  see also recall interviews
intuitive inquiry model, 83–4

Jacobson, N.S., 134–5
Johnson, J.M., 95
Jones, P., 87
*Journal of Consulting and Clinical
    Psychology*, 52, 101, 189
Journal of Counseling Psychology, 100
journals, academic, 14–17, 38–9

Kagan, N., 148
Kazdin, A.E., 133
Kendall, P.C., 64
Kinn, S., 127
Kivlighan, D.M., 28
Krause, M.S., 135
Kuhn, T., 6
kurtosis, 46
Kvale, S., 74, 76, 96

Laing, R.D., 95
Lambert, M.J., 121–2, 135, 139
Landis, C., 118
laws of nature, 7
legitimacy of counselling, 3

Lewin, K., 190
Lewis, J., 81, 173
libraries, use of, 15
Liddle, B.J., 65
Lieberman, M., 136
Lietaer, G., 12, 79, 146
life history research, 104
Lincoln, Y.S., 93
Lipkin, S., 146
literature on counselling, 10–15
literature reviews, 13, 16, 18, 32, 56, 88–9
lived experience, 85, 88
Llewelyn, S.P., 79, 146
Lofland, J., 74
longitudinal studies, 29
Luborsky, L., 140–1, 160–1, 165, 188

Macaskill, N. and A., 65
McCann, D.L., 105–6, 112
McClelland, D.C., 66–7
McLeod, J., 76, 97, 103
Madigan, S., 187
Mahrer, A., 147, 154, 157–8
Malan, D., 12
maleficence, principle of, 167
Mallison, R., 186–7
Maluccio, A., 74, 159
Markow, R., 157
Marshall, R.D., 186
Martin, J., 146
Marxism, 6
Masters, K.S., 121–2
Mearns, D., 76, 103
Meehl, P.E., 52–3
Melisaratos, N., 61
Mellon, J., 160
Mellor-Clark, J., 141
meta-analysis, 19, 140
'methodolatry', 183
Mies, M., 76
Miles, M., 71, 92, 136
Miller, T., 19
mind-mapping, 25, 27
Minnesota Multiphasic Personality Inventory
    (MMPI), 61, 67–8
Mintz, J., 165
Mischel, W., 68–9
models, construction of, 26–7
moral principles, 167
Morgan, C.D., 103
Morrow-Bradley, C., 65, 184
Moustakas, C., 83
Mueser, K.T., 106
multiform method, 109
multiple baseline studies, 106

Murdock, M., 131–2
Murray, H., 11, 103, 108–10, 112, 181
mystery-mastery complex, 191–2

'n = 1' studies, 104–7, 113, 124–5
Nadler, W., 147, 157–8
narrative case studies, 101–4
narrative mode of thinking, 7–8
narrative processing coding scheme, 64, 149
naturalistic inquiry, 72
naturalistic outcome studies, 123
Nelson, R.O., 64
New, M.J., 169
'new paradigm' methods, 29
Nicholson, P., 76
nominal measurement, 42
normal distribution, 43–6
null hypothesis, 46–8, 51–4

objectivity, 83
observation of therapy sessions, 147–9
observational measures, 62–4, 68
O'Farrell, M.K., 100
Ogles, B., 67, 121–2, 135
O'Grady, K.E., 153
Omer, H., 51–2, 189
open-ended accounts of therapy, 146
operationalisation, 18, 56
OQ (Outcome Questionnaire), 60–1, 68,
    129–30
ordinal measurement, 42
Orlinsky, D.E., 135, 142, 163–4
outcome research, 11, 67–8, 97, 117–46
    difficulties with interpretation of, 119–21
    ethical issues in, 169–70
    historical development of, 118–21
    methodological issues for design of, 130–7
    relevance for practice of, 137–9
    types of, 122–5

paradigms, 6–8
parametric and non-parametric statistics, 36, 43,
    48
Parks, B.K., 163–4
Parloff, M.B., 129
participant observation, 80–1
Paterson, C., 126–7
Patterson, C.H., 152
Patton, M.Q., 137–8
Paul, G.L., 190–1
peer review, 38
personal contacts with researchers, 15
personal development for counsellors, 84
personal experience of researchers, use made of,
    83–4

personality change, core conditions for, 151–2
phenomenological reduction, 85–6
phenomenological research, 95, 97
philosophy of science, 5–6
pilot studies, 33–4
placebo factors, 132
planning of research, 27–8, 34–6
plausibility criteria for evidence, 110–11
pluralism, methodological, 73, 108–9, 178–83
policy-oriented studies, 24
politics of research, 187
Popper, Sir K., 5–6, 17, 52, 112, 189
positivism and positivist research, 7, 29, 71, 181
practice, relevance of research for, 184–7
practice-based evidence, 192
practitioner research, 173–5
practitioners' criticisms of research, 184–5
Prioleau, L., 131–2
probability, concept of, 47
process-experiential therapy, 156–7
process-outcome research, 163–5
process research, 145–66
 from psychodynamic perspective, 160–3
professional development of researchers, 2, 39
projective techniques, 12, 65–7, 79–80
Protestant ethic, 191
psychiatric status schedule, 127
psychoanalysis and psychoanalytic theory, 6, 189
psychodynamic theory, 12, 160, 188
psychological tests, 35, 55–6
 phases of, 56–7
 reliability and validity of, 55–8
psychometrics, 55
publication credit, 175

qualitative research, 17, 25, 30–1, 35–6, 41, 54, 71–98, 169, 179–83
 case studies, 101–4
 characteristic features of, 72–3
 data analysis for, 84–8
 data gathering for, 74–84
 definition of, 73
 efficacy studies, 110–11
 evaluation of validity, 93–6
 issues to be resolved in, 96–8
 outcome studies, 125
 use of researchers' personal experience in the course of, 83
quantitative research methodology, 41–54, 179–83

question-finding stage of research, 24–7
questionnaires
 on client experience, 158–60
 on client satisfaction, 125–6
 open-ended, 78–9
 for outcome research, 138–9
 self-report, 60, 66
 socially-desirable answers to, 68
 for specific surveys, 64–5
 as therapy process measures, 147–8

random sampling, 30
randomised AB designs, 106
randomised control trials (RCTs), 123–4
rating scales, 42–3, 60, 64
ratings
 of complaints or goals, 126–7
 by *significant others*, 128
 by therapists, 128
ratio scales, 43
Reason, P., 82–3
recall interviews, 148–50
refereeing of papers, 38–9
reflexivity, 26–7, 72, 95, 97, 186, 192
relevance of research for practice, 184–7
reliability
 of research results, 18
 of tests, 55–8, 68
reliable change in clients, 134–5
Rennie, D.L., 89, 91–2, 97, 145–6, 150, 159, 165, 169, 180–1, 189
replication, 96, 112
reports on research, structure of, 16–17
representativeness, 30–1
research
 contribution of counselling to, 187–8
 definition and nature of, 3–5, 9
 historical development of, 11–13
 on people, 6–7
 reasons for undertaking of, 1–3
 scepticism about value of, 1, 184–5
 tensions and dilemmas in, 5–8
research communities, 175
research instruments, 32–3, 55, 57
research papers
 reading of, 15–16
 structure of, 16–17
research participants, 95–6, 114, 187
 access to, 31–2
 protection of, 168–73
 researchers' personal contact with, 72
research-practice gap, 184–6
research projects, predictable crises in, 22–3
research proposals, structure of, 34
Revenstorf, D., 134–5

review articles, 13
Reynolds, S., 65
Rice, L.N., 155–8
Robinson, F., 147
Robson, C., 28
Rogers, C., 2, 63, 66, 99, 138, 146–7, 150–1, 154, 164–5, 183, 188
Rollnick, S., 22
Ronnestad, M.H., 74
Rorschach inkblot test, 65, 79
Ross, P., 24
Runyan, W.M., 103–4

sampling, 30–1
Sampson, H., 161
Sampson, J.P. Jr, 69
Saperia, E.P., 155–6
Sargent, M.M., 184
Schatzman, M., 103
Schreber case, 102–3
scientific method, 4–7
screening devices, 61
Sechrest, L.B., 184
self-report testing, 125
Seligman, M.E.P., 122–3
Serlin, R.C., 51–2
session evaluation questionnaire (SEQ) tool, 147, 159
Shapiro, D.A., 113, 133, 135, 142, 150, 154–5, 180
Shapiro, M., 126
Sheffield Psychotherapy Project, 49, 108
significant others, 128
single-case efficacy studies, 110–11
single-case experiments, 104–7, 113
single-case outcome studies, 124–5
single-case quantitative studies, 107
Skovholt, T.M., 74
Sloane, R.B., 119–21, 126, 134, 136
Sloboda, J.A., 130, 138
Smith, M., 19
'snowball' sampling, 30
social constructionism, 7, 29, 73
social psychology, 175
social responsibility, 175–6
sociological research, 181–2
sound files, 92
Spence, D.P., 62, 165
Spielberger, C.D., 56, 61
spontaneous recovery, 118–19, 133
SPSS, 51
standard deviation, 44–5
Stanton, A.L., 169
State-Trait Anxiety Inventory, 61, 67
statistical packages, 35–6, 43, 51

statistical significance, 47, 134
statistical tests, 29, 36, 51–3
  power of, 48
statistics
  descriptive, 43–6
  inferential, 44, 46–51
  misuse of, 51–2
Steenbarger, B.N., 20
Steier, F., 95
Stelmazonek, K., 146
Stiles, W.B., 72, 93, 96, 142, 154
stratified sampling, 30
Strauss, A., 88–9, 91, 188
Structured and Scaled Interview to Assess Maladjustment (SSIAM), 127
Strupp, H.H., 23, 100, 112, 129, 158, 170, 185
subjectivity, 83
'suspense' studies, 113

t-test, 48
tacit knowledge, 10
target complaint rating, 126–7
task analysis, 155–6
Taylor, J.A., 56
Taylor, L., 80
teams of researchers, 92–3
telephone counselling, 12
tests
  access to, 69
  computerised, 69
  doubts about, 69
  see also psychological tests; statistical tests
Thematic Apperception Test (TAT), 65–6, 79
theory
  development of, 87
  role of, 178, 188–90
therapist effects, 137
therapy session report questionnaire, 158
'thick' description, 86, 89
time-consuming forms of research, 29
timetabling of research, 34
Tingey, R.C., 134
Tomlinson, T.M., 63
Toukmanian, S.G., 180–1
training of therapists, 3
  manual-guided, 136–7
transference, 161
Treacher, A., 12
triangulation, 85–7, 95, 109, 181–2
trustworthiness of research, 83
truth value, 4, 52
Type I error, 47, 52
Type II error, 48

validity
  catalytic, 96
  internal and external (in outcome research),
    121–2
  of qualitative research, 93–6
  of questionnaire content, 65
  of tests, 55–8, 67–8
Van Gogh, V., 103
Vanderbilt Psychotherapy Process Scale, 149
Vanderbilt study, 108
variability in statistics, 44
variance, 44–5
verbal response modes, 149
Viens, M.J., 104–6
Von Wright, G.H., 7

waiting lists, patients on, 119–20, 131–2
Wallach, M., 158
Wampold, B.E., 28

Waskow, I.E., 129
Watson, D., 56
Watson, J.B., 99
Watson, N., 152
Weiss, J., 161
West, M., 65
West, W.S., 80, 84
Wilson, S.R., 81
Wing, J., 168
Wogan, M., 158
Wolcott, H.F., 27
working alliance inventory, 147, 149
writing up of research, 27, 36–7, 91,
    112–13

Yalom, I., 101–2, 136
Yin, R.K., 112–14

z-scores, 44–5